# SOCIAL WELFARE AND SOCIAL WORK

## IN SOUTHERN AFRICA

Ndangwa Noyoo

**EDITOR**

SUN PRESS

*Social Welfare and Social Work in Southern Africa*

Published by African Sun Media under the SUN PReSS imprint

This publication was subjected to an independent double-blind peer evaluation by the publisher.

The editor and the publisher have made every effort to obtain permission for and acknowledge the use of copyrighted material. Refer all enquiries to the publisher.

Views reflected in this publication are not necessarily those of the publisher.

First edition, first print 2021

ISBN 978-1-928480-76-1
ISBN (e-book) 978-1-928480-77-8
https://doi.org/10.18820/9781928480778

Set in Warnock Pro 10.5/16
Cover design, typesetting and production by African Sun Media

SUN PReSS is an imprint of AFRICAN SUN MeDIA. Scholarly, professional and reference works are published under this imprint in print and electronic formats.

This publication can be ordered from:
orders@africansunmedia.co.za
Takealot: bit.ly/2monsfl
Google Books: bit.ly/2k1Uilm
africansunmedia.store.it.si (e-books)
Amazon Kindle: amzn.to/2ktL.pkL

Visit africansunmedia.co.za for more information.

# TABLE OF CONTENTS

# MORE ABOUT THE EDITOR

**Ndangwa Noyoo** is an associate professor and the former head of the Department of Social Development at the University of Cape Town (UCT), South Africa. He previously worked for the University of Johannesburg (UJ) as an associate professor in the Department of Social Work and before that, for the South African Government, as a senior social policy specialist/chief director in the National Department of Social Development. Before this, he was a senior lecturer in the Department of Social Work at the University of the Witwatersrand (Wits). He has published widely in the context of Africa and Southern Africa in the areas of social policy, social development, and related fields. He has presented papers at various symposia in Africa and abroad. He holds a Doctor of Philosophy (PhD) degree from the University of the Witwatersrand (Wits), a Master of Philosophy (MPhil) in Development Studies from the University of Cambridge and a Bachelor of Social Work (BSW) degree from the University of Zambia (UNZA). He was a post-doctoral fellow at the Fondation Maison des Sciences de l'Homme, Paris, France from 2005–2006.

# CONTRIBUTORS

**José Ivo Correia** is a senior researcher and coordinator at the Centre for Mozambican and International Studies in Maputo. He is responsible for a joint project with the Department of Social Work of the Kassel University, Germany, and the Pontífica Universidade Católica do Rio Grande do Sul, Department of Sociology, Brazil. Before this, he was the Joint United Nations Programme on HIV/Aids (UNAIDS)'s Gender and HIV/Aids Joint Programme Coordinator in the Ministry of Women and Social Action. He worked as a research assistant at Oxford University's Queen Elizabeth House Project on the Economic and Social Costs of the War in Mozambique. He holds a Master of Public and Development Management degree from Wits, a BA in International Relations from the Higher Institute of International Relations (Instituto Superior de Relações Internacionais), Maputo, and a Certificate in International Conflict Resolution from the University of Uppsala, Sweden. His areas of interest are social policy; gender development; and African International Relations.

**Rachel Johanna Freeman** is a social work graduate from the University of Namibia (UNAM). She holds a Master of Arts (MA) of Social Behaviour Studies in Sociology (Cum Laude) degree from the University of South Africa (Unisa). She obtained a PhD in Sociology from Unisa in 2018. She has 22 years of social work practice experience. She is a social work lecturer at UNAM and is a passionate educationalist who finds pleasure in transforming minds through education, research and community service, and tasks she professionally undertakes. She received the UNAM's Faculty of Humanities and Social Sciences Meritorious Award in 2016 in recognition for her outstanding service and performance in the areas of research, community services and teaching. Her research interests are social work; palliative care; employee health and wellness promotion; combating gender-based violence; HIV/Aids; social justice; and human rights.

**Asrani Gopaul** is a senior lecturer in Social Work and Social Policy at the University of Mauritius (UOM). He holds an undergraduate degree in Social Work, a Master of Social Development degree and a postgraduate Certificate in Research from UOM. In his career, he has worked with various government departments in Mauritius before joining UOM as a full-time academic. He collaborated with the Commonwealth Secretariat to review the Vulnerability Index of Small States in the field of social resilience and social protection. He has published articles in areas related to social development, social protection, and social policy. His areas of research interest are social work, social development, social protection, shock responsive social protection, the informal sector and social resilience in small states islands. He is currently doing research in the field of social capital, social policy and climate change, family values, youth and health hazards, social policy for healthcare and development. Asrani is a member of Applied Socio-Economic Research and Analysis of UOM.

**Loveness Mwayi Imaan** is a lecturer and head of the Department of Social Work at the Catholic University of Malawi (Cunima). Previously, she worked as a senior care assistant at St Mary's Nursing Home, Rugby, England, and before that, she worked as a nurse-midwife technician at Malawi's premier hospital, the Mwaiwathu Private Hospital. Loveness's research interests that she has written articles about are older persons' issues and health. She holds a Master of Science (MSc) degree in Health Studies and a Bachelor of Science (BSc) (Honours) degree in Health Studies minoring in Social Work from the Coventry University, England, and a Certificate in Nursing Midwifery Technician from the Nkhoma Nursing College, Lilongwe, Malawi.

**Ndumba Jonnah Kamwanyah** is a multidisciplinary professional, currently lecturing at the Faculty of Humanities and Social Sciences at UNAM. He is the deputy director at UNAM's Centre for Professional Development, Teaching and Learning Improvement. His PhD in Public Policy was obtained from the University of Massachusetts, Boston. He holds an MSc in Public Policy and a MA degree in Conflict Studies from the University of Massachusetts Boston, and BSW from UNAM. A political analyst and social commentator on the news, he writes a weekly column for a Namibian newspaper, a widely read newspaper in the country, on politics, social and economic issues and culture.

**Alain Kambale Maboko** holds postgraduate qualifications in environmental and sustainable development sciences. He is an International Visitor Leadership Program alumnus of the USA's State Department Sustaining Civic Engagement. Alain is a passionate advocate of social work and is engaged in civic leadership, community organisation and sustainable development. Alain has successively worked in community social mobilisation with the United Nations (UN) agencies and non-governmental organisations in emergency programmes implemented in eastern Congo. He has worked as a lecturer in the Rural Development College of the Great Lakes Regions and with civil society organisations and the private sector on governance issues. He initiated the Young African Leaders Initiative branch and the Promoting Youth Education programme in the North Kivu region, where he is a volunteer social worker. His interests and areas of expertise include community organisation; youth participation; empowerment and resilience; rural development; social exclusion; injustice; marginalisation; civic participation; social change; and human rights. He holds postgraduate qualifications in environmental and sustainable development sciences. He is an International Visitor Leadership Program alumnus of the USA's State Department Sustaining Civic Engagement. Alain is a passionate advocate of social work and is engaged in civic leadership, community organisation and sustainable development. Alain has successively worked in community social mobilisation with the United Nations (UN) agencies and non-governmental organisations in emergency programmes implemented in eastern Congo.

**Lungile Mabundza** is a lecturer in the Department of Sociology and Social Work at the University of Eswatini (UNESWA, formerly known as the University of Swaziland). She holds a PhD from the University of KwaZulu-Natal (UKZN), South Africa, a Master of Social Work (MSW) degree from the University of Kansas, USA, and a Bachelor of Arts degree in Social Science (BASS) from UNESWA. She was a Fulbright Scholar between 2007-2009. She previously was an intern with the Counselling and Psychological Services at the Watkins Memorial Health Centre, University of Kansas, USA, from August 2008 to May 2009. From August 2007 to May 2008, she interned at the Douglas County Aids Project, Lawrence, Kansas, USA. Her research interests include gerontology; disability; children in difficult circumstances; policy and development; HIV/Aids; gender studies; and play therapy.

**Delipher Magola** is an assistant lecturer in the Social Work Department at Cunima. She previously worked as a volunteer at Make Me Smile, Kenya, where she participated in data management and information systems and provided life skills and counselling services for girls; and facilitated programmes on psychosocial support, poverty eradication and community mobilisation. She made follow-up visits to children at schools and homes; and facilitated Make Me Smile HIV/Aids support groups. She holds a BA degree in Sociology with IT from the Maseno University, Kenya.

**Tšepang Florence Manyeli** is a senior lecturer in the Department of Sociology and Social Work at the National University of Lesotho, in Lesotho. She previously worked as a social worker in the then Department of Social Welfare (DSW), currently known as the Ministry of Social Development. Before this, she worked as a director of programmes in the Lesotho Red Cross Society. She has published in the context of Lesotho in the areas of community care; child welfare; social development, and related fields. She has presented papers at different fora locally and internationally. She holds an Honours Degree in Social Work and an MSW degree in Social Development and Planning from the Nelson Mandela University (formerly known as the University of Port Elizabeth).

**Rodreck Mupedziswa** is a professor in the Department of Social Work, University of Botswana (UB) where he served as head of the department for six years. He holds a PhD from the University of Zimbabwe (UZ); an MSc from the London School of Economics; a BSW and a Diploma in Social Work from UZ. The previous positions he held include deputy director, School of Social Work, UZ, and director of the Forced Migration Studies Programme, Wits. He has published nine books as well as numerous journal articles, book chapters, occasional papers, and monographs. He has presented academic papers at over 120 gatherings in 45 countries. He was Editor-in-Chief for ten years of the International Bibliography of the Social Sciences accredited Journal of Social Development in Africa. He sits on editorial boards of four international journals, including the International Social Work, and Ethics and Social Welfare. He consulted for many international agencies, including those in the UN system. His research interests focus essentially on the theme of social development issues.

**Mildred Mushunje** holds a PhD degree from UKZN, South Africa; a Master's of Gender and Development Studies degree from the University of Manchester, UK; and a Bachelor of Social Work degree from UZ. Her experience includes work with the Food and Agriculture Organisation of the UN, where she worked as a specialist on gender, HIV/Aids and social-protection. She lectured at UZ's School of Social Work. Before, she worked as a probation officer with the DSW in Zimbabwe. She has vast experience in civil society work, focusing mainly on issues related to women and children's rights and social protection. Her country experiences include Tanzania, Namibia, Botswana, and Zimbabwe.

**Cheila Mutombene** is the executive director of Zayrah Africa Mozambique, a youth platform for youth rights and development. She previously worked as a mentor for the Civil Society Support Mechanism in the Gaza Province, and a gender and development programme officer at the Centre for Mozambican and International Studies. Before this, she was a research and advocacy programme officer at the Centro de Estudos para o Desenvolvimento da Juventude ('Youth Development Studies Centre') and programme officer at the Mozambican Youth Parliament, a national non-governmental organisation. She holds a BA Honours in Political Science from Eduardo Mondlane University. Her research interests are human rights; public policy; democratic politics; gender and human rights; social inclusion; and Africa Studies.

**Lengwe-Katembula Mwansa** was a professor at UB's Department of Social Work and recently retired. He taught various courses at the undergraduate and postgraduate levels. He started his teaching career at UNZA in 1979 as a staff development fellow. He continued lecturing after completing his MSW degree at the McGill University in Canada and PhD degree at the Heller Graduate School, Brandeis University, USA. He has held various portfolios including the head of Social Work at the Universities of Botswana and Zambia. He was the founding president of the Association of Schools of Social Work in Africa, by the same token as the vice president of the International Association of Schools of Social Work. He has received several academic awards and was the first recipient of the Catherine Kendal award in 2005. He has researched topical issues and published widely in professional journals, books and presented papers at conferences, workshops, and seminars. His interests were youth and children, and Social Work Education in Africa.

**Daniel Kabunduli Nkhata** is an assistant lecturer in the Department of Social Work at Cunima. Currently, he is at Wits studying for a MA degree in Industrial Sociology. He holds a BASS degree in General Sociology (Honours) from Africa University in Zimbabwe and a BA degree in Development Sociology (Honours) from Wits, South Africa. His current research interests are in labour policy; precariousness in Southern Africa; occult economies; experiences of capital in rural communities; black markets for human organs; and articulations of class formation in rural Malawi.

**Dolly Ntseane** completed her undergraduate degree at UB in 1981 and then proceeded to pursue a postgraduate Diploma in Youth Development at the Commonwealth Youth Programme, Chandigarh, India, in 1982. She obtained her MSW degree in Social Policy and Administration from the Columbia University, School of Social Work, New York (1985-1987) and in 1997 obtained a PhD in Social Welfare Policy from the Brandeis University. In 2016, she completed certificate training in Bioethics at the Johns Hopkins Fogarty African Bioethics Training Programme. She is one of the founding members of the Department of Social Work. Before teaching at UB, she worked in the Department of Social and Community Development, Ministry of Local Government. In the area of research and publications, she has published numerous journal articles, book chapters, monographs, and unpublished reports. She has presented academic papers at conferences in the areas of social protection, HIV/Aids, gender-based violence, marriage and family issues, and human security. She has served in numerous policy evaluation studies aimed at policy change and reforms in Botswana.

**Leah Natujwa Omari** is an assistant lecturer, head of the Quality Assurance and Control Unit, and the head of the Links and Cooperation Unit at the Institute of Social Work, Tanzania. She is an external examiner at the Mwalimu Nyerere Memorial Academy. She has several publications related to the social work profession, especially on teenage pregnancy in Tanzania and the use of case management as a means of reducing the problem in Tanzania. She is currently pursuing her PhD studies in Sociology at the University of Dar es Salaam, Tanzania. She holds a MA degree in Sociology from the University of Dar es Salaam, Tanzania, a postgraduate Diploma in Development Studies from Kimmage Manor, Dublin, Ireland, and an advanced Diploma in Social Work from the National Social Welfare Training Institute (currently known as Institute of Social Work), Kijitonyama, Dar es Salaam, Tanzania.

**Fabiola Ramsamy** is a lecturer in Social Work at the UOM. She has extensive experience after working as a practitioner in the social sector, including working with vulnerable groups, in government poverty alleviation and community empowerment programmes. Fabiola has held managerial positions in funding bodies for social development projects and locally based international institutions. She has been involved in human rights advocacy work with civil society organisations and has been providing social development consultancy services.

**Morena J. Rankopo** (PhD) is a senior lecturer and coordinator of graduate social work programmes at the UB. He joined the department as a staff development fellow and rose through the ranks to become a senior lecturer. He has co-edited a book, HIV/Aids and Social Welfare: Issues in Prevention Management and Care, 2010, and published several book chapters and journal articles on social work and community development. He is actively involved in research on community development; indigenous social work education and practice; volunteerism; HIV/Aids; disaster risk reduction and management; and gender development. His latest book chapters are on community development in Botswana and health fortunes of Botswana, issues of sustainability.

**Cristina Udelsmann Rodrigues** is a senior researcher at the Nordic Africa Institute in Sweden. She holds a PhD in Interdisciplinary African Studies from the University Institute of Lisbon, where she was a post-doctoral fellow. She was a post-doctoral fellow at the University Bordeaux IV in African Studies and Development. Previously, she worked for the University Institute of Lisbon as a senior researcher and lecturer of the Master's programme in African Studies (African Sociology; Globalisation and Development in Africa) and the Agostinho Neto Universiteit (Universidade Agostinho Neto), Angola, as an invited lecturer in the Doctorate in Social Sciences programme. She has published widely in the areas of urban studies; social development; and related fields; especially, in the context of Africa and the Portuguese speaking countries. She has presented papers at various symposia in Africa as well as abroad. She participated in different collaborative research projects and coordinated a number of them, namely: Poverty and Peace in the Portuguese Speaking African Countries; Identity and Borders in Africa; Sociospatial Reconfigurations in Cities of Angola and Mozambique; Urban to Rural Migration and Settlement in Angola and Mozambique.

**Hetty Rose-Junius** holds a PhD in Social Sciences and a BA degree from Unisa, MSW and a Master's of Sociology from UCT; a BSW (Honours) from the University of the Western Cape (UWC). She was a lecturer and senior lecturer at UWC before returning to Namibia to hold a position of chief social worker in the government's service and as a probation officer in the youth and children's courts of Windhoek. She began her career as a lecturer at the then Academy for Tertiary Education and Children's Courts in Windhoek. She then lectured at UNAM in Windhoek where she was the head of the Department for Social Work for 12 years and simultaneously acted as Dean of Students. She participated in international research on Intimate Partner Violence under the auspices of the World Health Organisation.

**Corine Saupin** currently works as a lecturer in the field of Social Work in the Faculty of Social Sciences and Humanities at UOM. She has more than 12 years' experience at this level. Her areas of interest are the following: socially disadvantaged populations; ethnic relations; intercultural social work; teaching practices and sharing of knowledge in social work; advocacy and animal rights and welfare. Before her academic career, she was involved in market and social research in a leading private research organisation in Mauritius. She holds a BSW (Honours) degree from UOM, and a MA degree, with specialisation in Sociology, by research, from Griffith University, Queensland, Australia.

**Boitumelo Seepamore** is a lecturer in the Department of Social Work at UKZN and obtained a PhD from UKZN, South Africa. She previously worked at the Speaker's Office at the City of Johannesburg and the Perinatal HIV/Aids Research Unit at the Chris Hani Baragwanath Hospital in Johannesburg. She obtained her BSW and MSW from Wits.

**Mzwandile Sobantu** is a lecturer in the Department Social Work at UJ and has a PhD from UJ as well. He also has a BSW and a Master of Housing degree from Wits. He has worked in the non-governmental and government sectors. In government, he worked at the Department of Social Development in Gauteng. His research niche areas include housing; social development; social policy; and older persons. He has presented several papers on housing and: decolonising spatiality; older persons; human rights; social development in South Africa at conferences in Africa and overseas.

**Vilanti Tambulasi** is a public health lecturer at Cunima in the Social Work Department with research interests in the areas of public health; gender and women's rights; disability; education; early childhood development; child protection and welfare; and reproductive health. Previously, she worked as a staff associate and lecturer at the Lilongwe University of Agriculture and Natural Resources, and before that as a secondary school teacher with the Government of Malawi at Likangala Secondary School. She has published articles and presented papers at international conferences. She holds a Master of Public Health degree from the College of Medicine at the University of Malawi and a Bachelor of Education (B.Ed.) degree obtained from the Chancellor College at the University of Malawi.

**Agnes Wizi** is an experienced qualitative social researcher, communications specialist, educator, development practitioner and social worker. She has eight years' experience working in tertiary education supplemented with an extensive academic background in social work; development studies; qualitative social research; participatory (action) research framework; policy and evaluative research; education; sociology; social policy; youth work; international development; communication; community practice and policies. Agnes holds an MSW from Durham University, UK, and a B.Ed. Degree from the University of Malawi. She currently teaches in the Social Work Department at Cunima, where she is the department's research coordinator.

**Mpumelelo Ncube** holds a PhD in Social work. He is current the Head of Department and Senior Lecturer of social work at the University of the Free State. He further supervisees post graduate research students. His areas of academic interest include supervision in social work, developmental social welfare, research and social policy. He has previously been an academic at the University of Johannesburg. He also worked in the public, private and NGO sectors prior to joining academia.

# FOREWORD

In this book, African scholars, academics, and practitioners provide a deep and critical reflection of social welfare, social work, and related disciplines during the colonial and post-colonial era, a period characterised by a deliberate move by Africa's political administrations to focus on nation-building and to attempt to make Africa a global player. Despite being endowed with rich natural resources like minerals; arable land; and solid family and extended family life, the continent is weak globally. Furthermore, the book focuses on the pre-colonial period – a golden thread running through the chapters. The book discusses the colonial era when Western countries' capture and oppression of Africa characterised the continent's history.

In Southern Africa and other regions, the colonialists sometimes went to war for ownership and control of the continent's gold, diamonds and other mineral resources and arable land. In the process, the indigenous Africans and local communities were stripped of their lands and became cheap migrant labourers in the industrial and strategic economically viable parts of the region. In the African countries mentioned in the book, there was a deliberate exclusion of indigenous Africans, particularly as benefactors of the wealth they generated and could not control. Africans were subjected to selective education, low investment in local human capital development and limited access to social welfare systems. This strategy was a tool to control and guarantee cheap labour as well as have enough stability to safeguard colonial interests. Thus, regimes of selective and differentiated welfare, social security and social protection systems emerged in the colonial era in Southern Africa.

Interestingly, the post-colonial period, particularly the latter part of the twentieth century, is characterised by African political administrations committed to rebuild the African continent and to eliminate poverty on the continent. Thus, in the 1960s and 1970s, principles of inclusion; universal access to basic services; mutual accountability; good governance; human rights; non-discrimination; and communalism underpinned African welfare systems, and continental, and national social development and social security plans as well as declarations committed to these principles. Nevertheless, the noble agenda for development in Africa seems to be destabilised by covert and overt distractions.

This book is an appropriate publication at this point in our history; a resource that can be used to generate appropriate narratives and questions within the social welfare and social development sector, particularly on delivery, education and training.

Professor Fikile N.M Mazibuko
*University of KwaZulu-Natal*
*Former Head of Department*

# ACKNOWLEDGEMENTS

I would like to extend my heartfelt thanks to all authors who participated in this project.

# DEDICATION

This book is dedicated to the memory of the late Professor,
Brian William McKendrick (4/10/1938 – 1/05/2016),
a scholar, mentor and social work educator who touched many lives.
May his soul rest in peace.

# ACRONYMS

| | |
|---|---|
| Abako | Association Culturelle des Bakongo (DRC) |
| ACVV | Afrikaans Christian Women's Association (*Afrikaanse Christelike Vroue Vereniging*, South Africa) |
| ANC | African National Congress (South Africa) |
| ASSWOT | Association of Schools of Social Work in Tanzania |
| BEAM | Basic Education Assistance Module (Zimbabwe) |
| BSP | Basic Social Protection (Mozambique) |
| BSAC | British South Africa Company |
| BSW | Bachelor of Social Work |
| CBOs | Community Based Organisations |
| Cosatu | Congress of South African Trade Unions |
| CSOs | Civil Society Organisations |
| CSP | Compulsory Social Protection (Mozambique) |
| Cunima | Catholic University of Malawi |
| DRC | The Democratic Republic of the Congo |
| DSS | Department of Social Services (Zimbabwe) |
| DSSW | Department of Sociology and Social Work (South Africa) |
| DSW | Department of Social Welfare |
| GAPVU | Office for Support of Vulnerable Population (Mozambique) |
| GDP | Gross Domestic Product |
| GEAR | Growth Employment and Redistribution (South Africa) |
| HDI | Human Development Index |
| HIPC | Highly Indebted Poor Country |

| | |
|---|---|
| HIV/Aids | Human Immunodeficiency Virus / Acquired Immunodeficiency Syndrome |
| IFSW | International Federation of Social Workers |
| IMF | International Monetary Fund |
| INAS | National Institute for Social Action (*Instituto Nacional de Acção Social*, Mozambique) |
| INSS | National Institute for Social Security (*Instituto Nacional de Segurança Social*, Angola) |
| LP | Labour Party (South Africa) |
| MACOSS | Mauritius Council of Social Services |
| MNC | Congolese National Movement (*Movement National Congolais*) |
| MPI | Multidimensional Poverty Index |
| MSW | Master of Social Work |
| NCPA | National Costed Plan of Action (Tanzania) |
| NDP | National Development Plan |
| NGK | Dutch Reformed Church ('Nederduitse Gereformeerde Kerk', South Africa) |
| NGO | Non-Governmental Organisation |
| NP | National Party (South Africa) |
| OVC | Orphans and Vulnerable Children |
| PA | Public Assistance (Zimbabwe) |
| PF | Patriotic Front (Zambia) |
| PSA | Food Subsidy Programme (*Programa Subsídios de Alimentos*, Mozambique) |
| PWAS | Public Welfare Assistance Scheme (Zambia) |
| RDP | Reconstruction and Development Programme (South Africa) |

| | |
|---|---|
| RRS | Recruitment and the Retention Strategy (South Africa) |
| SADC | Southern African Development Community |
| SAP | Structural Adjustment Programme (Malawi) |
| SAVF | Suid-Afrikaanse Vrouefederasie ('South African Women's Federation', South Africa) |
| SDA | Social Dimension of Adjustment (Malawi) |
| SSW | School of Social Work (Zimbabwe) |
| SWO | Social Welfare Officer |
| TASWO | Tanzania Social Workers Organisation |
| TESWEP | Tanzania Emerging Schools of Social Work Programme |
| UB | University of Botswana |
| UCT | University of Cape Town (South Africa) |
| UJ | University of Johannesburg (South Africa) |
| UKZN | University of KwaZulu-Natal |
| UNAIDS | Joint United Nations Programme on HIV/Aids |
| UNAM | University of Namibia |
| UNDP | United Nations Development Programme |
| UNESWA | University of Eswatini (formerly known as the University of Swaziland) |
| UNICEF | United Nations Children's Fund |
| UNIP | United National Independence Party |
| Unisa | University of South Africa |
| UNZA | University of Zambia |
| UOM | University of Mauritius |
| UWC | University of Western Cape (South Africa) |
| UZ | University of Zimbabwe |

| WHO | World Health Organisation |
| Wits | University of the Witwatersrand (South Africa) |
| WNLA | Witwatersrand Native Labour Association (South Africa) |
| ZANU-PF | Zimbabwe African National Union-Patriotic Front |

# PREFACE

This book is written by Southern African social welfare, social work, social development, social security and social policy academics, practitioners and advocates who have varying degrees of experience. The authors who contributed chapters to this book added their perspectives to ongoing debates about academic areas in the region. Thus, the book's primary objective is to discuss the development of social welfare and social work in Southern Africa. In doing so, it endeavours to contribute to the existing body of knowledge on social welfare and social work in the region. The chapters are examined through different theoretical lenses and historical perspectives.

The Editor made a deliberate effort to include the perspectives of the Lusophone bloc and French-speaking spheres of Southern Africa. Thus, there are chapters in the book that cover Angola, the Democratic Republic of the Congo (DRC), Mauritius and Mozambique. Arguably, there is not much interaction between English, French and Portuguese speaking countries of the region when it comes to academic work and research endeavours. Indeed, it seems like academics and practitioners in Southern African countries continue to work in their inherited colonial academic silos several decades into the post-colonial era. Therefore, when initiatives of this nature are undertaken in the English-speaking countries of the region, usually the voices of academics and practitioners in the former Portuguese, French and Belgian colonies are rarely or seldom considered. The fact that Southern Africa is dominated by former British colonies partly explains this distorted scenario.

Lastly, the finalisation of the chapter on the Democratic Republic of the Congo (DRC) deserves special mention. Alain Kambale Maboko, the author of this chapter, had to escape to safety when there was a rebel insurgency in his hometown. He is based in the eastern DRC, which is still the most volatile part of this conflict-ridden country. For the better part of writing his chapter, an Ebola epidemic ravaged the eastern DRC as well. Maboko must specifically be mentioned for his efforts and the heroic act of writing a chapter amid chaos, death, and human misery. As a young civil society actor, Maboko was undeterred and finished writing his chapter. He even followed through and corrected his work in dangerous conditions after I reviewed his first draft. What he did was not an easy feat, and I duly recognise his courage and steadfastness. Therefore, after he submitted his chapter, I was even more than convinced that I had made the right decision to include young social development practitioners like Maboko in this book. Maboko's resilience should give all in Southern Africa, and Africa, the hope that one day the DRC and our continent will be an oasis of peace and prosperity because there are young people like him, committed to making a difference in the lives of ordinary Congolese and Africans.

I hope that this book will bring forth fresh perspectives on social welfare and social work in Southern Africa. This book is intended for a wide audience of social welfare and social work students, academics, and policymakers in Southern Africa and on the African continent. It seeks to cater to social scientists, academics, and students of allied disciplines of social development; social policy; public policy; social security; sociology; and development studies.

Ndangwa Noyoo

*University of Cape Town*

*January 2020*

# Introduction

*Ndangwa Noyoo*

Southern Africa is a unique part of Africa, endowed with large deposits of mineral resources such as cobalt, coltan, copper, diamonds, gold, iron ore, silver, tin, uranium, zinc; semi-precious stones like amethyst, emeralds, rubies; and many more. It has large tracts of arable land, a temperate climate and abundant water sources, in some parts. Partly due to this, Southern Africa attracted a disproportionately large number of European settlers in comparison to other parts of Africa. These Europeans wanted to not only exploit the region's resources but establish permanent settlements for themselves. A unique feature of this colonial foray is how colonialism had deeply penetrated Southern Africa. In some countries like Angola, Mozambique and South Africa, colonialism spanned several centuries. In others, such as Zambia, colonial rule had lasted only 40 years. Hence, colonial rule had different nuances in Southern Africa.

Nevertheless, European settlers attempted to carve out their own countries in this region and sever ties with their mother countries in Europe. They had also attempted to completely exist separately from most indigenous African populations in the territories they subjugated. The large numbers of European settlers choosing to create their own countries in Southern Africa depicted a situation not obtained in other parts of Africa. This situation probably only resembled that of Kenya, where there was a large settler population. In most of Africa, there was usually a small European population that did not seek to create permanent settlements but saw colonies as outposts, needing to be exploited, for their natural resources to be exported back to Europe.

1

Before colonial domination, Southern Africa was ruled by different indigenous and in some instances, highly organised polities for thousands of years. In many parts of the region, powerful kingdoms, equally overseen by strong, powerful kings and queens, were in charge of land and people's lives. Some of these indigenous polities were re-configured during the great dispersion or *Mfecane or Difaqane* – meaning 'destroyed in war' or 'forced removals' in the Nguni or Sotho languages of South Africa. These upheavals stemmed from the rise of the Zulu nation and Shaka's wars of conquest, leading to various Nguni and Sotho tribes migrating northwards, roughly between 1815-1840. Nevertheless, it is noteworthy that the antecedent of these upheavals was the settlers' encroachment on the indigenous people's land. The Europeans had already started annexing the lands of the indigenous polities and thus fuelled intra-ethnic warfare resulting in the *Mfecane/ Difaqane*. These ethnic groups later influenced changes in the countries they settled, such as Malawi, Mozambique, Namibia, Tanzania, Zambia, and Zimbabwe. The island nations of Madagascar, Mauritius and Seychelles are part of Southern Africa and were drawn into the mercantile and transatlantic slave trade, with first the Portuguese and Dutch playing leading roles in this arena, before France and Britain took over. Slaves were forcefully removed from mainland Africa and Indonesia to provide work in, among other things, the burgeoning sugar industry on these islands. Later, indentured labour was brought in from India to work on the sugar plantations of Mauritius and South Africa's former British Natal Province, now called KwaZulu-Natal.

For purposes of this book, Southern Africa represents countries that belong to the regional economic bloc of the Southern African Development Community (SADC). These are Angola, Botswana, the Democratic Republic of the Congo (DRC), Lesotho, Malawi, Madagascar, Mauritius, Mozambique, Namibia, Seychelles, South Africa, Swaziland, Tanzania, Zambia, and Zimbabwe. In 2015, the estimated population of the SADC was 318.9 million, and in 2016 it had increased to 327.2 million, representing a 2.6 per cent annual population growth rate. The largest population share in the region in 2016 was in the DRC (26.6 per cent) followed by South Africa (17.1 per cent) and Tanzania (15.3 per cent). Today, all countries in the region are sovereign nation-states.

Nevertheless, it can be noted that all Southern African countries exhibit colonial imprints and are still contending with the legacy of colonialism. These countries' political and administrative systems still mirror those of their former colonial masters in many respects.

The existing political and administrative systems of Southern Africa are derivatives of their former colonising countries from Europe, *viz*: Belgium, the United Kingdom, France, Portugal, the Netherlands and South Africa (a mixture of British and Dutch traditions and itself a local coloniser). The League of Nations mandated South Africa to oversee Namibia (then known as South-West Africa) after the defeat of Germany in the First World War. Namibia had been a German colony since 1884. Inevitably, this colonial history of the region shaped the development of formalised social welfare systems and gave birth to the social work profession.

Therefore, when discussing the origins of social welfare and work in Southern Africa, it is important to remember the European religious factor, as many missionary organisations were the first to offer rudimentary social welfare and social work services to indigenous populations. However, this is not to say that there were no existing indigenous social welfare or social security systems in Southern Africa before the advent of colonial rule. They did exist, however, the colonialists and bizarrely even the region's post-colonial governments never formalised and mainstreamed them.

## Rationale for the book

Many of the authors of this book wanted to provide scholarly work about this book's focus: the development and evolution of social welfare and social work in Southern Africa. They took cognisance of the challenges they faced in teaching social welfare and social work in their respective countries due to, among others, a lack of information about social work's and social welfare's development in the Southern African context. There are still gaps and missing links about social welfare's and social work's origins in former British, Belgian, French and Portuguese territories. Thus, this book endeavours to provide scholarship on social welfare and social work in Africa by indigenous Southern African academics, practitioners, and other experts.

## Aim of the Book

This book aims to provide information on the historical and contemporary social welfare and social work, and by extension, social security and social protection trends of different countries of Southern Africa. Specifically, it attempts to respond to the needs of Southern African academics, policy- and lawmakers, practitioners in the social development sector, and students, among others.

## Conceptualising Social Welfare and Social Work in Southern Africa

Normative positions on social welfare anchor this work, and moving from a normative premise, social welfare is conceived in its most progressive and inclusive form. Therefore, a definition of social welfare befitting this perspective emphasises the idea of it being a state or condition of human wellbeing. It denotes a condition of being or doing well.[1] According to Segal (2016), in the term 'social welfare', 'social' speaks to the collective nature of society, as citizens are part of many systems.[2] Thus, systems combine to form the larger society. Furthermore, Zastrow (2010) observes that the goal of social welfare is to fulfil the social, financial, health, and recreational requirements of all individuals in a society.[3] Social welfare seeks to enhance the social functioning of all age groups, both rich and poor.

Therefore, when other institutions in society, for example, the market economy and the family, fail to meet the basic needs of individuals or groups of people, social services are needed and demanded.[4] In Africa, the extended family and kin still fulfil social welfare functions, just as they had responded to the needs of individuals in the pre-colonial era. Despite being eroded by colonialism, urbanisation and modernisation, the extended family system is still functioning in most of Africa and meeting the needs of its members. In the same vein, due to the former forces, African societies followed almost the same trajectory of European countries, where the meeting of needs was based at a formal level. Therefore, formal systems and in this case, the formal social welfare systems of the region are by-products of colonial rule. They were imported from Europe and superimposed on Africa. That is how social welfare systems took on their institutional character in Africa. In this regard, social welfare refers to a system of arrangements, programmes, mechanisms – formal or informal, governmental or non-governmental – that try to meet the needs of individuals and families who cannot fulfil such needs with their resources.[5]

---

1     Midgley, 1997; Burch, 1999.
2     Segal, 2016:2.
3     Zastrow, 2010:2
4     Ibid.
5     Johnson, Schwartz & Tate, 1997.

Typically, social work in Africa is a result of social welfare systems, and its development was dependent on the establishment of the latter in colonial Africa.

Midgley (1997) points out that a major innovation in the promotion of social welfare was the emergence of professional social workers in the mid-nineteenth century. Social work was an entirely new approach to dealing with social problems. For the first time, professionally trained personnel were available to assist individuals and their families to deal with their problems. It is important to note that social welfare systems need policies to govern them. Therefore, social welfare policy refers to the principles, activities or action frameworks adopted by a government to ensure a socially defined level of the individual, family, and community wellbeing.[6] Social welfare policy is thus one type of public policy and gives effect to social welfare programmes.[7] It is an essential part of any social worker's repertoire because it defines and shapes social welfare programmes such as income support, employment, housing, healthcare and food.[8] In some measure, social welfare policy covers 'the fields of practice' or 'welfare provision' in "social security, education and training, housing, health and community care services, work and training services, criminal justice services and policy, and personal services".[9]

Social welfare and social work are primarily related to the level of practice.[10] Social welfare seeks to mobilise financial resources needed for social workers to intervene on behalf of vulnerable groups. Thus, social welfare is a discretionary spending choice that provides necessities for the poor through taxes.[11] According to the International Federation of Social Workers (IFSW) and the International Association of Schools of Social Work (IASSW), social work is a practice-based profession and an academic discipline that promotes social change and development, social cohesion, and the empowerment and liberation of people.[12] Principles of social justice, human rights, collective responsibility and respect for diversities are central to social work. Underpinned by theories of social

---

6     Blau & Abramovitz, 2010:21.
7     Ibid.
8     Ibid.
9     Walsh, Stephens & Moore, 2000:19.
10    Zastrow, 2010.
11    Burch, 1999.
12    IFSW & IASSW, 2014.

work, social sciences, humanities and indigenous knowledge, social work engages people and structures to address life challenges and enhance wellbeing.

Social work emerged in nineteenth-century Europe, specifically Victorian England, to respond to social problems of that era and it then spread to North America and other Western countries. In Africa and Southern Africa, social welfare and social work cannot be discussed in isolation of colonial rule. Both are inextricably linked to the colonial mission. Like all the chapters in this book show, colonialism had brought new ways of organising society and responding to human needs. Thus colonialism was inimical to the wellbeing of the indigenous peoples of Africa. Hence, the formalised form of social welfare in Africa can be traced back to the colonial order, legitimised by the philosophy of race superiority and enforced through a highly hierarchical socio-political system. At the apex of this order were the Europeans, accorded all the social, economic, and political advantages.

Africans always occupied the lowest rung of the colonial social ladder, while Asians or the mixed-race population had certain privileges. Colonial society was extremely patriarchal and not open to the advancement of women. Women, just as the 'natives', had to know their place in this society and were not expected to aspire any higher than the colonial socio-political and economical ceiling. In instances where social welfare services were provided to women, they sought to maintain the 'good native wife', in her place, catering to her husband's needs. The husband was, in turn, expected to provide cheap labour to various commercial ventures in the colony. Women were not educated above a certain level; a move meant to curtail their upward social mobility.

The creation of welfare systems in the African colonies was heavily dependent on certain specific developments. Significantly, the Great Depression of the 1920s and 1930s, and the Second World War stand out as main catalysts behind the creation of welfare systems in the colonial territories. These two dislocating forces inadvertently triggered positive responses from European states in the form of comprehensive and high-quality social welfare systems for their citizens. Governments in Europe began to provide better social welfare services, and they were compelled by circumstances, to respond humanely to their colonial subjects. This changed attitude was tempered by two realities: economic and security. Firstly, the Great Depression had led to a fall in prices of many of the colonies' commodities on European markets. An outcome of this was dwindling revenues, critical to both the imperial countries' and the colonies' social and economic development pursuits. Social problems were increasing in the colonies and burdening their already politically volatile urban environment. Colonial subjects were getting disgruntled and began to demand better living conditions.[13] Therefore, colonial authorities' provision of social welfare services started to be crucial to the lives of colonial subjects. The Second World War had fundamentally transformed imperialism and led to a re-think of the European countries' imperial desires. Against Nazi and fascist threats, Western Europe had galvanised its colonial subjects towards the war effort under the banner of justice and freedom. This colonialists' stance had the unintended consequence of raising African people's desire to search for and demand self-rule.[14]

Britain and France were able to mobilise millions of Africans and Asians to fight against Nazi Germany and its allies. Africans were agreeable to fight this 'common enemy' and were even misled into believing that their sacrifices were for the good of all humanity. When the war was over, African veterans returned to their homes with high expectations. The war experiences served to raise political consciousness amongst Africans and made them realise that the concept of racial superiority was fallacious and could be challenged. Some colonial subjects had proved themselves more valiant on the battlefield than their European counterparts. Others had even earned themselves medals of valour; despite the racist conditions in colonial armies. Later, some of these individuals would become fierce opponents of colonial rule and add momentum to the drive for independence. Their ability to use modern weapons was an important factor for armed revolution and guerrilla warfare in colonial territories. In Kenya, for example, Dedan Kimathi, who fought in the Second World War for the British Empire would later lead the famous Mau-Mau rebellion. The uprising was instrumental in sowing the seeds against British rule in that country. It helped to galvanise the nationalists around the call for independence, which was eventually achieved in 1963.[15]

During this process, there arose dissenting voices against the status quo in Europe as well as the continued colonial occupation of African and Asian territories, because the post-war European continent was experiencing critical changes that threatened the old order. Many sections of European nations made strident demands for the State to entrench

---

13   Midgley, 1995; Noyoo, 2013.
14   Noyoo, 2013.
15   Ibid.

the notion of 'inclusive citizenry' and to uphold, people's rights. In the same vein, some progressive Europeans challenged their governments over their colonial agendas and began pushing them to relinquish their colonies. They called on their governments to make provision for better entitlements for their citizens. Thus, colonialism began to be a past relic, and the establishment of welfare states in Europe characterised this period. In this atmosphere, the African people's call for self-determination resonated with some sections of Europe and the United States. Increasingly, many imperial governments found themselves with no choice but to undertake reforms in their colonial territories, in some cases, to 'prepare' the indigenous people for self-government. Again, one instrument regarded as critical to the advancement of colonial subjects was social welfare.

It is important to note that social welfare systems were patterned differently in different colonial territories because they usually mirrored the political and administrative systems of the colonising powers.

## Different Colonial Regimes in Africa's Social Welfare Agendas

In this section, the colonial welfare regimes in different African countries inherited at independence, are closely examined.

### The British Experience

The British Empire's initial efforts regarding social welfare activities in its colonies can be traced back to the *Colonial Development Act of 1929*. In the British colonial sphere, social welfare interventions were predicated on the understanding that only urban Africans in the 'detribalised' areas could qualify for such assistance. The British authorities had always believed that the extended family was the safety-net, crucial to Africans in need. By the 1930s, the Colonial Office had made concerted efforts to avail social welfare services to indigenous people. The gradual abandonment of the principle of passive colonial trusteeship in favour of a more active one characterised this period. Some officials at the Colonial Office had begun to identify themselves with ordinary local people and to regard themselves as true guardians of their humanitarian interests.[16] The Colonial Office's role had hitherto been largely reactive, shaped by ad hoc responses

---

16    Lewis, 2000.

to local developments, cemented by the idea of trusteeship, and limited by a concern to respect the substantial autonomy the colonial governments enjoyed under devolved British rule.[17]

In later years, the Colonial Office was compelled to stress 'development', necessitating the need for a combined approach to development problems. The education sector generally paid attention to this approach before other fields. For example, an official statement of policy that the Colonial Office issued in 1925, insisted that every department of government concerning people's welfare or vocational teaching to cooperate closely with educational policy, including the Departments of Health, Public Works, Railways, and Agriculture. By 1940, most of the African colonies, and a good number of those in the West Indies and Fiji, had either nutrition or development committees.[18] Therefore, the intervening war years added momentum to these initiatives, and hence, the Colonial Development and Welfare Act got passed in 1940. Consequently, the number of colonial civil servants increased after the war – known as the 'Second Colonial Occupation' – and guidelines were issued on the establishment of social welfare departments.[19]

Thus, social services and community development activities became the hallmarks of social welfare interventions in British colonial Africa. For the first time, social welfare was used to address the increasing social ills in the colonies. Though paternalistic or at times misplaced, this attitude was nonetheless crucial to changing the social and economic atmosphere in the colonies. Against the wartime mobilisation of the empire's resources background; metropolitan discussions on post-war reconstruction; and the advent of a Labour Government; two critical factors informed the Colonial Office's changed attitude towards the colonies: Firstly, the colonial state took on new responsibilities in directing local economies, mirroring the growth of collectivism in Britain, and prompting discussions on the State's role in future economic development. Secondly, during the 1940s, the Colonial Office increasingly, if temporarily, became the driving force in colonial policy initiatives, disturbing the traditional balance of power between London and the colonial governments and further exposing weaknesses in local development machinery.[20] In this regard, the vagaries of indirect rule finally had to make

---

17    Butler, 1997.

18    Mair, 1944.

19    Lewis, 2000.

20    Butler, 1997:3.

way for the rhetoric of welfare and development to show that the imperial mission was neither finished nor a failure. The dialectical relationship between war and welfare in metropolitan Britain began a new phase in empire state-building in Africa.[21]

Afterwards, the Colonial Office was obliged to be more assertive and above all, to anticipate local developments and devise new policies, methods, and machinery, centred around the goal of achieving controlled decolonisation at the time London deemed appropriate. Britain was at this time under increasing pressure to justify its colonial role to domestic, colonial and international opinion.[22] The indigenous peoples' agitation against colonial rule through protest, civil unrest and warfare contributed to general uncertainty in metropolitan countries. The drive for self-rule was gaining momentum, and it was not coincidental that countries like Britain were ready to make concessions.

However, some African nationalist organisations had not wholly rejected the colonial set-up, and they had only sought to reform and not radically transform it. Negotiated independence was the route taken by a good number of nationalist independence movements. There would be an almost transplant of metropolitan institutions through entrenched constitutional provisions and a Westminster type of democracy, in the case of British colonies once self-rule was achieved. Encouraged to modernise trusteeship but to enjoy little in the way of an extensive state structure or easy access to civil society, empire administrators looked to improve African welfare as the metropolitan launched its welfare state. Conditions overseas were different, however. Colonies had fewer resources, no single moral authority and little in the form of a waged labour force that could afford to contribute to national welfare.[23]

## The French Example

While the British were more concerned with protecting the extended African family, the French essentially applauded its dissolution, viewing the demise of the 'traditional' collectivists as the liberation of the individual. Due to this and other things, the French metropole subsidised social service provision in the colonies through the Investment Funds for Economic and Social Development (*Fonds d'Investissement pour le Development*

---

21    Lewis, 2000.
22    Butler, 1997.
23    Lewis, 2000.

*Economique et Sociale*) as early as 1928.[24] However, social service delivery was only one branch of French social policy. The other was social security, namely, retirement and invalidity pensions, accidents and sickness benefits, family- and maternity allowances. The French and British practices diverged sharply here. In most British colonies, the only benefit available at independence covered occupational injury – a provision instituted in the 1940s at the employers' expense.[25] Most French colonies, by contrast, legislated provisions during the 'compassionate' 1950s for sickness, maternity, employment injury, family and sometimes retirement benefits – generally financed from employers' and workers' contributions. The benefits covered only a relatively small group – urban workers in large enterprises, rarely more than 10 per cent of the economically active – and therefore did little to alleviate poverty directly. However, their 'trickle down' effects may have been considerable.[26] The French had a more expansive provision of social services and had discussed the need for a broader social insurance system as early as 1910.[27]

As with Britain, significant reforms took place in the French colonies during and after the Second World War. Inevitably, developments in France had implications for the colonies. For instance, the establishment of the French social security system in 1945 profoundly influenced events in the French colonies. The French welfare state had attributes of both the British and German Bismarckian models. It was characterised by state-funded social services as well as a compulsory insurance system. Thus, social welfare in the French colonies focused more on the provision of health and social security programmes. As noted above, although several nationalist parties challenged colonial rule in the French African colonies, some colonial subjects in these areas were not keen on independence but wanted citizenship rights within the French state. They wanted to be citizens of France, and their demands were not for severance of ties with their colonial 'master'. Nonetheless, the demands for self-government only received favourable attention from the government of the Free French, that replaced the Vichy administration, a surrogate of Nazi Germany during the German occupation in the Second World War.

---

24    MacLean, 2010.
25    Iliffe, 1987.
26    Ibid:208.
27    MacLean, 2010.

## The Belgian Case

After the Berlin Conference of 1884-1885, dubbed the 'Scramble for Africa', other European nations granted King Leopold II of Belgium the area known as the Congo. He named it the 'Congo Free State' as he wanted to keep this place as a 'free-trade zone'. Initially, the Congo was the only territory falling under the Belgian sphere and as a private estate of Leopold II (essentially regarding the Congo as his investment). Due to this and other issues, the Congo under Leopold II had experienced the worst forms of brutal oppression. He committed atrocious acts against the indigenous people such as decapitating their limbs if they did not 'work hard enough' in the rubber plantations. Leopold decimated the local population almost to half its size. By 1908 the Belgian Government had forced him to surrender the territory (after a huge outcry from some of the enlightened quarters of Europe), and it was renamed the Belgian Congo. The Belgian Government and the Catholic missionaries began to provide social services such as education to the local people. Later, German-colonised Ruanda-Urundi (Rwanda and Burundi), were added to the Belgian colonies after the defeat of Germany in the First World War. The extension of Belgium's political and social struggles, after the Second World War, promoted speedier reforms in the colonies and created sharp shifts in colonial policy. Between 1945 and 1947, the Belgians put through various improvement schemes. From 1947 to about 1954, the Belgians attempted to meet the new challenges by a policy of 'cautious assimilation' whereby 'advanced' Africans received privileges. At the same time, the Belgians vainly tried to force Africans into the Western way of life.[28]

After the Belgian elections of 1954, a liberal-socialist coalition came to power. After that, the Belgians allowed more freedom of speech and publications in their colonies, and Africans obtained a greater share in local government. In the Congo, there was a new social welfare dispensation coupled with the building of two universities in the country. The Belgians aimed for gradual emancipation, but they were overtaken by events as Africans stepped up the fight for self-rule.[29] It has been observed that an elaborate social welfare system was established in the Belgian Congo without significant trade union pressure as part of the general policy of paternalism and an attempt to stabilise Katanga's labour force. Union Minière du Haut Katanga instituted an accident compensation scheme as early as 1928. Most other forms of social security followed in the 1950s, while in 1957

28    Okoth, 2006.

29    Ibid.

the Belgian authorities created the first extensive old-age pensions in tropical Africa. By 1959 it covered nearly a million workers.[30] The Belgian thrust was more towards social security, as in the case of the French, rather than towards social welfare as in British colonies. It is interesting to note that the example of Congo has similarities with that of Northern Rhodesia, later known as Zambia. Due to the wealth generated from copper and other minerals in this territory, the mining companies availed a more comprehensive social welfare dispensation to their workers than what the colonial authorities were providing to the rest of Northern Rhodesia's population. Thus, Zambia almost followed the same pattern as the Congo, where the country's mineral wealth (copper) was crucial in creating a somewhat advanced social welfare system (for colonial standards) in the Copperbelt region.

## The Portuguese Example

The Lisbon Government regarded the Portuguese territories as provinces, and freedom came late in these parts of Africa. It was only after various territorial liberation movements waged long and bitter wars in Angola, Guinea Bissau and Mozambique, that they were finally granted independence. With an authoritarian regime in Portugal and no democratic atmosphere existing in this country, the Portuguese made no moves to reform conditions in the colonies. Even after the onset of the liberation struggle, Portugal would steadfastly hold on to its prized possessions in the form of colonies. Portugal's citizens placed no demands on the regime due to its undemocratic nature. Hence, social welfare initiatives were not pronounced even in the mother country and were not as elaborate as in Britain or France, for example. Portugal had a weak economy and was generally poor in comparison to other European powers. Portugal was notorious for the brutal suppression of the political and civil liberties of the indigenous populace in its colonies. In many respects, Portuguese colonial rule was considered 'backwards' by 'European standards' with forced labour only abolished in the early 1960s. The Portuguese colonies covered an area of about two million km² (about five per cent of the entire continent and larger than the combined areas of Spain, France, Germany, Italy, and England). According to Amilcar Cabral, the charismatic leader of the armed struggle against Portuguese rule in Guinea Bissau, a small country, the 'most backward in Europe', enslaved the African population of these colonies. Discrimination based on race was openly practised while

---

30    Iliffe, 1987.

Africans were driven from fertile regions so that European farms could be built there.[31] Political, social or trade union organisation was forbidden to Africans, who did not enjoy even the most elementary human rights.

Thousands of workers from Angola, Mozambique and the Cape Verde Islands worked twelve hours a day on the settlers' farms in São Tomé, the heart of the equatorial zone. There was forced labour for public works in Guinea Bissau, Angola, and Mozambique; but in the latter two, it extended to privately-owned companies as well. Every year, 250 000 Angolans were rented out to agricultural, mining and construction concerns. Every year 400 000 Mozambicans were subjected to forced labour, and a 100 000 were exported to the mines of South Africa and Rhodesia.[32] Up until the 1950s, the Portuguese did not invest in education and other social services. While they believed that education was necessary to 'civilise' Africans, they were afraid that educated Africans would endanger Portuguese interests. Even in Portugal itself, the government was not spending enough to educate its citizens resulting in an illiteracy rate in 1960 of 40 per cent – the highest in Europe. In Africa, progress in this area was slow. In Angola (the most developed colony as far as education was concerned) in 1950, there were only 13 000 children in elementary schools, about 3 000 in secondary schools, and less than 2 000 in technical schools, out of a population of close to four million. The Catholic Church dominated the school system, and it concentrated on rudimentary education of three years to teach Portuguese culture and language.[33]

## Spanish Colonial Rule: Introduction of Social Welfare/Social Protection Systems

The Republic of Equatorial Guinea is sub-Saharan Africa's only Spanish-speaking nation, making it somewhat of a linguistic curiosity, and contributing to its political isolation from neighbouring countries. At the same time, the role of the national, ex-colonial language is significantly different in Equatorial Guinea than in most of English, French and Portuguese-speaking Africa.[34] Previously, Equatorial Guinea was referred to as Spanish Guinea. According to Aixelà (2013), barriers were established in the colony between

---

31      Vambe & Zegeye, 2008.
32      Ibid.
33      Falola, 2002:275.
34      Lipski, 2000.

the white immigrant population, who emigrated from Europe to work and manage the affairs of the colony, and the indigenous Guinean population, and the black migrants, hired and transported from nearby African countries to work on the plantations.[35] The contempt for the African population and the hierarchy explicit in all spheres of social life were part of the Eurocentric vision exposed in the writings of the explorer Burton, while he was Consul in Fernando Poo (1861-1864).

Spain's twentieth-century African colonies were extremely small, limited to Spanish Guinea, a strip of territory along the northern Moroccan coast, and a sparsely inhabited region in Western Sahara. Nonetheless, Spain's African empire stood at the heart of Francoist ideology and foreign policy during the early years of the regime. The language of the empire had been central to the discourse of Spanish nationalist and right-wing movements since the 'Disaster' of 1898 when Spain had lost its remaining Latin American and Asian colonies.[36] Francisco Franco Bahamonde was a dictator and a military general who ruled Spain from 1939, after the Nationalist victory in the Spanish Civil War (1936-1939) to 1975. Equatorial Guineans became increasingly familiar with the phenomenon of political exile from the 1950s when the Spanish Colonial Government brutally repressed the first nationalist demonstrations demanding independence.

Notably, the birth of various liberation movements from the 1950s resulted in Spanish Government reprisals and many independence fighters going into exile. Nevertheless, after Independence ethnic rivalries which had been encouraged by the Spanish colonialists continued, even to this day.

Colonial policies led to segregation, hierarchy, and inequality. During the colonial era, whites were given priority over the black African population, except in the case of the black Fernandino elite, who held a position at the top of the black population and could even be more powerful than whites.[37] According to Lipski (2000), colonial education was predominantly in the hands of missionary groups, particularly the Claret Order. Still, Spanish government schools played a significant role in implanting Spanish as an effective language of communication. The missionaries played important roles in the early and rudimentary forays into social welfare and social work. However, after its independence

---

35    Aixelà, 2013:57.
36    Brydan, 2018.
37    Aixelà, 2013.

on 12 October 1968, the political goals of integration and greater egalitarianism came to nothing as Equatorial Guinea entered a dictatorial loop, still in place today, and the Fang were prioritised over other ethnic groups. The President's Fang origins provided advantages to some groups, detrimental to others, through a national identity construct with a homogenous and non-inclusive design.[38]

## Italian Colonial Rule: Introduction of Social Welfare Systems

Italian colonialism, in comparison with the experiences of Britain, Spain, France, the Netherlands and Portugal, was limited both in time and space. It lasted only 60 years and involved only a few African countries: Eritrea (1882), Somalia (1889), Libya (1911) and Ethiopia (1935). There was no colonial possession after the end of the Second World War when Allied forces conquered Germany and Italy. The desire to accumulate wealth and other advantages drove many Italians to emigrate to Africa. There is not a large footprint of Italian colonialism on the African continent. Suffice it to say, the same ethos of broad European colonialism informed Italy's colonial foray.

## German Colonial Imprints in Africa: Social Welfare Systems

Germany became part of the infamous 'Scramble for Africa' after it convened the Berlin Conference between 1884-1885 aimed at partitioning Africa and parcelling it out to European imperial powers. In this regard, Europeans apportioned themselves huge swathes of African territories. However, after the First World War, Germany lost its colonies, under the mandate of the League of Nations and with South Africa, Britain and France respectively assuming rule over the German territories. Particularly, the former can be attributed to the efforts of Chancellor Otto von Bismarck, who created an African empire for Germany, lasting about 30 years from 1884-1918. Germany's 'possessions' included Togoland, Cameroun, German South-West Africa and German East Africa incorporating, at the time, the Kingdoms of Rwanda and Burundi. With time, a grandiose plan evolved: to merge these disparate possessions to form one contiguous empire stretching from the Atlantic coast in the west to the Indian Ocean sea-line in the east, in what became known as *Mittelafrika*, i.e. 'Middle Africa' in a literal English translation.[39]

---

38    Ibid.

39    Mambo, 1990.

According to Mambo (1990), during their three-decade rule in Africa, the Germans, like the other European colonial masters, were confronted with stiff resistance from their African subjects.[40] Perhaps the best-known upheavals are those of the Herero and Nama in 1903-1907 in German South-West Africa, and the Maji Maji Rebellion in German East Africa, 1905-1907. Mambo (1990) further observes that in the wake of these uprisings, the German colonial 'masters' argued, among other things, that perhaps these disturbances had been difficult to quell because their empire was not compact but spread in patches all over the African continent. Would it not have been much better if all these possessions made a contiguous body of territory which, military officials had argued, would have been easy to defend both internally and externally?

## Colonial-Apartheid Social Welfare in South Africa

After the initial Dutch and later British occupation, South Africa morphed into a settler colony. In this regard, the large European population in the country had eventually taken its own form of occupation by diluting ties with the imperial countries and carving out a niche for itself. The colonialism of a special type gave birth to a variant form of capitalism and later, welfare capitalism.[41] The colonial-apartheid social welfare system was founded upon four principles, namely: racial division in the provision of welfare services; a rejection of socialism; a partnership between the State and community; and movement from residential and therapeutic services towards community-based and preventative facilities.[42] State social welfare services were not only residual but fragmented; with apartheid policies and legislation heavily impacting upon the social welfare system of the country, in turn, influencing social work education and social work practice.

Two important factors contributed to the formation of the colonial-apartheid social welfare system: the discovery of rich mineral deposits of diamonds and gold, which then created conditions fostering the industrial development of South Africa, from the 1870s onwards; and the Anglo-Boer war (now known as the South African war) between 1899-1902. With industrialisation, the African peasantry was uprooted from its subsistent agricultural base, leading to many African communities losing their land

---

40    Ibid:163.

41    Mhone, 2002; Noyoo, 2017.

42    McKendrick, 1987.

and precipitating an exodus to the cities where mining was taking place. However, white Afrikaner populations lost out in the industrialisation process as they had been mainly agricultural producers.

The discussions in this book are presented in thirteen chapters. In the Introduction, Ndangwa Noyoo introduces the book's rationale, aim and its contextual background. The section highlights the different welfare systems existent in Africa and the region. It shows that in most instances, countries of Southern Africa, which were not British colonies, had stronger social protection systems than social welfare institutions. In Chapter 1, Cristina Udelsmann Rodrigues discusses the social protection of informal economy workers in Angola: past and present challenges. The chapter touches on social welfare and social work from a social protection perspective, because in Angola, the colonialists established formal social security systems before the social welfare mechanisms were put in place. In Chapter 2, Morena J. Rankopo, Dolly Ntseane and Lengwe-Katembula Mwansa plot the evolution of social welfare and social work in Botswana. In Chapter 3, Alain Kambale Maboko traces the origins of social welfare in the DRC. Chapter 4 focusses on Lesotho, with Tšepang Florence Manyeli providing insights into the development of social welfare and social work in that country. Loveness Imaan and her colleagues examine the history of social welfare and social work in Malawi in Chapter 5.

Chapter 6 looks at the trajectory of social welfare and social work in Mauritius. Asrani Gopaul and his colleagues discuss in detail how social welfare and social work evolved in different colonial systems of that country, until the present time. José Ivo Correia and Cheila Mutombene examine the history of social welfare and social work in the context of Mozambique in Chapter 7. In Chapter 8, Ndumba Jonnah Kamwanyah, Rachel Johanna Freeman and Hetty Rose-Junius focus on social welfare and social work in Namibia. Ndangwa Noyoo and his colleagues discuss social welfare and social work in South Africa in Chapter 9. After that, Lungile Mabundza discusses social welfare and social work in Eswatini formerly known Swaziland in Chapter 10. In Chapter 11, Leah Natujwa Omari examines social welfare and social work in Tanzania. Then Chapter 12 looks at Zambia with Ndangwa Noyoo providing the historical and contextual perspective to social welfare and social work in that country. In Chapter 13,

Rodreck Mupedziswa and Mildred Mushunje discuss the development of social welfare and social work in Zimbabwe. Ndangwa Noyoo then wraps up the book's discussions with a Conclusion section.

## References

Aixelà, Y. 2013. Of Colonists, Migrants and National Identity: The Historical Difficulties of the Socio-Political Construction of Equatorial Guinea. *Nordic Journal of African Studies*, 22(1&2):49-71.

Blau, J. & Abramovitz, M. 2010. *The Dynamics of Social Welfare Policy.* 3rd Edition. New York: Oxford University Press.

Brydan, D. 2018. Mikomeseng: Leprosy, Legitimacy and Francoist Repression in Spanish Guinea. *Social History of Medicine*, 32(3):627-647.

Burch, H. A. 1999. *Social Welfare Policy Analysis and Choices.* New York: The Haworth Press.

Butler, L.J. 1997. *Industrialisation and the British Colonial State, West Africa 1939-1951.* London: Frank Cass.

Dobelstein, A.W. 1986. *Politics, Economics, and Public Welfare.* 2nd Edition. Englewood Cliffs, NJ: Prentice-Hall.

Du Toit, P. 1995. *State Building and Democracy in Southern Africa.* Washington, DC: United States Institute of Peace Press.

Falola, T. 2002. *Key Events in African History - A Reference Guide.* Westport, CT: Greenwood Publishing Group, Inc.

Gil, D.G. 1992. *Unravelling Social Policy: Theory, Analysis, and Political Action Towards Social Equality.* 5th Edition. Rochester, VT: Schenkman Books.

IFSW (International Federation of Social Workers) & Association of Schools of Social Work (IASSW). 2014. *Global definition of social work.* [https://bit.ly/3krvBrU].

Johnson, L.C., Schwartz, C.L. & Tate, D. S. 1997. *Social Welfare: A Response to Human Need.* 4th Edition. Boston, MA: Allyn and Bacon.

Lester, A., Nel, E. & Binns, T. 2014. *South Africa, past, present and future: Gold at the end of the rainbow?* London: Routledge.

Lewis, J. 2000. *Empire State Building. War and Welfare in Kenya 1925-52.* Columbus, OH: Ohio State University Press.

Lipski, J. 2000. The Spanish of Equatorial Guinea: Research on La Hispanidad's Best-Kept Secret. *Afro-Hispanic Review*, 19(1):11-38.

MaClean, L.M. 2010. *Informal Institutions and Citizenship in Rural Africa: Risk and Reciprocity in Ghana and Côte d'Ivoire.* Cambridge: Cambridge University Press.

Mair, L.P. 1944. *Welfare in the British Colonies.* London: The Royal Institute of International Affairs.

Mambo, R.M. 1990. Mittelafrika: the German dream of an empire across Africa in the late 19th and early 20th Centuries: An overview. *Transafrican Journal of History*, 20(1991):161-180.

McKendrick, B.W. 1987. *Introduction to Social Work in South Africa.* Pretoria: HAUM.

Midgley, J. 1995. *Social Development: The Developmental Perspective in Social Welfare.* London: SAGE Publications.

Midgley, J. 1997. *Social Welfare in Global Context.* Thousand Oaks, CA: SAGE Publications.

Noyoo, N. 2013. *Social Welfare in Zambia: The Search for a Transformative Agenda.* London: Adonis & Abbey.

Noyoo, N. 2017. Social policy and welfare regimes typologies: Any relevance to South Africa? *Sozialpolitik.CH*, 2(2):1-16.

Okoth, A. 2006. *A History of Africa (Vol.2) - 1915-1995.* Nairobi: East African Education Publications.

Segal, E.A. 2016. *Social Welfare Policy and Social Programmes: A Values Perspective.* Boston, MA: Cengage.

Southern African Development Community. 2016. *Towards a common future: SADC Selected Economic and SocialIndicator, 2016.* [https://bit.ly/33Eq5eO].

Vambe, M.T. & Zegeye, A. 2008. *Unity and Struggle - Selected Speeches and Writings. Amilcar Cabral.* Pretoria: University of South Africa (UNISA) Press.

Walsh, M., Stephens, P. & Moore, S. 2000. *Social Policy & Welfare.* Cheltenham: Stanley Thorne.

Zastrow, C. 2010. *Introduction to Social Work and Social Welfare: Empowering People.* 10th Edition. Belmont, CA: Brooks Cole.

# SOCIAL PROTECTION OF INFORMAL ECONOMY WORKERS IN ANGOLA: PAST AND PRESENT CHALLENGES

*Cristina Udelsmann Rodrigues*

## Introduction

Informal economy workers in Angola, like in many parts of the world and specifically the African continent, are among the most vulnerable when it comes to jobs, safety, and protection. Not only because the informal economy is characterised by higher levels of uncertainty about integration; profits and income; protection from job performance threats; but because the systems in place do not respond to specific features and conditions of informal work and do not consider the significance of the informal economy today. Particularly, in a context of accelerated urbanisation, the informal economy does not require much initial capital; implies less investment in infrastructure, schooling and professional qualifications; and is, therefore, adapted to both the conditions of poor families and urban migrants. In Sub-Saharan Africa, 66 per cent of employment is in the informal economy, with a predominance of self-employment.[1] However, incomes are generally, low, irregular and insufficient.[2]

---

1    Vanek, Chen, Carré, Heintz & Hussmanns, 2014.
2    Lund, 2009; Udelsmann Rodrigues, Lopes & Feliciano, 2006.

Work-related uncertainty and vulnerability have for years been the ordinary conditions and context for urban livelihoods. Organisations, like the World Bank, have been devoting substantial work to address social protection and include in it informal workers, especially those of the global south.[3] The effort leading to more inclusive systems has been central in the work of the International Labour Organisation. However, worldwide, the social protection coverage, in terms of the numbers of informal workers catered for, in developing countries is still low. In Angola, with important economic transformations taking place, such as the acute decrease in oil prices, starting in 2014, and consequently limiting access to foreign currency, important new challenges add up to the already unfavourable situation of informal economy workers. Therefore, a bolder response from social protection mechanisms is needed. This chapter analyses social protection mechanisms in Angola, particularly those related to the informal economy; and argues that this sector still relies largely on informal, traditional systems and mechanisms, confirming the low significance of existing formal, private or public alternatives. It serves as one way of contributing to the development of knowledge in social welfare and social work in Angola.

Significant percentages of the Angolan population live in poverty and are dependent on the informal economy. With a population of about 25.8 million, unequally distributed between rural and urban areas (62.6 per cent urban), the Angolan economically active population over 15 years old – working both in the informal and formal economy – represents 40 per cent of the total population, according to the last 2014 General Census.[4] According to the Survey on the Population Wellbeing (*Inquérito Integrado sobre o Bem-Estar da População*), 37 per cent of the population lives below the national poverty line.[5] In rural areas, this is as high as 58 per cent. The informal economy in Angola is an important source of security and livelihoods, but it:

> ... triggers perverse effects on the structure and coverage levels of social protection, the standards of decent work, the effectiveness of public policies and can, potentially, give rise to poverty and forms of social exclusion among its actors.[6]

---

3    Kabeer, 2014.

4    UNFPA Angola, 2016.

5    INE, 2010.

6    Udelsmann Rodrigues et al., 2006:150.

Social protection may include national schemes and modalities of social security or social insurance aimed at protecting both those exposed to risks and generally everyone in situations of vulnerability. Broadly, it includes interventions of public, private and voluntary organisations and informal networks to support individuals and communities in their efforts to prevent, manage and overcome risks and vulnerabilities.[7] While workers in Angola over the years have relied on protection systems based on social or traditional dispositions and mechanisms, a small number of workers relied on systems that the colonial system developed – for a short period. Later, a limited number of workers were covered by social systems under the pro-socialist state. The post-colonial and post-war context of today's Angola has inherited few prerogatives of the colonial and post-Independence schemes and, given the levels of poverty and precarity, there are calls for profound revisions of available and functioning systems:

> Public social protection has very limited coverage because of the small proportion of the active population working in the formal sector and also due to the many institutional and organisational problems resulting from the relatively rapid changes which took place in political and economic management in these countries over the last few decades.[8]

Formal social protection, involving regular formal contributions, covers a limited number of people. Over the years, the available formal and informal systems have changed, from traditional family-based pre-colonial mechanisms to colonial exclusion of non-formal workers from protection systems.

After Independence, attempts to implement an egalitarian distributive system proved ineffective. After Angola's civil war, redefinition of social protection faced several challenges, due to a number of reasons: the extent of the informal economy; the need to address poverty and vulnerability; and a changing economy that could no longer rely on the wealth of oil. Angola did not build a welfare state like other post-World War II countries did, during the colonial period. The unified management of insurance, benefits and social services was never achieved or the universalisation of coverage as well as the prevention of future risks and compensations. In fact, by absence, the Angolan system is based on reduced social expenditures; absence of universal social protection schemes; and the reliance on alternative compensation schemes; making it closer to a

---

7      Kabeer, 2004.

8      Udelsmann Rodrigues et al., 2006:152-153.

neoliberal model. After Independence, Angola opted for a development line based on socialist models, with a state economy of central planning and a single party-political regime. During the long civil war (1975-2002), Angola channelled a substantial part of its financial resources to warfare, leaving all social protection areas practically uncovered. During this period, the country relied on non-governmental and emergency aid to cover important sectors of social protection and provide security to the population.

Several programmes addressing poverty and vulnerable groups were developed in Angola after Independence. The most central, focusing on fighting poverty, were consecutively reviewed to address the changing conditions of the country in terms of the prevalence of war and emergencies, available national budgets and variable international support. The Social Action Fund (*Fundo de Apoio Social*), a government programme that the World Bank and the Government of Angola funded and established in 1994, aims to support communities through the creation of social and economic infrastructure. Other prominent funds that the two major state companies created over the years are the Sonangol oil company's fund and the Endiama diamond company's Brilhante fund. Other domestic and private Angolan social funds are the Eduardo dos Santos Foundation (*Fundação Eduardo dos Santos*) and the Lwini Fund (*Fundo de Solidariedade Social*). The main government strategy for poverty reduction is the National Poverty Strategy (*Estratégia de Combate à Pobreza, Crescimento e Estabilização Económica*) of 2010. Its key objectives are promoting the rapid and sustained reduction of poverty, focusing on ten main sectors including social reintegration; civil security and protection; food security; rural development; education; health; basic infrastructure; employment; vocational training; governance and macroeconomic management. The National Development Plan for 2013-2017 establishes a commitment towards strengthening social assistance and in this sense, identifies several objectives, such as implementing cash transfer programmes and, more broadly, improve the social protection system. It indicates an intention to create an Institute for Social Services. Also, the National Development Plan, 2018-2022, places emphasis on Social Assistance and Protection as key policies of Human Development and Well-being. Despite the existence of these programmes and a series of other sectoral, bilateral, private programmes and projects, social protection has not been comprehensively addressed in Angola.

An assessment of the existing social assistance policy that the World Bank and the United Nations Children's Fund (UNICEF) Angola conducted in 2012, shows that:

> ... social assistance has mainly consisted of small scale social transfers programmes targeting war-veterans, basic food packages for the most vulnerable, items to support people with disabilities, occupational therapy for the elderly and professional training and reintegration of the poor and unemployed.[9]

Furthermore, the European Union and UNICEF launched a project, the Support Project for Assistance and Social Protection Interventions (*Projecto de Apoio às intervenções de Assistência e Proteção Social*), in line with the government's intentions to expand the social protection of the poorest. The Ministry of Public Administration and Social Security (*Ministério da Administração Pública, Trabalho e Segurança Social*) is currently responsible for the national social security system of public sector workers through the National Institute of Social Security. This institute manages, among others, contributory insurance schemes and coverage of retirement pensions; maternity subsidies; funeral subsidies; family subsidies; subsidy for deaths; and survival pensions. The Ministry of Social Assistance and Reintegration (*Ministério da Assistência e Reinserção Social*), in turn, manages the bulk of social protection under non-contributive schemes. Main target groups include vulnerable populations, including the elderly; children; adolescents; disabled not covered by social security; families in need; and a broad scope of community development actions. The Institute of Reintegration of Social Combatants (*Instituto de Reintegração Social dos Ex-Militares*), within the Angolan context, is one of the main branches of the Ministry of Social Assistance.

In August 2001, the draft of the Basic Law on Social Protection was sent out for public discussion. The document structured social protection at three levels, namely, basic social protection; compulsory social protection, covering both employed and self-employed workers; and supplementary social protection. It stipulated the following social protection objectives:

▻ To mitigate the effects of reducing the income of workers in situations of shortage or loss of work capacity, maternity, unemployment, and old age and ensuring the survival of their family members in the event of death.

---

9    EU, 2013:3.

▷ To compensate, at least partially, the increase in the burdens inherent in family situations of special fragility or dependency.

▷ To ensure the means of subsistence for the needy resident population, as far as the economic and social development of the country is concerned, and promote, together with individuals and families, their insertion in the community, in the full guarantee of their responsible citizenship.

The Social Protection Law 7/04 of October 15 was approved in 2014 and based on the drafted objectives' established three modalities of assuring social protection:

▷ Basic social protection: funded by taxation, it covers situations of deprivation and is targeted to the most vulnerable by providing the minimums of subsistence.

▷ Compulsory social protection: based on a logic of insurance and funded by contributions of employers and employees, it covers employees and self-employed in situations of lack or decrease of working capacity, maternity, work accidents and professional disease, unemployment, old age and death, and aggravation of family expenses.

▷ Complementary social protection: based on optional membership and in a logic of insurance, it covers those with an active compulsory social protection plan and is based on specific private accords between workers and providing entities.

Public expenses with social protection constitute 0.61 per cent of the Gross Domestic Product (GDP). According to the Ministry of Finance, taxpayer numbers for the social security system was 123 685 in 2016, and the number of people the compulsory social protection schemes covered was 1 147 471, according to the CIP.[10]

Along with the new law, Angola currently has a range of structures and mechanisms addressing social protection, including public social security and various private, community and family social protection mechanisms. The public systems include a contributory component, to which citizens/workers contribute a percentage of their formal income and social assistance; and non-contributory, essentially providing more vulnerable groups minimum levels of basic social needs. These mechanisms of basic social protection and eventually voluntary complementary social protection schemes, cover

---

10    CIP, 2017.

the social protection of informal economy workers in case of vulnerability. In practice, however, these formal mechanisms do not cover the population whose livelihoods depend on the informal economy.

## Origins and Evolution of Social Protection

Overall, the Angolan social protection reality today is substantially defined by its colonial past of an economy based on the primary sector with low investment in human capital and markedly unequal regional development. There are few references or studies about internal mechanisms of social protection before the colonial regime started to control all aspects of the economy and work. However, dispositions of the socio-cultural and economic matrices still inform the informal economy and its structures, how it works, as well as associated social mechanisms with safety functions.[11] *Kixiquila*, an Angolan expression that identifies rotating savings and credit associations, is a mechanism based on traditional mutual aid institutions that allow traders to raise funds to increase their level of business. Simultaneously, it is related to social functions, like, among others, financing family events and religious ceremonies. The groups' sizes vary, members participate voluntarily and mutually, defining the frequency and value of their respective contributions and how these funds are used, in turn, by each member. Its functioning is based on the principles of trust and solidarity, and the control mechanism is based on social peer pressure. *Kilapi*, which refers to loans, is an expression of unknown origin but widespread as a concept and mechanism of economic support. The term is used to identify credit transactions, based on trust and consensus, between sellers and consumers. In the informal trade, it has become common practice in situations where someone does not have the capital needed for investment or to cover unexpected expenses and resorts to a loan. It is assumed to be a compromise between individuals, with delayed re-payments dependent on the possibilities of the borrower. *Kilapi* has become an alternative for many due to possible delayed re-payment and as a way to support unexpected expenses. Both mechanisms have a historical social and economic background that, with modifications, subsisted through the colonial times. There is, however, not much knowledge of how they were structured and worked before.

---

11    Ducados & Ferreira, 1998; Lopes, 2010.

During the centuries of Portuguese colonial rule, the primary sector was the basis of the Angolan economy, with emphasis on commercial agriculture. Although the economy grew impressively during the colonial period, the social benefits were not evenly distributed across the population, with a clear detriment to the indigenous population; not counting the slave trade and the terrible impacts on forms of work and work relations. For an extended period of colonial rule, most of the population lived and worked within systems, not formally protected, with only a few social benefits associated with their work. Moreover, poverty and vulnerability issues were not included in social policies, except for a few charity institutions. Labour-intensive agriculture, absorbing most of the population for many years, did not have an associated system of social protection. In addition to the conditions of a society where access to resources and opportunities was discriminatory, there was the marginalisation of most of the population from the few formal labour protective systems. The establishment of a general social protection system that would meet the needs of an overwhelming minority was never even pondered at the policy level.

In the last decades of the colonial period, between the 1940s and 1970s, some initiatives and systems aimed at the protection and mitigation of economic and social risks were constituted, for instance, the cooperative *Lar Do Namibe*, created in the 1940s in the Namibe province. It was a mutualist agreement focusing on financing housing. The funds came from the contributions of members, and every month, one or two associates would be allocated funds to build a house through a system of a lottery. Charities and religion-related institutions mainly carried out social work. Specialised entities and systems, like the *Casa-do-Gaiato*, for instance, supported abandoned children. Angola had two such homes in the 1960s and 1970s, one founded in Benguela in 1962 and another in Malange the next year. The colonial government's Institute of Social Assistance and Integration (*Instituto de Asistencia e Integración Social*) of Luanda created the third old-age home, Lar Beiral in 1953, to host former Portuguese civil servant pensioners. Formal training of social assistants, however, only began in 1962 and social services remained an area of both the State and the Catholic Church. Social protection, under the designation of social providence (*previdência social*), was linked to formal work. In the 1960s, when social providence started to be implemented in a few organisations and firms as mutualist schemes, it only reached the urban workers. It did not cover unemployment, old-age pensions, or disability. Support was only granted to sickness, maternity (up to three months), work accidents and disease. These institutions, with a vocation for social protection of vulnerable groups, functioned more as charities and were dependent on voluntary contributions; however, mostly targeting the colonial state staff and, at a much smaller scale, the African communities. Social Action at Work (*Acção Social no Trabalho*) was created in 1962 by decree together with the Social Action Fund at Work (*Fundo de Acção Social no Trabalho*) dedicated to the maintenance of kindergartens and similar institutions for the protection of vulnerable children through orphanages and asylums. With it, the Institute of Education and Social Service Pio XII (*Instituto de Educação e Serviço Social Pio XII*) was created, a private entity that the government, the Church and private contributions funds, and in 1963 the first social assistants concluded the course. The institute continued to train assistants until after Independence but in 1977 ceased its work.[12]

After Independence, some social structures from the colonial era were inherited and continued to function. The secretary of the assistance of social services (afterwards, the Ministry of Assistance and Social Reinsertion) started to assist the Lar Beiral home, for instance. However, few remained active and, with the cumulative impact of war affecting a large percentage of the population, their work became increasingly narrow. In the post-Independence period, the effects of a long-armed conflict and the leadership of a single-party regime with a Marxist orientation, dictated the way the social protection systems evolved or did not. In 1975, Angola attained Independence after an unprecedented war of devastating proportions. The newly independent country followed (by then) a line of socialist redistribution and equality aimed at social and economic protection for all but only catering for a few, and it was absorbed by the expansion of the public sector with its associated welfare system. Again, this system touched only a small number of urban dwellers. In rural areas, the population was increasingly affected by civil conflict and the erosion of economic and social structures. The current state of social protection development institutions still leaves many unprotected, as mentioned. The limited scope of the formal economy geographically, with an advantage to urban areas with higher numbers of people, leads to the conclusion that the number of those protected by formal systems and mechanisms is low in national terms. Even among those covered by formal social protection within the national anti poverty programme and several increased

---

12    Monteiro, 2015.

social protection of the most vulnerable initiatives, the benefits are limited, in real terms, not covering individuals' exposure to risks.

The Kikuia Card (*Cartão Kikuia*) programme was started in 2013 and later expanded to address the negative impacts of other reforms such as the existing fuel subsidies reform. The programme prioritises widows with orphans or relatives with disabilities, chronically ill persons, and ex-combatants. With the card, beneficiaries can buy basic goods (food, school materials and farming tools) on a monthly basis, in adhering stores up to 5 000 Kwanzas, even though the amount was reduced in 2016. Private companies are spending significant resources on social projects in Angola for the benefit of the poor and general development.[13] Social work has only recently become an area of specific training again. The Higher Institute of Social Services (*Instituto Superior de Serviço Social de Angola*) has since 2009 been training social assistants and childhood educators with the first graduates concluding their courses in Luanda in 2013. The aforementioned UNICEF and World Bank funded programmes have also started to enrol a number of vulnerable populations in social protection schemes.

## Social Protection in the Informal Economy

Before Independence, informal activities played a strictly subsidiary role in the dominant formal sector of the economy, structured and equipped with the necessary control and regulation mechanisms. The informal economy of the capital city, Luanda, and other cities was restricted to traditional artisanal activities from the provision of services – in particular, domestic services – to street vending, small local markets and construction activities, particularly in the peripheries of cities. The informal economy, as it is now known, began to grow a couple of years after Independence in 1975, still under the socialist system, and quickly informal practices – then called 'schemes', *candonga* – spread to different sectors of the economy. Economic centralism, as part of the process of transition to a market economy (1987-1991), did not produce substantial changes in the fast-growing dynamics of the informal sector. Sectors such as transport, urban markets and the exchange market became more complex and gradually involved more individuals and families. The informal economy has not, however, developed systems to protect the workers from risks and vulnerability. There are today some informal associations

---

13   Amundsen & Wiig, 2008.

connected to the informal economy that manage common funds to cover certain risks and provide investment funding. Most of these associations organise informally, and they are based on relations of personal trust, involving a group of individuals connected by professional and economic relations, family and neighbourhood ties, friendship or long-term relations. In some cases, sectors of specific activities in the informal economy have created organisations – some of them informal too – that, among others, focus on social and professional protection.[14] Some of these associations support members on legal matters.

References to a long African tradition of mutual aid schemes, namely the rotating use of savings and credit – known as Rotating Savings and Credit Associations – are frequent in specialised literature. In Angola, such schemes have been documented, particularly among women in the informal economy.[15] Over the years, there have been some initiatives to organise and empower these networks. Non-governmental actors are usually the key persons responsible for these initiatives, acting essentially around microcredit. The projects and programmes are varied, from long-term well-established organisations to smaller and shorter-term organisations. They usually manage participants' contributions to supply renewable credit, manage a common fund used in special circumstances, like, among others, the loss of merchandise, illness, family obligations, and the rebuilding of housing. Microcredit, in this case, functions as a social protection mechanism. In the Angolan context, there is an accelerated growth of micro-credit institutions, becoming an increasingly important resource for the people involved in the informal economy, and even for those with formal occupations, to have access to income. Credit not only guarantees the ability to meet basic needs but also access to funds to meet unexpected situations.

## Vulnerability in the Informal Economy

While poverty and developmental challenges are a central concern in Africa, in general, and in Angola in particular, the informal economy workers are among the most vulnerable and exposed to changing situations in their social and domestic lives and the economy. It can be argued that access to resources and income through the

---

14    Lopes, 2010.

15    Ducados & Ferreira, 1998.

informal economy is many families' solution to unemployment and lack of opportunity in the formal economy and therefore represents a form of mitigation of vulnerability. The conditions that informal workers develop their activities in, mostly do not have protection mechanisms. Considering the Angolan population, and particularly the urban population, groups constituting the bulk of the informal economy, are by nature and condition highly exposed to risks. The youth, unprepared for the labour market, with low levels of education and significantly coming from the rural areas to the cities in search of opportunities, constitute one such group most dependent on resources generated in the informal economy. According to the last General Census of 2014, 76.63 per cent of the urban population in Angola is unemployed, and over 30 per cent of them are youth and young adults between 15 and 29 years old. Of significance, is the fact that youth and young adults under 24 years old head around 14 per cent of Angolan households. A second group includes women, to whom the informal economy constitutes the principal means of livelihood.[16] The percentage of households headed by single women are, according to the 2014 census, 58 per cent. Typically, given the socio-cultural matrix of the country, these women heading households constitute those separated, divorced or widowed or involved in polygamous relationships, placing them in an increasingly vulnerable position. A third group includes those households headed by elderly people (60 and older). Of the Angolan households, as the 2014 census indicated, more than seven per cent were headed by individuals of 65 years old or older. These three groups together represent a large proportion of potentially vulnerable individuals in the population and a high number of individuals in vulnerable positions in a population of almost 26 million, in 2014.

Among the risks and vulnerable situations workers are exposed to, informal economy workers in Angola face challenges of illness; access to subsistence, funerals or marriages; risk of unemployment; lack of old-age pension; lack of proper housing; and access to credit or education.[17] In the absence of institutions dedicated to mitigating or alleviating the vulnerability of families that depend almost entirely on informal activities, solidarity networks, both intra-family and inter-family networks are frequently mobilised as means of social protection. However, in contexts of poverty and vulnerability and especially in the urban centres where family and social networks are challenged, there is a tendency

---

16    EU, 2013.

17    Udelsmann Rodrigues et al., 2006.

for decreased reliability on these systems.[18] Family support is a crucial mechanism in providing protection. While other networks, like churches, or neighbourhood solidarities, can play an important role, family-based relations remain at the centre of the economic and social life of many, both in the rural areas and in the cities.

## Conclusion

The first conclusion is that in the context of Angola, the phenomena of poverty, social exclusion and the informal economy are intimately linked to a series of socio-economic processes that, throughout history, interact dynamically and whose contours can be linked to three important periods. First, the legacy of about five centuries of Portuguese colonial rule, characterised by restricted and exclusionary systems of social protection. Secondly, the post-Independence period, marked by a long-armed conflict with deep socio-economic repercussions and an incipient development of social protection mechanisms, with few workers in the formal economy benefiting from these mechanisms. Currently, there are transformations taking place in the panorama of social protection systems, with a line of development addressing poverty and most of the population depending on the informal economy. Coverage, however, is still limited and in this context, the informal workers continue to be the most vulnerable, and are exposed to several risks and have an additional burden of having to depend on fluctuating, uncertain and increasingly reduced income opportunities. The large sector of informal economy activities represents a vast proportion of uncovered workers.

---

18    Robson & Roque, 2002.

# References

African Development Bank. 2013. *Democratic Republic of Congo: 2013-2017 Country Strategy Paper.* [https://bit.ly/2REJZRe]. (Accessed 21 May 2014).

Amundsen, I. & Wiig, A. 2008. Social Funds in Angola: Channels, Amounts and Impact. Working Paper 8, Christian Michelsen Institute.

Cain, A. 2003. *Civil Society and Community Reconstruction in Post-War Angola.* Paper presented to the Roundtable Discussion on International Donors and Civil Society Implications for Angola's Recovery and the Displaced at Luanda, Angola, 16-17 July 2003. [https://bit.ly/3kvXOhA]. (Accessed 21 June 2016).

CIP (Social Protection Information Centre, *Centro de Informação em Protecção Social*). 2018. *São tomé e príncipe: país adota política nacional de proteção da criança.* [https://bit.ly/2EfLqTi]. (Accessed 21 May 2019).

Ducados, H. & Ferreira, M. 1998. O financiamento informal e as estratégias de sobrevivência económica das mulheres em Angola: a Kixikila no município do Sambizanga – Luanda). *Documentos de trabalho – CEsA*, 53:1-14.

EU (European Union). 2013. Project to support the Government of Angola to define and implement an effective policy for Social Protection and Social Solidarity. [https://bit.ly/33U774f] (Accessed 21 May 2014).

EU & Afonso, A. 2010. *Angola Gender Country Profile. Action Plan for Gender Equality and the Empowerment of Women in Development (2010-2015).* Luxembourg: Publications Office of the EU. [https://bit.ly/3iJRToj]. (Accessed 2 September 2011).

INE (National Institute of Statistics). 2010. *Inquérito Integrado sobre o Bem-Estar da População (IBEP), 2008-2009.* Luanda, Angola: National Institute of Statistics.

International Bank for Reconstruction and Development, World Bank & Gorza, D. (ed). 2016. *Pobreza e Análise de Impacto Social: Reforma de Subsídio e Extensão do Programa de Protecção Social.* [https://bit.ly/2ZN1TG5]. (Accessed 2 September 2017).

Kabeer, N. 2014. *Gender and Social Protection Strategies in the Informal Economy.* London: Routledge.

Lopes, C.M. 2006. Candongueiros, kinguilas, roboteiros e zungueiros: uma digressão pela economia informal de Luanda. *Lusotopie*, XIII(1):163-183.

Lopes, C. 2010. Dinâmicas do associativismo na economia informal: os transportes de passageiros em Angola. *Análise Social*, XLV(195):367-391.

Lund, F. 2009. Social Protection and the Informal Economy: linkages and good practices for poverty reduction and empowerment. In: *Promoting Pro-Poor Growth: Social Protection. Paris, France: Organisation for Economic Cooperation and Development.* pp.69-88. [https://bit.ly/3hHHmJ9] (Accessed 2 September 2011).

MAPESS (Ministry of Public Administration, Employment and Social Security). 2001. *Ante-Projecto da Lei de Bases da Protecção Social*. Luanda, Angola: Ministry of Employment and Social Security (MAPESS).

Monteiro, A.A. 2015. Natureza do Serviço Social em Angola: génese, formação, concepções e práticas profissionais dos assistentes sociais nos serviços de saúde das forças armadas angolanas, Masters dissertation. Masters dissertation. São Paulo: Pontifical Catholic University of São Paulo.

Republic of Angola. 2014. *Lei de Bases da Protecção Social, Lei 7/04, October 15*. [https://bit.ly/35NFwnC]. (Accessed 2 September 2011).

Robson, P. & Roque, S. 2002. Aqui na Cidade Nada Sobra para Ajudar. Buscando A Solidariedade e a Acção Colectiva em Bairros Peri-Urbanos de Angola. Development Workshop, *Occasional Papers*, 3.

Udelsmann Rodrigues, C., Lopes, C. & Feliciano, J. 2006. Social Protection and the Informal Economy: the experiences and challenges of Portuguese speaking countries. In: *Social Protection and Inclusion: experiences and policy issues*. Geneva: International Labour Office. pp.149-164.

UNFPA Angola (United Nations Population Fund). 2016. General Population and Housing Census Final Results Published. [https://bit.ly/35Q5TJE]. (Accessed 2 September 2017).

Vanek, J., Chen, M.A., Carré, F., Heintz, J. & Hussmanns, R. 2014. *Statistics on the Informal Economy: definitions, regional estimates and challenges. Women in Informal Employment: Globalizing and Organizing (WIEGO)*. Working Paper, 2. [https://www.wiego.org/sites/default/files/publications/files/Vanek-Statistics-WIEGO-WP2.pdf]. (Accessed 2 May 2018).

# 02

# EVOLUTION OF SOCIAL WELFARE AND SOCIAL WORK IN BOTSWANA

*Morena J. Rankopo, Dolly Ntseane*
*& Lengwe-Katembula Mwansa*

## Introduction

It is 54 years ago since Botswana attained political Independence from Britain on 30 September 1966 and became a republic. The country was initially called Bechuanaland after it became a Protectorate of Great Britain in 1885. The understanding then was that Britain would protect Bechuanaland from the Boers in South Africa advancing from the south to encroach on this country. On her own, Bechuanaland could not stop the Boers and therefore entered into an arrangement with Britain to 'protect' the country. Although this arrangement was most welcome because the country needed protection, Bechuanaland at that time had virtually no known wealth such as minerals to offer Britain. It was regarded as an outpost of less value, with Britain wanting to exert its territorial claims to secure more land to the north. Notably, Botswana coming under British influence brought about intense political, social, and economic changes in the country. The protection of Bechuanaland meant the introduction of colonialism, a liberal economic system and the process of urbanisation.[1] The introduction of free-market enterprise brought unprecedented changes in the economic life of the people; from a

---

1    Hedenquist, 1992.

subsistence, communal and self-sufficient type of economy to a free-market enterprise with individualism; competition; profit; laissez-faireism; and reliance on money as a mode of transaction. People had to leave their familiar environment to look for paid jobs in newly established urban centres. The process of urbanisation resulted in the emergence of towns that consequently brought about the rural-urban drift.

The movement of people from rural to urban areas meant that urban areas grew much faster than development could allow. Problems of overcrowding in urban areas led to the mushrooming of unplanned areas of living such as the shanty towns. Those who trekked to the towns were not guaranteed paid jobs or accommodation. Thus, unemployment was a direct outcome of this rapid urbanisation leading to other unwanted developments, especially a rise in crime and urban poverty. The social changes brought about by urbanisation, and the liberal economy required new relationships or arrangements from the extended family system "and the role that it played in providing for the welfare of families and the communities".[2] The new capitalist values were not in consonant with the traditional social norms that embraced communalism and the extended family structure. Extended family arrangements were weakened and could not pose as much influence as before. This situation created conditions for social problems such as troubled youths; high rates of unemployment; destitution; marital problems; alcoholism; and a general breakdown in social norms with the attendant social ills. The colonial administrators introduced social welfare and community development in Botswana because of the increasingly negative effects of the market economy and urbanisation on the local populace.

Botswana fits well in the proverbial saying of 'from rags to riches'. This young democratic nation has evolved from absolute poverty and one of the least developed and poorest nations in the world to an upper-middle-income country today. At Independence in 1966, Botswana's per capita income was barely 83 US dollars, but by the turn of the century, it had improved to 7 300 US dollars. Exports are said to have grown from about 2 million US dollars after Independence to over 2 billion US dollars in 2007.[3] According to the World Bank, the country's Gross Domestic Product (GDP) per capita was reported to be 7 234.23 US dollars by 2015.[4] Botswana stands out from most African countries in

---

2      Ibid:12.

3      Mills, 2012.

4      World Bank, 2015.

terms of its human development index. This achievement and democracy growth has been largely attributed to, among others, the wise stewardship of diamond revenues as a commodity. In Botswana, revenues from diamonds have been wisely directed towards human development, and today Botswana has emerged from absolute anonymity to the heights of prominence and accomplishment. The country provides an example of positive transformation from poverty status to one of commodity-driven development. This chapter examines the country's development paradigm that sets it apart from many other African states. It interrogates factors that may account for the difference in developmental success and the roles that the social work profession performs in this regard. Meaningful discourse is promoted through the examination of social welfare and community development evolution in the pre-colonial and colonial era, and the emergence of social work after Independence.

## Indigenous Social Welfare Services in the Pre-Colonial Era

From time immemorial, Batswana (local people) lived in small communities, and people's basic needs were fulfilled in direct and indigenous ways. Farming was the main source of livelihood. Extended families, relatives and neighbours lived close by and were obliged to support those in dire need. Three types of indigenous social supports were common among Batswana: family and kin obligations; community support networks; and mutual aid groups. These approaches continue to exist in contemporary society alongside formal social welfare provisions.[5]

## Extended Family and Kin Support Systems

Historically, the extended family system was the closest and most accessible response system in pre-colonial Botswana to provide support to household members experiencing diverse personal needs.[6] For example, extended families' members provided care to orphans and vulnerable children, people with disabilities, the sick and elderly. There was a fixed order of responsibility within the extended family, with the most senior male elder having authority over all his extended family members and automatically assuming the

---

5   Mwansa, Lucas & Osei-Hwedie, 1998; Apt, 2002; Shaibu & Wallhagen, 2002; Maes, 2003; Foster, 2007; Ntseane & Solo, 2007; Mpedi, 2008; Emmanuel, Maundeni & Letshwiti-Macheng, 2011.

6   Mwansa et al., 1998; Foster, 2007.

position of family headman because of birth-right. He would convene extended family meetings to address issues of need and get family members to play their roles as assigned by culture. Grandparents, parents, uncles, and aunts understood their social obligations to the extended family. Following the introduction of the money economy, able-bodied men were encouraged to migrate to the South African mines and farms in search of job opportunities. Such assistance took the form of regular urban-rural and inter-household income transfers.

Further, when crops failed, family members in town purchased food and sent cash to needy relatives in rural areas. When a relative in town became unemployed, food was sent from the rural areas to towns or the unemployed relative was received back into the rural homestead. Nowadays, households experiencing income stress due to HIV/Aids may send their children to live with relatives who become responsible for feeding the children in their care.[7]

The extended family was a major source of support to orphans and vulnerable children who lost one or both parents. Aunts, uncles, grandparents, and other relatives fostering children was common in Botswana. Consequently, there were no homeless children because of the strong communitarian ethic that existed in those times. Relatives could also offer couples, unable to have children, children to foster or adopt as their own (*go tsalelwa*). To date, these traditions continue to be practised in contemporary Botswana and Africa, although to a lesser extent. In Sub-Saharan Africa, it is estimated that 90 per cent of orphaned children in households live with extended family members.[8] Households that can afford to, provide several forms of support such as food, access to education, shelter, clothing, psychosocial support and other basic needs.[9]

During the pre-colonial era, the extended family system was the first point of contact to cushion individuals who encountered diverse life crises such as hunger, sickness, disability, death, old age, unemployment, injuries, and other risk factors. The principles of solidarity and generalised reciprocity guided such responses. According to Schapera (1970), the extended family system comprised a group of families closely united by blood or marriage. Members acted collectively to discharge important domestic as well

---

7    Foster, 2004; Miller, Gruskin, Subramanian, Rajaraman & Heymann, 2006; Foster, 2007; USAID, 2010.

8    Miller et al., 2006.

9    Foster, 2004; Miller et al., 2006.

as economic activities including construction and thatching of huts to provide shelter; clearing the fields for ploughing; weeding; harvesting; as well as assisting one another with gifts, livestock and other commodities during social events. Although the concept of *botlhoki* or destitution always existed in the Setswana vocabulary, the extended family took it upon itself to provide for the needs of relatives without any expectations of rewards. It was a civic duty to care for one's relatives.[10] Furthermore, the two pillars that buttressed the indigenous social security system in pre-colonial Botswana were community support networks and mutual aid groups.

## Community Support Networks

These networks played a significant role in meeting the critical needs of the destitute. Village chiefs were the custodians of community assets. The chiefs coordinated two commonly practised social protection systems that buffered the destitute:

- *masotla* (large tribal pastures) and

- *kgamelo* (cattle's milk).

*Masotla* were large tribal farms that fell under the custody of the chief. During the ploughing season, age regiments or family clans would be invited to take turns ploughing the fields. The harvest would be stored in large granaries (*difalana*) under the care of the chief. *Difalana* would be used to support needy families and were a safety net in times of food insecurity. Thus, the disadvantaged were assured of food, especially where the extended family was unable to meet their needs. The practice of *kgamelo* was another traditional practice that fell under the purview of the chief. Under this system, the chief would direct that cattle's milk from selected households be used to feed identified poorer members of the community. The chiefs would often entrust a herd of cattle to selected prominent commoners to support the needy.[11] The cattle belonged to the community with the chief serving as the custodian.

---

10    Schapera, 1970.
11    Ibid.; Denbow & Phenyo, 2006.

## Mutual Aid Groups

Indigenous social welfare systems relied heavily on the goodwill of neighbours, age regiments or the community at large. For example, the *mafisa* system (lending cattle to the poor) was a special arrangement whereby wealthy relatives or community members entered a contract with the destitute to care for a small herd of cattle. These poorer individuals in the community would use the livestock for ploughing and milk production as though they owned them. However, they were not allowed to sell or slaughter the livestock. However, they could eat the meat of an animal that died or was killed on account of injury. Under the *mafisa* system, the poorer individual or family receiving the cattle would be given a proportion of new-born calves as agreed in the contract. It was hoped that one day, the cattle would have multiplied, and the poorer family would be given enough livestock to start to support themselves and return the *mafisa* cattle to their owner.[12]

Another system, known as *majako*, allowed poor people working in the fields of the rich to share in the harvest. This system may be compared to the practice of 'gleaning' in the Bible. The difference lies in the fact that with *majako*, the poor would work full-time on the farm during weeding and harvesting seasons and they would be given an agreed portion after the work was completed. Likewise, *go tshwara teu* or *bodisa* accorded the able-bodied poor an opportunity to break the cycle of poverty by looking after cattle and each year receiving a cow in return for their labour.[13] It was expected that after some time, the poor would accumulate enough livestock to start to support themselves. Every village has its stories about poor individuals that benefited immensely from such systems and how their lives were transformed. *Letsema* or *molaletsa* was another community-based intervention that enabled neighbours to perform voluntary work on behalf of a deserving family. This was a tradition that was based on the principle of physical proximity to the poor family and implored neighbours to care for the poor in their neighbourhoods. It is not clear whether such neighbours would consult each other before help could be offered. The practice was, however, that a neighbour would just inform the poor family of the date that they would come to plough their field or assist in the construction of a home. Neighbours would bring food and traditional beer and at the end of the work, there would be a celebration.

---

12    Schapera, 1970.

13    BIDPA, 1997.

## Social Welfare in the Colonial Era (1885-1966)

According to the historian, Ramsay (1998): "... the British announced their intention to occupy southern Botswana in an Order-in-Council in January 1885".[14] It was done to safeguard British interests against the rival Germans, who colonised South-West Africa (Namibia) in 1884 and to thwart any German plans to join the Transvaal Boers in South Africa. Based on Ramsay's account, the three kings commonly associated with asking for British protection were only consulted after the decision had been made. It is clear that only King Khama III welcomed the protection while Kings Gaseitsewe and Sechele 'reluctantly accepted it'. It was only in 1890 that the British began to exercise full control over the 'protectorate'. Bechuanaland was perceived as a 'barren land', and as such, it did not offer any prospects for mineral exploitation, unlike other African colonies. Thus, initially, colonial rule did not interfere in the domestic affairs of the *merafe* ('tribes'), the Colonial Office rather adopted a policy of indirect rule. However, that approach was short-lived once Cecil John Rhodes came up with the strategy of building the Cape to Cairo railway line. It was this English expansionist project that ultimately led to the Orders-in-Council of 1890 and 1891 that gave the High Commissioner and representative of the Queen of England, based in Cape Town, legal powers to enact laws for "the administration of justice, the raising of revenue and generally for peace, order and good government of all persons within this order, including the prohibition of acts tending to disturb the public peace".[15]

The police service was the first formal institution to be established in 1885 with the formation of the Bechuanaland Mounted Police, renamed the Bechuanaland Border Police in 1886, under Lieutenant Colonel Frederick Carrington and further renamed the Bechuanaland Protectorate Police in 1902.[16] Initially, the 500 men of the Bechuanaland Mounted Police comprised of migrants from Basutoland (Lesotho) and Southern Rhodesia (Zimbabwe). Based on historical accounts, the main purpose of the police was to serve the interests of the Colonial Administration, initially by policing the chiefs in the southern part who were resistant to 'protection'. Later, the police service shifted its focus to fighting crime and maintaining peace and order. At Independence in 1966, the police service was renamed the Botswana Police Force and the English continued to lead it until

---

14    Ramsay, 1998:62.
15    Ibid.
16    Republic of Botswana, 2010.

1971 when the first Motswana Commissioner, Mr Simon Hirschfeld, was appointed. It was during this time that the first batch of eight women police officers enlisted. In 2009 the Botswana Police Force was renamed the Botswana Police Service after merging with the Local Police, whose jurisdiction fell under the Tribal Administration, and working with the Customary Courts.

The first major social welfare service was introduced in 1897 following a devastating outbreak of rinderpest that killed an estimated 90 per cent of cattle in the 'protectorate', followed by famine and fever that resulted in the high mortality of people. The missionaries used these catastrophes to promote migration labour, especially to South Africa. It is reported that by 1897, the protectorate witnessed many migrant labour agents in search of male labourers. While the actual figures remain unknown, the Colonial Office observed at the time that a significant number of men left to the extent that many villages appeared deserted.[17] Subsequently, a Bechuanaland Relief Committee was formed under the influence of both the Colonial Office and missionaries. Only tribal people in the southern and south-central parts were able to receive food rations during that time. The construction of the railway line from Mafikeng in South Africa to Bulawayo in Southern Rhodesia, passing through Botswana, created employment for many men in 1897-1898. Unfortunately, there are no statistics on the magnitude of jobs that were created. By the end of the year, the railway line had been completed. Another employment opportunity emerged from selling timber to Kimberley in South Africa. It appears that chiefs benefited from selling timber as they had to be approached to permit the timber to be harvested from their territories. In the north-western part of the protectorate, Batawana chief Sekgoma Letsholathebe had to impose travel restrictions within his region to control rinderpest. The chief asserted his authority over the distribution of locally available food to alleviate the famine as there were no job opportunities for his tribesmen. Orphaned children were relocated to parts of the region that had cattle so they could be fed with milk.[18]

## Introduction of 'Hut Tax'

In 1899 'hut tax' came into force after four years of famine with most able-bodied young men having left the villages to go to South African farms and mines in search

---

17    Ramsay, 1998.

18    Ibid.

of jobs. The missionaries and the Colonial Office widely celebrated the move they saw as an opportunity to promote the value of labour. A hut tax was collected through the chiefs. Due to high default rates resulting from famine, there were increased cases of tax defaulters at the magistrate courts. As migrant labour increased, chiefs began to enter into contracts with the recruitment agencies committing recruits to pay the tax from their wages. Defaulters and those the courts found guilty were forced to get jobs. The hut tax generated money for the recognised chiefs as they collected 10 per cent of the hut tax annually received from their reserves. The chiefs could use the money for public projects if they wished. By 1938, the Colonial Office began to establish treasury offices in every major village for collecting the hut tax and other public revenue.[19]

## Establishment of Formal Social Welfare Services in the Colonial Era

Formal social welfare services began to emerge after 1920 with the establishment of primary schools in major villages, commonly referred to as 'national schools' that the chiefs initially ran, for example, the Bakgatla National School in Mochudi, the Batlokwa National School in Tlokweng, and the Bakwena National School in Molepolole. Throughout the colonial era, it was common for children to go to school for two to four years before transferring to a bigger village to complete primary school education. Missionaries played an important role in the education sector with the church running secondary schools such as Moeding College, St. Josephs College, and Mater Spei College. Moeng College may be the only one that Bangwato tribe's contributions established. Health services developed along with similar patterns as the education sector. The first few public hospitals were established in the 1920s, namely: the Athlone Hospital in Lobatse, the Scottish Livingstone Hospital in Molepolole and the Sekgoma Memorial Hospital in Serowe. The Seventh Day Adventists in Kanye, the Lutherans in Ramotswa, and the Dutch Reformists in Mochudi initiated mission hospitals. These marked the introduction of Western healthcare models in the protectorate. Unlike many other African colonies, Bechuanaland did not have a strong formal economy sector, requiring similar provisions in the health and education sectors. Most of the people continued to rely on indigenous healthcare systems.

---

19    Ibid.

The first social welfare officer, Jack Leech, was appointed in 1946 and remained the only staff member until 1964. The position covered the emerging poor neighbourhoods in Lobatse and Francistown, where there were small businesses. This position involved working with youth groups such as the Boy Scouts and Girl Guides; the destitute; Second World War veterans; explaining government policies to the people; and adult literacy.[20] In 1964, four community development assistants were sent to Tanzania for basic training, and upon their return, community development was piloted at a village called Bokaa, some 30 km from the capital, Gaborone. According to the Bechuanaland Protectorate Plan (1963): "... community development was viewed as relevant for the rural areas to encourage local responsibility and initiative at the village level."[21] However, social welfare was not considered for the rural areas as the focus was on urban areas where a new social order with attendant problems was emerging.[22]

The budget allocation for community development was 39 000 pounds sterling and included salaries of the staff members. Further, no planning was done for community development in urban areas. The Transitional Plan (1966) identified community development as a vehicle for rural development and specifically a response to the devastating drought of 1965-1968. Community development assistants became the drivers of the Food-for-Work programme (*Ipelegeng* in Setswana, meaning self-help or self-reliance), which has remained an integral part of contemporary social welfare programmes in Botswana.[23] A community development department was established in 1968 under the Ministry of Local Government and Lands, and its staff grew to 100 officers. It was through community development that basic social service infrastructure such as primary schools, health clinics and staff houses, for extension workers were completed.[24]

## Independence and Post-Independence Era: Expansion of Social Welfare; Emergence of Social Work

It has been demonstrated above that social welfare in pre-colonial Botswana relied heavily on indigenous social protection schemes. During colonial rule, there was a dearth

20   Wass, 1969; Hedenquist, 1992; Ferguson-Brown, 1996; Jongman, 2014.
21   Bechuanaland Protectorate Plan, 1963:54.
22   Ibid.
23   Ramchandani, 1970.
24   Hedenquist, 1992.

of social welfare infrastructure as the Colonial Administration focused on maintaining law and order to protect its economic interests. Therefore, the local tribes pulled their resources to create health and education services with the support of the missionaries. After Independence, in 1966, the government decided to expand social welfare services, initially in response to the devastating drought of the late 1960s. The first social welfare programme was launched in 1965 with the assistance of the World Food Programme.[25] Community development assistants were employed in the rural areas to identify and provide food rations to vulnerable population groups, including lactating mothers, pregnant women, pre-school children, primary school-going children and TB patients. It was during this time that the Food-for-Work programme was introduced to target able-bodied community members. The villagers were given food rations in exchange for labour in community development projects. The common community development projects then included, among others, the construction of village dams, housing for extension workers, school classrooms, health clinics and rural roads.[26]

At Independence, national development planning was adopted as a critical approach to social welfare. Planning of social welfare services was centralised within the Ministry of Local Government which provided leadership in policy formulation, while local authorities were the implementing agencies. Since Independence, National Development Plans were guided by four national principles:

▻ development (*ditlhabololo*),

▻ democracy (*puso ya batho ka batho*),

▻ self-reliance (*boipelego*), and

▻ national unity (*Popagano ya Sechaba*).[27]

The National Development Plan 3 (1970-1975) was the first to mention the need to promote social justice and equal opportunity explicitly and to aim to improve health services, education, housing, water supply and to create income generation through community development projects.[28] Between 1966 and 1979, indigenous social protection schemes

---

25    Ntseane & Solo, 2004; Ntseana, 2007; Botlhale, Lekorwe, Mothusi & Motshegwa, 2015.
26    Wass, 1969; Rankopo, 1996.
27    Republic of Botswana, 1968.
28    Republic of Botswana, 1970.

were the major source of support to those in need. The early social welfare programmes were intended to cushion citizens against the negative effects of recurring drought.

After Independence, the Department of Community Development, established in 1968 following the pilot project at Bokaa, demonstrated that citizens could contribute towards the development of social infrastructure in their communities.[29] A Social Welfare Unit was established in 1973 to coordinate the provision of mainly food-rations and clothes to poor families, pregnant women and malnourished children.[30] In 1974-1975, the Department of Community Development was dissolved, and a new Department of Social and Community Development was established under the Ministry of Local Government.[31] This Department was subsequently renamed the Department of Social Services (DSS) in the mid-1990s, and later renamed the Department of Social Protection in 2012. Local authorities have a Department of Social and Community Development, implementing all policies and programmes the Department of Social Protection develops. In Botswana, local authorities do not have much leeway to develop policies and programmes; rather, they depend on the central government for policy direction. The following characterises the social welfare system of Botswana:

▷ Destitute and Orphans and Vulnerable Children Programmes

The first social welfare programme for the destitute was launched in 1980 and subsequently reviewed in 2002. The primary goal of the programme was to provide minimal assistance to the deserving poorest of the poor, officially known as the destitute, to ensure good health and welfare.[32] Target beneficiaries are means-tested and must not own assets beyond the set limit. Mostly, the programme's beneficiaries are the elderly; people with mental and physical disabilities; orphans and vulnerable children; and survivors of natural disasters or other temporary hardships. Destitute able-bodied persons are placed in public works programmes where they can earn an allowance. Generally, the benefits of the destitute programme include a food basket, shelter, medical care, transport, protective clothing, funeral expenses, exemption from service levies and other related services. School-going children under the age of 18 years are assisted with

---

29    Hedenquist, 1992; Ntseane, 2007; Rankopo, 1996; Wass, 1969.
30    Ntseane, 2007.
31    Hedenquist, 1992; Rankopo, 1996.
32    Republic of Botswana. DSS, 2002.

school uniforms, toiletries, transport, clothing, boarding facilities, and tuition fees.[33] About 40 000 people enrol in this programme every year with an annual budget of at least 40 million pula (Botswana's currency).[34]

Parliament adopted the first policy to protect children in 1981, the Children's Act, that aimed to protect children from ill-treatment, neglect, and other social vulnerabilities.[35] The Act primarily addressed issues of custody, care, juvenile justice, and aspects of child protection and prescribed the small amount of 100 pula as fines for offences against children. This law was subsequently reviewed in 2009 to embrace a human-rights approach. However, child abuse cases rarely reach the courts apart from sex-related ones. Traditionally, leaving a child home alone or under the care of other children is quite acceptable. Many parents consider it an embarrassment to report child abuse cases. Following the onset of the HIV/Aids epidemic, the Government of Botswana introduced a programme for orphans and vulnerable children (OVC) in 1999. The epidemic had caused such a significant increase in the number of OVC that the indigenous support systems of informal adoption or foster care were unable to cope with the care of affected children. The Short-Term Plan of Action for OVC aimed to mitigate the impact of the HIV/Aids crisis on orphans and their caregivers.[36] By 2004, Botswana was estimated to have the highest rate of orphan-hood in Sub-Saharan Africa.[37] The National Situation Analysis on OVC conducted in 2007 estimated the number of OVC at 130 000, with nearly 95 000 being orphaned due to HIV/Aids.[38]

Other factors contributing to OVC's vulnerability were the abusive environments in which children found themselves. Many children became heads of households, lived in child-headed households or cared for a sick parent or guardian. It emerged that an increasing number of children were living with HIV in addition to a disability, and a large number lived outside family care. All of these conditions made the children vulnerable to abuse and exploitation, poor health, to be withdrawn from school and have emotional

---

33    Ntseane & Solo, 2007.

34    IMF & World Bank, 2013.

35    Republic of Botswana, 1981a.

36    Republic of Botswana, 1999; 2009.

37    UNAIDS, UNICEF & USAID, 2004.

38    UNICEF et al., 2009.

distress, and trauma.[39] In Botswana, an orphan is a child younger than 18 years who lost an only parent (in the case of a single parent) or both parents (a married couple). According to this definition, 51 806 orphans were living in Botswana in 2007.[40] However, the number increases to 130 000 if the international definition of orphan-hood is used. The United Nations Children's Fund (UNICEF) defines an orphan as any child below the age of 18 years who has lost one or both parents. In Botswana, children from married families are excluded if they lost one parent. Benefits for orphans which the Ministry of Local Government and Lands, and the Ministry of Health developed, include a nutritionally balanced monthly food basket worth 216 Pula; clothing; toiletry; assistance with educational needs; and psychosocial support. In 2002, 39 571 children were on the government's register, the figure increasing to 47 964 by 2004. By 2008-2009, the figure had risen to 48 119.[41]

▷ Vulnerable Groups and School Feeding Programmes

The Vulnerable Groups and School Feeding programmes distribute meals and nutritional supplements to people susceptible to malnutrition. Beneficiaries include pregnant and lactating mothers, nutritionally at-risk under-fives, and tuberculosis patients. Supplementary feeding is provided to all under-fives, while food rations are distributed to lactating mothers. The School Feeding Programme provides all school children in government schools with at least one meal per day. In 2009-2010, the number of registered beneficiaries in primary school stood at 261 513, while the figure for secondary school children stood at 165 097. The Vulnerable Group Feeding Programme, targeting adults and pre-school children at nutritional risk, has been quite popular; in 2009-2010, the number of beneficiaries stood at 239 985.[42]

▷ Universal Old-Age Pension Scheme

This scheme was introduced to curb the increasing vulnerability of older people – a result of rural-to-urban migration, severely weakening the extended family structure. All older persons, irrespective of their socio-economic backgrounds are eligible. Those registered under other schemes such as the Programme for Destitute Persons are still eligible to

---

39    UNICEF, 2008.

40    Republic of Botswana. DSS., 2008a.

41    RHVP, 2011.

42    Ibid.

receive their pension benefits if they qualify on account of age. The cash transfer is made through beneficiaries' bank accounts or at the post offices.[43] The number of beneficiaries steadily increased from 84 577 in 2003 to 86 859 in 2006. In 2010, 91 446 beneficiaries received 220 pula per month each.

▻ Remote-Area Dwellers Programme

This programme is rolled out in designated settlements through the DSS, targeting over 90 per cent of remote-area dwellers in 64 settlements in seven districts.[44] Virtually all remote-area dwellers are eligible to receive rations and allowances based on their destitution, and to create employment opportunities for them, the government established the Economic Promotion Fund. This Fund provides seed money for business-oriented activities, including game ranching, handicrafts and agricultural activities such as poultry rearing and livestock production and related activities like a tannery.[45] An estimated 43 070 beneficiaries are currently enrolled in this programme.[46] The Remote-Area Dwellers Programme was reviewed and renamed the Remote Area Communities Development programme. An important element of this programme today is that it promotes increased access to education for students from remote communities through affirmative action. The government also funds a beauty pageant for young women from remote communities as a way of promoting their dignity. The Remote Area Communities Development Programme is led by an officer at the Permanent Secretary level, demonstrating the government's commitment to the indigenous peoples. The Government of Botswana does not adopt the term 'indigenous peoples' because it regards all citizens as indigenous. The fact of the matter is that the Basarwa are the first inhabitants of Botswana and constitute the main beneficiaries under the Remote Area Communities Development Programme.

▻ *Ipelegeng* Programme

*Ipelegeng* is a nationwide government-sponsored programme that targets unskilled and semi-skilled labour. It is envisaged as a supplementary income source and involves carrying out essential development activities across the country to provide short-term

---

43    Republic of Botswana. Ministry of Local Government, 2010.
44    BIDPA, 1997.
45    Seleka, Siphambe, Ntseane, Mbere, Kerapeletswe & Sharp, 2007.
46    Republic of Botswana. Ministry of Local Government, 2010; Republic of Botswana & UNDP, 2010.

employment support and relief. Local authorities assign public works activities to beneficiaries; these tasks include, among others, litter collection; minor construction; clearing of fields; maintenance of buildings and secondary roads. Current wage rates are pegged at 18 pula per day for casual labourers and 24 pula per day for their supervisors. An estimated 19 431 people benefited from the programme in 2010, compared to 14 363 in 2008.[47]

## Social Work Training and Education

Social work training in Botswana started in 1972 with a one-year-long Certificate in Community Development at the Botswana Agricultural College. Two years later, a few social work courses were added, the programme extended to two years and was renamed a Certificate in Social Welfare and Community Development until 1984. In 1985, a two-year Certificate in Social Work and a two-year Diploma in Social Work were launched at the University of Botswana (UB), followed by the addition of a Bachelor of Social Work degree in 1986, a Master of Social Work in 1999 and a Master of Philosophy (MPhil) and a Doctor of Philosophy (PhD) in Social Work in 2010. These programmes have graduated at least 100 students annually between 1986 and 2016. The first PhD graduate was in 2015. Today, three tertiary colleges offer certificate and diploma programmes in social work in the country.

Social work training and education at UB has produced graduates with Master's and PhDs from many countries across the globe. This feat proves that the young social work programme has stood the test of time by drawing on expertise from abroad and the region to strengthen its curriculum. The newly formed Botswana National Association of Social Workers has been accredited with the International Federation of Social Workers since 2012 and has started engaging with the government to establish a statutory body for regulating the profession. There is no official statistics yet on the number of social workers in the country. Social workers in Botswana are employed across the central government, local authorities, parastatals, private and civil society sectors, respectively. They have contributed tremendously to the growth of social welfare and social work practice in the country.

---

47    Republic of Botswana. Ministry of Local Government of Botswana, 2010.

## Conclusion

Botswana stands among few countries in the world emerging from a poverty status to significant development in almost all of the human development indices; made possible because of diamonds discovered in 1972. The poverty status in the 1960s stood at 65 per cent, but to date, the poverty rate is around 21 per cent, demonstrating fundamental development in the quality of life. The growth of the country's GDP has been phenomenal. Generally, economic development has always grown at an average annual rate of about 8 per cent, resulting in improvements in social development. Botswana's phenomenal growth dispels the myth about commodity resources not being used to bring about social development, partially true, as commodity resources of the world have brought about misery in some nations. In this case, Botswana has directed its mineral resources into human development, contributing to phenomenal growth in social services.

At Independence, the country had little or nothing to boast about in terms of physical infrastructure such as roads, bridges, water, power, or primary, secondary and tertiary institutions; clinics, hospitals, stadia, airports, and telecommunications. To date, the country has seen remarkable development in social amenities. For example, after Independence, the health infrastructure, almost non-existent, has evolved from a 30-40 km radius of health facilities to 5 km. The same can be said of the education sector that has witnessed similar success. For example, the Education Policy and Data Centre (2014) stated:

> In Botswana, the gross enrolment rate in primary education is 106 per cent for girls and boys combined, decreasing to 90 per cent in lower secondary, with a student transition rate to secondary school of 97 per cent. The primary net enrolment rate is 84 per cent, and the primary completion rate is 95 per cent.[48]

Therefore, it is quite apparent that Botswana stands well in terms of the human development index. If the trend continues, Botswana, an upper-middle-income country, will attain the upper-income status in a foreseeable future that will translate into a higher quality of life for its people. Botswana will then be in a strong position to achieve most of the sustainable development goals.

---

48    Statistics Botswana, 2015:5.

# References

Apt, N.A. 2002. Ageing and changing role of the family and community: An African perspective. *International Social Security Review*, 55(1):39-47.

Bechuanaland Protectorate. 1963. *Bechuanaland Protectorate: Development Plan, 1963-1968*. Gaborone: Bechuanaland Press.

BIDPA (Botswana Institute for Development Policy Analysis). 1996. *Study of poverty and poverty alleviation in Botswana: Inception report*. Working Paper, 3. Gaborone: BIDPA.

Botlhale, E., Lekorwe, M., Mothusi, B. & Motshegwa, B. 2015. *A Political Economy Analysis of Social Protection in Botswana*. Working Paper, 1. Nairobi, Kenya: Partnership for African Social and Governance Research. [https://bit.ly/32EE3OE]. (Accessed 12 December 2016).

Denbow, J. & Phenyo, C. 2006. *Culture and Customs of Botswana*. London: Greenwood Press.

DSS (Department of Social Services) & Ministry of Local Government of Botswana. 2005. *Guidelines for provision of social safety net for community home-based care patients*. Gaborone: DSS and the Ministry of Local Government.

Ellis, F., Devereux, S. & White, P. 2009. *Social Protection in Africa*. Cheltenham: Edward Elgar Publishing Limited.

Ellis, F., Freeland, N., Ntseane, D., Seleka, T., Turner, S. & White, P. 2010. *Preparation of a Social Development Policy – Phase 1: Situation Analysis*. Gaborone: Ministry of Local Government's DSS.

Emmanuel, J., Maundeni, T. & Letshwiti-Macheng, P. 2011. Child protection issues in HIV and AIDS burdened countries: The case of Botswana. *Thari ya Bana: Reflections on children in Botswana 2011*. pp.44-48. Gaborone: University of Botswana and United Nation's Children Fund.

Ferguson-Brown, H.A. 1996. The origins of the welfare and community development programmes in Botswana. *Pula: Botswana Journal of African Studies*, 10(2):66-82.

Foster, G. 2004. Safety nets for children affected by HIV/AIDS in Southern Africa. In: R. Pharaoh (ed). *A generation at risk? HIV/AIDS, vulnerable children and security in Southern Africa*. Cape Town: Institute of Security Studies. pp.65-92.

Foster, G. 2007. Under the radar: community safety nets for AIDS-affected household in sub-Saharan Africa. *AIDS Care*, 19(Supplement 1):54-63.

Gray, M. 1996. Towards understanding of developmental social work. *Social Work Practice*, 1(96):9-12.

Hedenquist, J. 1992. *Introduction to Social and Community Development Work in Botswana*. Gaborone: Ministry of Local Government, Lands and Housing.

Holzmann, R. & Jorgensen, S. 1990. Social risk management: A new conceptual framework for social protection, and beyond. *International Tax and Public Finance*, 8:529-556.

Jongman, K. 2014. *A history of social work in Botswana and why the future looks bleak*. [https://bit.ly/2HdruBC]. (Accessed 15 December 2016).

Kaseke, E. 2004. Social Protection in SADC: Developing an Integrated and Inclusive Framework-Social Policy Perspective. In: M.P. Olivier & E.R. Kalula (eds). *Social Protection in SADC: Developing an Integrated and Inclusive Framework*. South Africa: Centre for International and Comparative Labour and Social Security Law, Rand Afrikaans University & Institute of Development and Labour Law, University of Cape Town. pp.1-11.

Maes, A. 2003. Informal economic and social security in sub-Saharan Africa. *International Social Security Review*, 56(3-4):39-58.

Midgley, J. 1994. Social security policy in developing countries: integrating state and traditional systems. *Focaal*, 2(22/34):219-230.

Midgley, J. 1995. *Social Development: The Developmental Perspective in Social Welfare*. London: Sage Publications.

Midgley, J. 2013. Social development and social protection: New opportunities and challenges. *Development Southern Africa*, 30(1):2-12.

Midgley, J. & Tang, K. 2001. Introduction: Social Policy, Economic Growth and Developmental Welfare. *International Journal of Social Welfare*, 10(4):244-252.

Miller, C., Gruskin, S., Subramanian, S., Rajaraman, D. & Heymann, J. 2006. Orphan Care in Botswana's Working Households: Growing Responsibilities in the Absence of Adequate Support. *American Journal of Public Health*, 96(8):1429-1435.

Mills, G. 2012. *Why Africa is poor and what Africans can do about it*. Rosebank, Johannesburg: Penguin Group.

Mosene, O. 2002. Informal credit demand in Botswana: micro-lending industry in Gaborone. MA thesis, Gaborone: University of Botswana.

Mpedi, L.G. 2008. The role of religious values in extending social protection: A South African perspective. *Acta Theologica*, 28(1):105-125.

Mwansa, L., Lucas, T. & Osei-Hwedie, K. 1998. The Practice of Social Policy in Botswana. *Journal of Social Development in Africa*, 13(2): 55-74.

NACA (National Aids Coordinating Agency). 2009. *The Second Botswana National Strategic Framework for HIV and AIDS, 2010-2016*. Gaborone: NACA.

Ngwenya, B.N. 2003. Redefining Kin: Burial Societies in Botswana. *Journal of Social Development in Africa*, 18(1):85-110.

Nkabinde, V.C. & Schoeman, N.J. 2007. *Does Social Security Enhance Growth in SADC Countries?* Unpublished conference paper. Pretoria: Department of Economics, University of Pretoria.

Ntseane, D. 2007. *Welfare Regime, Social Protection and Poverty Reduction.* Geneva: United Nations Research Institute for Social Development.

Ntseane, D. & Solo, K. 2004. Social Protection in SADC: Developing an Integrated and Inclusive Framework – the case of Botswana. In: M.P. Olivier & E.R. Kalula (eds). *Social Protection in SADC: Developing an Integrated and Inclusive Framework.* Johannesburg: Centre for International and Comparative Labour and Social Security Law, Rand Afrikaans University & Institute of Development and Labour Law, University of Cape Town. pp.73-96.

Ntseane, D. & Solo, K. 2007. *Social Security and Social Protection in Botswana.* Gaborone: Bay Publishing.

Okurut, N. & Botlhole, T. 2010. Informal Financial Markets in Botswana: A Case of Gaborone City. *Development Southern Africa*, 26(2):255-270. [https://doi.org/10.1080/03768350902899561]. (Accessed 11 October 2011).

Olivier, M. & Dekker, A.H. 2003. Informal social security. In: M. Olivier (ed). *Social Security A Legal Analysis.* Durban: Butterworth/Nexis Lexis.

Olivier, M., Kaseke, E. & Mpedi, L.G. 2008. Informal Social Security in Africa: Developing a Framework for Policy Intervention. Paper presented at International Conference on Social Security, 10-14 March, Cape Town.

Partnership for African Social & Governance Research. 2011. Scoping study on social protection in Africa. Nairobi. Unpublished handout.

Patel, L. 2005. *Social welfare and social development in South Africa.* Cape Town: Oxford University Press.

Patel, L. 2008. Getting it Right and Wrong: An Overview of a Decade of Post-Apartheid Social Welfare, Practice. *Social Work in Action*, 20(2):71-81.

Patel, L., Kaseke, E. & Midgley, J. 2012. Indigenous welfare and community based social development: Lessons from African innovations. *Journal of Community Practice*, 20(1):12-31.

Ramchandani, J.C. 1970. *Community development in Botswana.* New York: United Nations.

Ramsay, J. 1998. Twentieth-century antecedents of decolonising nationalism in Botswana. In: W.A. Edge & M.H. Lekorwe (eds). *Botswana: Politics and society.* Pretoria: Van Schaik Publishers. pp.101-117.

Rankopo, M. 1996. Community participation in self-help projects in Botswana. In: M. Hutton & L. Mwansa (eds). *Social work practice in Africa.* Gaborone: PrintConsult. pp.43-58.

Republic of Botswana. 1970. *National Development Plan 3 1970-1975.* Gaborone: Government Printing Works.

Republic of Botswana. 1981a. *Children's Act 5 of 1981*. Gaborone: Government Printing Works.

Republic of Botswana. 1981b. *National Policy on Destitute Persons*. Gaborone: Government Printing Works.

Republic of Botswana. 1999. *Short-term Plan of Action for the Care of Orphans in Botswana 1999-2001*. Gaborone: Ministry of Local Government: Social Welfare Division.

Republic of Botswana. 2009. *Children's Act 8 of 2009*. Gaborone: Government Printing Works.

Republic of Botswana. 2015. *History of the Botswana Police Service*. Gaborone: Botswana Police Service.

Republic of Botswana. DSS (Department of Social Services). 2002. *Revised National Policy on Destitute Persons*. Gaborone: DSS, Ministry of Local Government.

Republic of Botswana. DSS (Department of Social Services). 2008a. *National Guidelines on the Care of Orphans and Vulnerable Children*. Gaborone: Ministry of Local Government, DSS.

Republic of Botswana. DSS (Department of Social Services). 2008b. *National Situation Analysis on Orphans and Vulnerable Children in Botswana*. Gaborone: Ministry of Local Government, DSS.

Republic of Botswana. Ministry of Local Government. 2010. Data obtained from the Department of Social Services (DSS). Leaflet. Received from the DSS Headquarters in Gaborone.

Republic of Botswana & United Nations. 2010. *Botswana: Millennium Development Goals: Status Report 2010*. Gaborone: Botswana Printing & Publishing Company.

Republic of South Africa. National Department of Social Development. 2010. *Evaluation of Retirement: Systems of Countries within SADC*. Pretoria: Government Printing Works.

RHVP (Regional Hunger and Vulnerability Programme). 2007. *Social transfers: Experiences and evidence from Southern Africa*, 1(Case Studies 3, 16, 18). Johannesburg: RHVP.

RHVP (Regional Hunger and Vulnerability Programme). 2010. *Social Protection in Africa: Where are we, and how did we get there?* Johannesburg: RHVP.

RHVP (Regional Hunger and Vulnerability Programme). 2011. *Social Protection in Botswana – A Model for Africa?* Johannesburg: RHVP.

Schapera, I. 1970. *A Handbook of Tswana Law and Custom*. London: Frank Cass.

Seleka, T., Siphambe, H., Ntseane, D., Mbere, N., Kerapeletswe, C. & Sharp, C. 2007. *Social Safety Nets in Botswana: Administration, Targeting and Sustainability*. Gaborone: Botswana Institute for Development Policy Analysis.

Shaibu, S. & Wallhagen, M. 2002. Family caregiving of the elderly in Botswana: Boundaries of culturally acceptable options and resources. *Journal of Cross-Cultural Gerontology*, 17(2):139-154.

Statistics Botswana. 2013. *Botswana Core Welfare Indicators (Poverty) Survey 2009/10*. Gaborone: Statistics Botswana.

Statistics Botswana. 2015. *Primary School Stats Brief 2015*. Gaborone: Statistics Botswana.

Tesliuc, C., Marques, J.S., Lekobane, K.R., Mookodi, L., Bezhanyan, A., Braithwaite, J., Mohan, A., Otsuka, M., Scheja, E., Sharma, S., Ntseane, D., Tsirunyan, S. & Schmalzbach, M. 2013. *Botswana Social Protection Assessment*. Gaborone: BIDPA & World Bank.

UNAIDS (Joint United Nations Programme on HIV/Aids), UNICEF (United Nations International Children's Fund) & USAID (United States Agency for International Development). 2004. *Children on the Brink 2004: A Joint Report of New Orphan Estimates and a Framework for Action*. Washington, DC: UNICEF.

UNAIDS & UNICEF. 2004. *The Framework for the Protection, Care, and Support of Orphans and Vulnerable Children Living in a World with HIV and AIDS*. New York: UNICEF.

UNICEF, UNAIDS, UNFPA (United Nations Fund for Population Activities) & WHO (World Health Organisation). 2009. *Children and AIDS: Fourth Stocktaking Report, 2009*. New York: UNICEF.

USAID. 2010. *Assessing the implementation of Botswana's programme for orphans and vulnerable children*. Washington, DC: USAID.

Wass, P. 1969. A case history: Community development gets established in Botswana. *International Review of Community Development*, 2(21/22):181-198.

# 03

# SOCIAL WELFARE AND SOCIAL WORK IN THE DEMOCRATIC REPUBLIC OF CONGO

*Alain Kambale Maboko*

## Introduction

This chapter examines social welfare and social work in the context of political instability, poor governance, corruption, accountability bottlenecks and social fragility in the Democratic Republic of Congo (DRC). It discusses the main internal and external factors that influenced this country's social welfare and social work endeavours while considering the prevailing political chaos, poor governance and social discord after 58 years of independence. On 30 December 2018, the people of the DRC, during colonial rule known as the Belgian Congo and later Zaire, went to the polls after a two-year delay. It is a sovereign nation-state, nearly 80 times larger than the whole of Belgium. The DRC is the southernmost country of Central Africa. In 2017 it had a population of 81 339 988.[1] With 80 million hectares of arable land and over 1 100 minerals and precious metals, the DRC has the potential to become one of the richest countries in the world and a driver of African growth if it can overcome its political instability. Despite a decreased poverty rate – 71 per cent to 64 per cent of the population (2005-2012) – the DRC still ranks among the world's poorest countries.[2] The DRC has a total area of 2 345 858 km$^2$

---

1    UNDP, 2019

2    Ibid.

in terms of landmass; a tropical climate, with monthly average temperatures of between 23-27 degrees Celsius across 90 per cent of the country; unparalleled natural resources to Africa and the world. The United Nations Environment Programme reports that the DRC has the highest level of biodiversity in Africa, with tropical rainforests extending over 1.55 million km$^2$ (half of Africa's forests) and accounting for more than half of Africa's forest resources and half of Africa's water resources and trillion-dollar mineral reserves.[3] It makes the DRC a critical global ecosystem service provider and a potential source of 900 million US dollars in annual revenue up to 2030.

The DRC is strategically located on the Equator, practically the centre of the African continent and shares borders with nine other countries: Angola, Burundi, the Central African Republic, the Republic of Congo, Rwanda, South Sudan, Tanzania, Uganda and Zambia. The country has about four hundred different ethnic and linguistic groups after the Belgian colonialists introduced the French language as the official language. However, most of the Congolese are fluent in the dominant indigenous languages such as Swahili, Lingala, Kikongo, and Tshiluba. In terms of religion, approximately 50 per cent is Roman Catholic, 35 per cent Protestant (including evangelicals), 5 per cent Kimbanguist (a Congolese Christian church), and 5 per cent Muslim. Religious groups with small populations include Jehovah's Witnesses; the Church of Jesus Christ of Latter-day Saints (Mormons); Greek Orthodox Christians and Jews; and the remainder of the population generally adheres to indigenous religious beliefs.[4] The relationship between the Church and state has varied over time. In the colonial era, the mostly Catholic Belgian colonial administrators cooperated closely with Catholic missionaries.

In contrast, Protestant missionaries were sometimes critical of colonial practices, as can be seen in the international movement, the mostly Protestant churches organised against the Red Rubber Regime. Under the regime of the dictator Mobutu Sese Seko, all mainstream Protestant groups and the Kimbanguists were closely allied with the government.[5] At the same time, the Catholics were often at odds with the totalitarian regime. The Catholic Church provided essential support to the pro-democracy movement in the 1990s, with a Bishop serving as president of the National Conference.

---

3    UNEP, 2017

4    Global Security.Org, 2018.

5    Ikambana, P. 2007. *Mobutu's totalitarian political system: An Afrocentric analysis.*

Both Catholic and Protestant leaders played important roles in promoting peace during Congo's various armed conflicts.[6]

The DRC's economy slowed from 6.9 per cent in Gross Domestic Product (GDP) in 2015 to hovering around 3.4 per cent in 2017, driven by increases in commodity prices and national mining production, particularly of copper and cobalt, accounting for 80 per cent of export revenue.[7] Many of the DRC's social indicators are not encouraging, for example, its human development profile. An indicator such as the Human Development Index (HDI) is useful in providing a clearer picture of the quality of life of a particular country's citizens, as is the case with the DRC. According to the United Nations Development Programme (UNDP), the HDI is a summary measure for assessing long-term progress in three basic dimensions of human development: a long and healthy life, access to knowledge and a decent standard of living.[8] The DRC's HDI value for 2017 was 0.457 – putting the country in the low human development category – positioning it at 176 out of 189 countries and territories (UNDP, 2017).

Nevertheless, between 1990 and 2017, the country's HDI value increased from 0.356 to 0.457 – an increase of 28.5 per cent. DRC's HDI of 0.457 is below the average of 0.504 for countries in the low human development group and below the average of 0.537 for countries in Sub-Saharan Africa. From Sub-Saharan Africa, countries close to its 2017 HDI rank and some extent in population size, are Ethiopia and Nigeria, having HDIs ranked 173 and 157, respectively (UNDP, 2017). Another dimension that shows the quality of life of the people is the Multidimensional Poverty Index (MPI). According to the UNDP (2015), the MPI identifies multiple deprivations in the same households in education, and health and living standards.[9] The most recent survey data that were publicly available for the DRC's MPI estimation refer to 2013-2014, whereby 72.5 per cent of the population (50 312 people) were multidimensionally poor. In comparison, an additional 18.5 per cent lived near multidimensional poverty (12 836 people). The breadth of deprivation (intensity) in the DRC, the average of deprivation scores experienced by people in multidimensional poverty, was 50.8 per cent.[10]

---

6    Global Security.Org, 2018.
7    Global Security.Org, 2018.
8    UNDP, 2015:2.
9    Ibid:6.
10   UNDP, 2015.

Despite the preceding, the DRC has potential: "Africa is like a revolver whose trigger is in the Congo. If the trigger is pulled, the whole of Africa will explode", a quote attributed to Frantz Fanon as a summary to his struggles for the African revolution meaning the DRC could be the trigger for African development.

However, political misrule, extensive corruption, weak institutions and human incapability, coupled with a lack of basic infrastructure, means that the pace of development for the average citizen remains slow or even non-existent.[11] Arguably, many of these challenges emanate from a brutal colonial history.

## Historical Context: Colonial Rule in the Belgian Congo

Colonial rule in the DRC began in the late nineteenth century. The Congo Free State, from 1885-1908, included the present DRC's area and fell under Leopold II, King of Belgium. His administration exploited rubber, called 'red rubber' because of the Belgians' brutality towards indigenous people working on the rubber plantations. Due to this, the Belgian colony became a humanitarian disaster. John Cox (2014) wrote in his book that in pursuit of ivory and rubber, as well as the status afforded a major colonial power, Leopold's authorities, complemented by a motley assortment of adventurers, inflicted terrible violence upon the Congolese people. Cox further points out that most of the population was enslaved as Leopold's men imposed production quotas for harvesting rubber while the hapless slave labourers who failed to meet these quotas had their hands chopped off. Beatings, lashings, and periodic massacres characterised Leopold's rule, and starvation and disease were the predictable consequences of the Belgians' destruction of community life (torture or holding wives and children hostage, for example) and commerce. As many as 10 million Congolese ultimately perished under Leopold's rule. Europeans, in this case Belgians, engaged in the scramble and conquest of Africa committed atrocities and abuses, but the atrocities committed in the Congo were far beyond anywhere else. Leopold's exploitation of the territory and its peoples was merciless to the point of genocide. Leopold himself created a Crown Estate (*Domaine de la Couronne*) from where the profits of the rubber regime went to him personally. The local inhabitants were forced to collect rubber for minimal returns and were subjected to a variety of compulsions if they failed to deliver the quotas demanded. Hostages were

---

11    DFID, 2014.

taken against deliveries, chiefs killed or intimidated, individuals slaughtered and whole villages razed. A potentially lethal whip of dried hippopotamus hides, the *chicotte*, was widely used, and the regime's soldiers were ordered to produce severed hands, to prove that they had used their weapons effectively. The rubber-producing areas' populations were decimated, partly as a result of these practices and flight; malnutrition and disease that followed.[12]

Leopold extracted a fortune from the Congo, initially collecting ivory, and after a rise in the price of rubber in the 1890s, forcing labour from the natives to harvest and process rubber. Under his regime, millions of Congolese people died: modern estimates range from 1 million to 15 million, with a consensus growing around 10 million. Human rights abuses under his regime contributed significantly to these deaths. Reports of deaths and abuse led to a major international scandal in the early twentieth century. By 1908, public pressure and international diplomatic pressure led to the end of Leopold II's rule and the annexation of the Congo as a colony of Belgium in Central Africa, known as the Belgian Congo, from 1908-1960.

## Violent Colonial Administration

When the Belgian Government took over the administration of the Congo in 1908, the situation in the country improved in certain respects. The colonialists' and concessionary companies' brutal exploitation and arbitrary use of violence against the people were curbed. The crime of 'red rubber' was put to a stop. Article 3 of the Colonial Charter of 18 October 1908 establishes that: "Nobody can be forced to work on behalf of and for the profit of companies or privates." Forced labour, in differing forms and degrees, would not disappear entirely until the end of the colonial period. Through forced labour, Leopold II was able to amass billions of Belgian francs while the Congo was left in economic ruin and debt:

> King Leopold II used the anti-slavery excuse to introduce into Congo forced labour and modern slavery. Besides, all Europeans had derived ideas of racial and cultural superiority between the 15th and 19th centuries, while engaged in genocide and the enslavement of non-white peoples.[13]

---

12    Ewans, 2002.

13    Rodney, 1973:216.

The 1908 Colonial Charter arranged the Government of the Belgian Congo, that would not recognise or promote any indigenous elite, and its parliament, exercised legislative authority over this territory. The Congo had a high degree of racial segregation. Large numbers of white immigrants, moving to the Congo after the end of the Second World War, came from across the social spectrum but were always treated as superior to blacks. On many occasions, the indigenous population tried to resist the colonialists' ill-treatment. However, this was in vain because the interests of the colonial government and private enterprise were closely tied together.

## *Les Évolués*: Step to Europeanisation

From the 1920s, both Britain and France produced colonial educators and education commissioners who urged the relevance of teaching programmes in Africa. They suggested the use of local languages in primary schools, more education for girls, and an end to the white-collar orientation of schooling. However, the seemingly progressive nature of those recommendations could not change the fact that colonial education was an instrument to serve the European capitalist class in the exploitation of Africa.[14] During the 1940s and 1950s, the Congo experienced rapid and extensive urbanisation, and the colonial administration put in place various development programmes aimed at making the territory into a 'model colony'. One of the results was the development of a new middle class of Europeanised Africans or *évolués* ('educated ones') in the cities. By the 1950s the Congo had a 'wage labour force' twice as large as that of any other African colony. The Belgian Congo developed the most extensive and thorough colonial administration in Africa, based upon the idea of direct rule (i.e., by Belgians) and intense paternalism. The Belgian Congo was characterised by a high degree of coordination between the three sectors of penetration, called the 'Trinity': the colonial administration (government), the Church (Roman Catholic) and private companies. The background to this penetration can be attributed to the Kongo (here meaning the Kingdom of Kongo before Congo) becoming globalised, having already incorporated outside influences.

Nevertheless, Kongo culture remained resolutely Kongolese throughout colonial rule. This experience of pluralism and cultural retention would put the societies of West-Central Africa in good stead, to retain their vitality when colonialism began almost two

---

14    Rodney, 1973.

centuries later. Post-colonial nations such as Angola and the DRC grew from a core of a strong, deep-rooted, and yet globalised peoples and cultures.[15]

By then, the Jesuit missionaries (*'Père Jesuite'*), created social infrastructures and educational systems - a model still used today in the country. The first secondary education school that was made available to the indigenous population was in 1954. However, in 1960 there was only a handful of Congolese holding a university degree. The colonial administration implemented a variety of economic reforms that focused on the building of infrastructure: railways, ports, roads, mines, plantations, and industrial areas. The Congolese people, however, lacked political power and faced legal discrimination.

The DRC, contrary to European assumption and thought, was a complex society linked by chiefs, kings, and trade. Gann and Duignan (1979), say that "An African Aristotle would have been found in the Congo in every conceivable form of constitution, from small stateless neighbourhood societies to powerful monarchies." Some of these powerful kingdoms were the Luba, Lunda, and Kongo kingdoms. People in these kingdoms consisted of farmers, hunters, and fishermen.[16] However, Adam Hochschild's book, *King Leopold's Ghost* (one of the most seminal studies on the Congo), shows that the Congo had just as much civilisation as most European countries during the sixteenth century until the horrendous slave trade period.[17] Also, Jan Vansina, in his book *Kingdoms of the Savanna*, points out that in the Congo, "several villages together formed a chiefdom, some of these powerful kingdoms were the Luba, Lunda, and Kongo kingdoms and all the provinces together made up the kingdom."[18] Murphy explains in his book, *History of African Civilisation*, that members of a lineage possessed the quality of *Bulopwe*, the sacred right of leadership, and could legitimately organise a revolt if the king became unpopular.[19]

---

15    Toby, 2015:17.
16    Gann & Duignan, 1979.
17    Hochschild, 1998.
18    Vansina, 1966:37.
19    Murphy, 1972.

## Questionable Evangelisation: A tool for Colonialists' Control of Wealth and Local Communities

Since the colonial period, the Catholic Church priests worked with political and administrative authorities mostly in the health and education sectors. The colonialists' strategy of deep control of the population was their evangelisation through the *Père Jesuite*, the catholic missionaries who were supposed to care for the indigenous communities. Even after Independence, these missionaries founded social projects and centres, for example, the Social Action Study Centre (*Centre d'Etudes pour l'Action Sociale*, CEPAS) in 1965. Today CEPAS demonstrates social work impacts in the country: the social apostolate had to provide society's poor, underprivileged classes with the temporary and spiritual goods required to lead a proper life. While indigenous people were considered not civilised by the colonialists, the economic exploitation of the Congo was the coloniser's top priority, and one important tool was the construction of the railways to open the mineral and agricultural areas. However, because of the inability of the colonial government to introduce radical and credible changes, the Congolese elites began to organise themselves socially and soon politically.

The colonialist system suppressing and opposing any local initiative, resulted in the first local organisation being founded in 1950. Joseph Kasa Vubu headed the Bakongo Cultural Association (*Association Culturelle des Bakongo*, Abako), initially a cultural association that soon turned into a political organisation. From the mid-1950s, a major ethnoreligious organisation, the Kimbanguist Church, was extremely popular. It comprised of a group of Catholic *évolués* who were fighting for social community development. These confessional organisations and many other indigenous organisations started to engage in the social welfare of the indigenous people. Education emerged as the new basis for social stratification and was limited to primary schooling; secondary schooling was denied until the late 1940s. The University of Lovanium, the first institution of higher educational opportunities, was established in 1954.

Nonetheless, those few Africans who were granted education beyond the primary level were the first to challenge the colonial system. The colonial administrators treated the *évolués*, the desired product of Belgium's assimilation policy, who insisted on better education for all, as an elite and privileged group. Socially, the *évolués* were between the Europeans and the masses and were conscious of their elevated status. By the end of the

Second World War, the number of *évolués* was large enough to constitute a distinct social group. Since the colonial system prohibited organisations with political overtones from operating, the *évolués* formed cultural organisations that had some ethnic connections. These ethnic associations began making pleas for self-government in the mid-1950s, ultimately resulting in the creation of political parties.

Overall, the result of King Leopold II's exploitation of the Congo and direct colonial rule set in motion the ethnic, political, and economic challenges that still prevail today. Towards the end of Belgian colonial domination in the DRC, relations between the colonial master and the local people worsened, a situation culminating in the formation of a radicalised nationalist movement. The Congolese National Movement (*Movement National Congolais*, MNC), led by Patrice Lumumba, demanded independence of the Congolese people and eventually led the Congo to Independence. The Belgians responded to the African appeal for self-governance by introducing political reforms that culminated in legislative elections in May 1960, and soon after, June 30 was proclaimed the Day of Independence and is the kept memorial date in the DRC's history.

## Political Instability, Corruption, Poor Governance: Internal Causes

In 1960, at Independence under Prime Minister Patrice Lumumba and President Joseph Kasa Vubu, the DRC became a Republic. Despite the MNC being popular, Kasa Vubu's Abako Party had also won significant seats in the National Assembly, and thus a compromise had to be made for both leaders to rule the DRC. The ideological differences between Lumumba and Kasa Vubu plunged the country into a political crisis. The pro-West Kasa Vubu, who was close to the former colonial master Belgium, accused Lumumba of being a communist. Due to this, Lumumba fired Kasa Vubu several months into Independence, but Kasa Vubu refused to be dismissed by Lumumba leading to a political impasse. This political arrangement was short-lived and precipitated a political crisis that saw the first democratically elected leader, Lumumba, being ousted and later assassinated. At the same time, another ethnic crisis erupted in the Katanga region when Katanga announced its secession from the DRC. The leader of Katanga, Moïse Tshombe, declared Katanga an independent state with the blessings of Belgium, the USA and other Western nations. After Lumumba's assassination on 17 January 1961, the Congo descended into a civil war.

Consequently, Colonel Joseph Désiré Mobutu ended the political impasse by seizing power in a coup d'état.[20] Mobutu renamed the Congo the Republic of Zaire in 1971 and launched a campaign of Congolese 'authenticity' called 'Zaïrisation' of the country in the mid-1970s, leading to an exodus of foreign workers and resulting in an economic disaster.[21] Consequently, all the social and economic conditions of the country became deplorable.

Mobutu remained the country's president until 1997. During his rule, living conditions had lost meaning, as the social and economic sectors were paralyzed. Mobutu's rule was oppressive and mostly chaotic. State coffers were looted at will while civil servants were not paid their salaries. Mobutu's regime had created disorientation in the public management system and compromised the country's future. Despite these shortcomings, in 1972, Mobutu banned all Christian names and nationalised the Catholic schools, starting the conflict between the Catholic Church and the State. Forbidding Christian names was known as 'authenticity' a process that extended to lifestyle with European models forbidden. Mobutu passed a policy to improve the disastrous indigenous social conditions on 30 November 1973, for the Zairianisation (nationalisation) of small and medium-sized foreign businesses; commerce; plantations; small industries; construction firms; transportation; and property-holding businesses.[22]

## Political Context and Social Crisis: External Causes

Today, the country is still recovering from a series of conflicts that broke out in the 1990s, creating a protracted economic and social slump. In 1997 a rebel force headed by Laurent-Désiré Kabila ousted Mobutu from power and renamed Zaire as the DRC. However; one of his bodyguards assassinated him in 2001 and his son Joseph Kabila Kabange immediately replaced him. In 2006 Joseph Kabila was confirmed as president through the first nationwide 'free' elections in the Congo since 1960, widely thought to have been rigged. The population also had not been involved in the political process. In 2011, Joseph Kabila and his party won the presidential and legislative elections despite concerns about the transparency of the electoral process. He declared himself president.

---

20  Ikambana, P. 2007. Mobutu's totalitarian political system: An Afrocentric analysis.
21  Ibid.
22  Ikambana, 2007.

After his father's death, Joseph Kabila unsuccessfully tried to work on the social and economic reforms.

Nevertheless, political instability continues to define the DRC with insurrections emerging almost yearly. Although different social actors are involved in the country, insecurity contributes enormously to social instability. The political situation remains tense in the DRC, particularly in the eastern provinces. Peacebuilding and economic recovery efforts are being carried out in a challenging social context. On top of this, Kabila became autocratic and cancelled the 2016 elections. The elections of December 2018 were a contentious issue with Kabila losing to Félix Tshisekedi from the Union for Democracy and Social Progress, who became president in January 2019.

## Provision of Social Services

This section will first provide a general description of the national commitment to basic services and social protection, before zooming in on the sectors under special scrutiny: health, education, transport, water and sanitation, and social protection. Afterwards, this section will go into the various distinguishable interventions in these sectors, whether government-led, community-based, agency-led, or private sector-led, with a special focus on community participation.

According to the DRC Poverty Reduction Strategy Paper 2, 2011-2015, the International Monetary Fund's (IMF) Pillar 3, it is a government's responsibility to allow access to quality basic social services to all.[23] In March 2010, the government adopted a new educational policy, the *Development Strategy of Primary, Secondary and Vocational Education 2010/11-2015/16*, targeting three major strategic goals:

▷ To increase access, affordability, equity, and retention in the different levels of education and particularly basic education.

▷ To improve the quality and relevance of education.

▷ To strengthen the governance of the sector.

---

23    IMF, 2013:73.

These goals were defined and designed to help the DRC advance towards achieving its development vision and converting to a middle-income country.[24] The role of the State in policy formulation, providing supervision and support, as well as indirect service provision, is in many cases limited. For example, only 10 per cent of primary education is State provided. The religious and private sector deliver the rest and in the sectors of health and water and sanitation, non-governmental organisations (NGOs) provide 50 per cent of services.[25]

The provision of social services is of great importance in the DRC, notably provided by different actors involved in the welfare of the Congolese population. Many aid organisations, voluntary and private sector organs, have programmes and agency-led interventions directed at restoring people's livelihoods in the DRC. These agencies invest in infrastructure (transport and social), including the rehabilitation and construction of new schools, hospitals, and markets. However, the number of studies on the impact of livelihoods programmes in the DRC are limited, and no reports or articles have been found that present an overview of livelihoods interventions in this country. In fact, as Bailey (2011) notes: "... very little is known about the impact of assistance, but also, it is unknown to what extent use will be made of Congolese workers, and what employment opportunities will be generated for the Congolese."[26] Education and health in the DRC can broadly be divided into three categories: state, religious run and private. The religious-run schools represent a majority of almost 70 per cent, State-run less than 20 per cent, and private schools around 10 per cent, a system that can be historically traced back to colonial times when virtually all the schools were under missionaries' care. The Catholic denomination is the largest and educating approximately 50 per cent of the student population, followed by Protestants (37 per cent), Kimbanguists (8 per cent) and Moslem (2 per cent).

There are a lot of community-based organisations and local civil society actors in the DRC, providing various community-based services to communities and working to address community issues. All these structures coordinate actions towards social recovery, improved social services and increased economic activity within the communities. Apart from the hard times of political instability in the country, churches play a major social

---

24  IMF, 2013.

25  Wejis, Hilhorst & Ferf, 2012.

26  Bailey, 2011:8.

role in the DRC, by controlling most of the social services offered at schools, hospitals and local economic market development. International non-governmental organisations play prominent roles in the social sector and offer tremendous services to the Congolese people. Most of them work in humanitarian, health, and educational services. To illustrate this, for instance, the International Rescue Committee and CARE International began the 'Tuungane' community-driven planning and reconstruction programme to improve stability and quality of life for communities in the eastern DRC (the Kivus, Maniema, Katanga regions). Tuungane had started as a three-year programme (2007-2010), to cover 1 780 000 people in 280 communities and including 1 266 (originally 1 400) villages. From a budget of 40 million US dollars, over 20 million was to be invested in villages and community projects (54 US dollars per household). After 2010, the programme was extended to 2014, with a 2011-2014 budget of 100 million US dollars. The goal:

▻ To foster social cohesion in eastern Congo (improved trust, confidence and cooperation between community members, including marginalised groups, and between people and their local institutions).

▻ To establish democratic governance (community members understanding the value of democratic local governance structures and experiencing active participation and transparent, accountable decision-making).

▻ To enhance social-economic recovery (improved social services and increased economic activity within the communities).[27]

The country benefits from the presence of United Nations agencies that coordinate actions through clusters matching their appropriated area of intervention. The United Nations Children's Fund (UNICEF) takes the lead in education and youth development programmes; the World Health Organisation (WHO) leads the health sector, the World Food Programme is at the forefront of food security. Other organisations, the Food Security and Inclusive Access to Resources for Conflict-Sensitive Market Development Programme, humanitarian agencies such as Mercy Corps and Search for Common Ground, for example, work together to give their actions impact. World Vision responds to food security and water governance with the International Rescue Committee and many more other humanitarian agencies conducting surveys (accountability in public

---

27    Weijs, Hilhorst & Ferf, 2012:24.

service delivery). One of these surveys' key findings revealed the dysfunction of public infrastructure to meet citizens' basic needs.[28] There is a vast array of national and international, governmental and non-governmental organisations involved in the development and social relief efforts in the DRC. These are traditionally divided into humanitarian and development aid.

Humanitarian financing amounted to approximately 600 million in 2010, according to Bailey, with the Humanitarian Action Plan, *Humanitarian Accountability Partnership-HAP 2011* governing the United Nations Office for the Coordination of Humanitarian Affairs coordinating interventions.[29]

Besides the political and economic aspects of the country's development, the country's social welfare plans intend to improve the policies to support economic growth as well as improve the different governance areas. They seek to provide basic social services, sustaining real progress on poverty reduction and combating corruption. However, the Ministry of Social Affairs offers social services through public institutions and other structures or individuals who may or may not be professional social workers and work in organisations such as community-based organisations like schools and particularly health centres. These local organisations are involved in the welfare sector of the DRC and perform well given their programme-led community participation aspect. Nevertheless, poor social welfare does not result from the lack of economic potential, but primarily because of an acute governance crisis: structures at various levels are often unable and at times unwilling to finance or provide basic services. Where services do exist, they are primarily financed by and provided by the UN and international and national civil society organisations on the one hand, and congregational denominations on the other.

The scale of the social welfare challenges in the DRC is enormous. Both conflict and poor governance like corruption mean that the DRC remains a challenging environment for development programming. However, the cost of failing to address the needs of the population are great if these issues are not sorted out.

---

28    Mercy Corps, 2016.
29    Bailey, 2011:11.

## Steps to Engage in Social Welfare Improvement

As formulated in the DRC's Poverty Reduction and Growth Strategy Paper, mentioned earlier, this strategy aims to improve the population's living conditions by laying a strong foundation for the diversification of the economy by strengthening infrastructure; improving governance and institutional capacity; and ensuring the rapid development of a greater private-sector contribution towards economic growth.[30] Given the country's geographic area, the implementation action plan in the government's 2012-2016 programme, adopts a spatial approach around five priority development zones to ensure the accelerated and coordinated realisation of their economic potential, mainly as a result of increased private sector mobilisation in the productive sectors. To reduce the levels of poverty in the country, the DRC Government embarked on IMF recommended reforms to improve its macroeconomic environment, initiate policies to support economic growth as well as improve its provision of basic social services. The results have been mixed.

## Conclusion

It is crucial to establish a new system of governance in the DRC and to elect a new, uncorrupted and disciplined government, capable of improving the living conditions of the average Congolese. A precondition for the DRC is that it must have good leadership and hold fair democratic elections as a turning point for the country's development. The future government must focus on education, healthcare, and child education should become the number one priority. After a decade of war and conflict, it is mandatory to shift the priorities from military/security and inter-ethnic conflicts to people's social welfare and sustainable development. Political instability and human rights violations must be dealt with, but everything depends on the eradication of poverty. The DRC offers challenges and opportunities that could determine its long-term social development path. Despite the international community's intervention, supply has been insufficient to meet basic social service demand. The national government is attempting to minimise international NGOs and the services they offer and amplify state interventions in the abovementioned sectors.

---

30    IMF, 2013.

# References

Africa News. 2019. *Can Tshisekedi's govt deliver free education in DRC?* [https://bit.ly/2Eglh6Q]. (Accessed 22 January 2020).

Bailey, S. 2011. *Humanitarian action, early recovery and stabilisation in the Democratic Republic of Congo.* London: Humanitarian Policy Group.

Bosch, B., Douma, P., Bolhuis, E., Klaver, D. & Zawadi, Y. 2009. *Public-Private Cooperation in Fragile States: Field Study Report: Democratic Republic of Congo.* Utrecht: Agency for International Business Cooperation & Conflict Research Unit.

Copperbelt Katanga News. 2020. *DRC? The potential to be Africa's richest country?* [https://bit.ly/3kxO8Dd]. (Accessed 22 June 2020).

Cox, J. 2016. *To kill a people, genocide in twentieth century.* London: Oxford University Press.

DRC (Democratic Republic of Congo). Ministry of Education. 2010. *Stratégie de Développement de l'Enseignement Primaire, Secondaire et Professionnel (2010/11-2015/16): Democratic Republic of Congo.* Paris, France: United Nations Educational, Scientific and Cultural Organisation. [https://bit.ly/33ICluX]. (Accessed 22 January 2011).

DRC. Ministry of Planning. 2011. *Document de Stratégie de Croissance et de Réduction de la Pauvreté (DSCRP).* Kinshasa: Ministry of Planning.

DRC. Ministry of Public Health & Ministry of Education. 2010. *Inf'Eau Congo: Bulletin d'information du secteur de l'eau, l'hygiène et l'assainissement en milieu rural et périurbain en République Démocratique du Congo.* Kinshasa: Ministry of Public Health & Ministry of Education. [https://uni.cf/35IrlQS]. (Accessed 2 May 2018).

Emizet, K.F. 1997. *Zaire after Mobutu: A Case of a Humanitarian Emergency.* Helsinki: United Nations University World Institute for Development Economics Research.

Ewans, M. 2003. Belgium and the Colonial Experience. *Journal of Contemporary European Studies,* 11(2):167-180.

Gann, L.H. & Duignan. L. 1979. *The Rulers of Belgian Congo 1884-1914.* Princeton, NJ: Princeton University Press.

Global Security. 2018. DR Congo - Religion. [https://bit.ly/3c7Tt0Y]. (Accessed 23 March 2019).

Green, T. 2015. *African Kingdoms: A Guide to the Kingdoms of Songhay, Kongo, Benin, Oyo and Dahomey c.1400 – c.1800.* Cambridge: Cambridge University Press.

Grega, P., Garbarino, S., Mata, G.T. & Eggen, M. 2008. *Citizens' Voice and Accountability-Democratic Republic of Congo Country Case Study Final Report.* Walhain, Belgium: Federal Public Department for Foreign Affairs, Foreign Trade and Cooperation for Development & Swedish International Development Cooperation Agency.

Hochschild, A. 1998. *King Leopold's Ghost: A Story of Greed, Terror and Heroism in Colonial Africa*. Boston, MA: Mariner Books.

Ikambana, P. 2007. *Mobutu's totalitarian political system: An Afrocentric analysis*. New York: Routledge.

IMF (International Monetary Fund). 2010. *Democratic Republic of Congo: Poverty Reduction Strategy Paper*. Country Report 10/328. Washington, DC: IMF. [https://bit.ly/35NkVzV]. (Accessed 22 January 2018).

IMF (International Monetary Fund). African Department. 2013. *Democratic Republic of the Congo: Poverty Reduction Strategy Paper 2 (2011-2015)*. Country Report 13/226. Washington, DC: IMF.

IMF (International Monetary Fund) & World Bank. 2013. *DRC's Growth and Poverty Reduction Strategy Paper*, 1. Washington, DC: International Monetary Fund Publication Services.

Jefferson, M.E. 1972. *History of African civilization*. New York: Thomas Y. Crowell Company.

Kabuya, K.F. & Cassimon, D. 2010. *Global Financial Crisis Discussion Series Paper 15: Democratic Republic of Congo Phase 2*. London: Overseas Development Institute.

Lucio, K.K. 2013. *Social work in the democratic republic of Congo*. Paper. Burundi: Hope Africa University. [https://bit.ly/35Ms1Vf]. (Accessed 22 January 2019).

Murphy, E.J. 1972. *History of African Civilisation*. New York: Thomas Y. Crowell Company.

Peter-Hans Kolvenbach, S.J. 2000. On the Social Apostolate. *Promotio Iustitiae*, 73(2000):20-28. [https://bit.ly/2RELUp6]. (Accessed 22 January 2019).

Programme Management Unit (FTF-ITT) National Institute of Agricultural Extension Management. n.d. *Demand Analysis Report of the Democratic Republic of the Congo*. [https://bit.ly/2Fxkj6Y]. (Accessed 22 January 2019).

Rodney, W. 1973. *How Europe Underdeveloped Africa*. London: Bogle-L'Ouverture Publications.

Socio-Economic Network. 2013. *BBC World Debate: Why Poverty?* [https://bit.ly/32ISzEQ]. (Accessed 12 December 2016).

UK (United Kingdom). DFID (Department for International Development). 2014. *Operational plan 2011-2016 DFID Democratic Republic of the Congo (DRC)*. [https://bit.ly/2ZPv2jV]. (Accessed 12 December 2015).

UN (United Nations). 2010. *Humanitarian Action Plan-HAP Annual report 2011*. Geneva, Switzerland: UN Office for the Coordination of Humanitarian Affairs (OCHA). [https://bit.ly/3mxWa0B]. (Accessed 10 July 2011).

UNDP (United Nations Development Programme). 2015. *Human Development Indices and Indicators: 2015 Statistical Update. Briefing note for countries on the 2018 Statistical Update: Burundi*. [https://bit.ly/2FEUsKc]. (Accessed 12 December 2019).

UNDP (United Nations Development Programme). 2017. Briefing note for countries on the 2017 Human Development Report, Congo (Democratic Republic of the). [https://bit.ly/2ZKx1pC]. (Accessed 12 December 2019).

UNEP. 2017. *UNEP Study Confirms DR Congo's Potential as Environmental Powerhouse but Warns of Critical Threats.* [https://bit.ly/32ITm8Z]. (Accessed 12 January 2018).

Vansina, J. 1966. *Kingdoms of the Savanna.* Madison, WI: University of Wisconsin Press.

Weijs, B., Hilhorst, D. & Ferf, A. 2012. *Livelihoods, basic services and social protection in Democratic Republic of the Congo.* Working Paper 2. London: Department for International Development, United Kingdom.

WHO (World Health Organisation). 2016. *Democratic Republic of Congo: National Health Planning Cycles.* [https://bit.ly/33G1QwP]. (Accessed 12 December 2016).

# 04

# SOCIAL WELFARE AND SOCIAL WORK IN LESOTHO

*Ts'epang Florence Manyeli*

## Introduction

In Africa, the emergence of social work and social welfare have been attributed to several factors but mainly the arrival of missionaries from Europe and other parts of the world. Chitereka propounds that the development of social welfare systems, social work practice and social work education must be understood within the historical context of each country's pre-colonial and post-colonial experience.[1] Western industrial social welfare models have largely influenced social work practice in the developing world, resulting in the adoption of approaches, inappropriate to prevailing conditions in developing countries.[2] Governments consequently established, what was considered as, organised welfare systems and further attempted professionalising social work. New systems of addressing the wellbeing of people and improving social ills were introduced, and these included the residual, institutional and developmental approaches, remaining in force in many African countries like Lesotho, with the most common being more curative or remedial; thus, the residual approach.[3] This form of intervention is more inclined to social casework, remaining predominant in the social work fraternity. Even after gaining

1    Chitereka, 2009:145.
2    Patel, 2005.
3    Kaseke, 2009:33.

Independence, most African countries are still using the residual approach in addressing social problems.[4] Regrettably, these approaches overshadowed the traditional social welfare systems, proven to be more responsive to the most vulnerable's welfare needs.

This chapter traces the origins and examines the development of social welfare and social work in Lesotho from the pre-colonial era to date, intending to augment the limited available literature on social welfare and social work in Lesotho. It concludes with a reflection on the contemporary challenges and prospects facing the Lesotho social welfare system and the profession of social work.

## Pre-Colonial Social Work and Social Welfare Practice in Lesotho

Before the arrival of missionaries and colonialists, tribal and mutual aid societies already existed in Africa. Indigenous and traditional educational programmes guided these arrangements, meant to teach everyone the importance of helping, being responsible members of the society and instilling the spirit of humanity. The Basotho had a distinct indigenous education system that they controlled. Kelleher believed that in this indigenous type of education, learning was tailored towards practical activities for boys and girls at home and in the fields.[5] As part of the socialisation process, young boys and girls between 10 and 15 years old were organised into peer educator groups, called *thakaneng* where older youth, with some adult guidance, arranged lessons to educate the younger ones on acceptable traditional practices, norms, values and good behaviour in general. As they grew up, they were then enrolled in initiation schools, preparing them to be responsible adults.

Principles and values of reciprocity, humanity, and mutual aid generally drove the indigenous social welfare practices in African societies, Lesotho included.[6] Such indigenous mutual aid systems have a close resemblance with the methods of interventions in social work, mainly emphasising the importance of helping, problem-solving and empowerment in the profession of social work. Family and other community structures like the chieftaincy were responsible for the protection of the most vulnerable

---

4     Darkwa, 2009:33.

5     Kelleher, 2011:58.

6     Bettman, Osei-Hwedie, Mmatli, Jacques, Jasperson, Rankopo & Maundeni, 2009:91; Abdi, 2013:68; Patel, Kaseke & Midgley, 2012:14.

and providing for their needs. Culturally, the entire family had an obligation of fending for its members through all possible means. Above all, the Basotho society has always upheld the principle of helping each other through certain culturally recognised societal structures, one of which is the extended family. According to Darkwa (2009) and Patel, Kaseke and Midgley (2012), the extended African family has always operated as a social welfare system and continues to address the needs of those who lack some form of social protection.[7] In Lesotho, like in many African countries: "... the extended family is regarded as an important social security institution, providing support to its members based upon culturally determined patterns of mutual assistance".[8] Darkwa and Patel et al (2012) further contend that children were a source of social protection against the contingency of old age, which explains why African families are so large. In the case where the family was failing to provide for its members, other social institutions like the chieftaincy or community members or structures would take over.

In the Basotho society, the Chief is the highest political authority and had a great role to play in providing for the social needs of everyone and ensuring social protection for all, but more especially the poor and most vulnerable. They had to develop strategies to improve people's general wellbeing and living standards. Amongst other strategies, they established a traditional communal agricultural system called *matsema* (work-parties), an arrangement whereby community development groups would collectively start community projects, with the most common being agricultural projects. This strategy allowed everyone to contribute with any form of resource they had, be it land, farming equipment or labour. It was aimed at providing a more inclusive response to social needs in a mutually supportive manner, but mainly to alleviate poverty. Like the *matsema*, the Basotho introduced *seahlolo* (sharecropping), whereby at least two households would collaborate to form a farming unit and agree on the terms of individual contribution. The last system was a patronage system called *mafisa* (the cattle loaning system) whereby an affluent cattle owner would loan one or more head of cattle to a poor person who had none. Such an individual would be responsible for taking proper care of the animals. Eldredge (1993) indicates that the person loaned had the right to produce milk and some offspring, in return for caring for the animals.[9] He could plough with them or use them

---

7    Darkwa, 2009:37; Patel et al., 2012:13.
8    Kaseke, 1999:21.
9    Eldredge, 1993:146.

for transport. These proved to be beneficial welfare systems whereby no member in the village, especially the needy, the old, the sick, widows and orphans, would go to bed on an empty stomach.[10]

Colonialism and its welfare approach greatly diffused and overshadowed these indigenous educational programmes and survival strategies. Except for sharecropping, the other two practices, namely, *matsema* and the patronage system, are no longer in practice. However, the above reflects the existence of what resembled indigenous social work practice in Basotho society. The next section looks at social welfare and social work in the colonial era.

## Social Welfare and Social Work in the Colonial Era

As Chitereka (2009) and Mhiribidi (2010) assert, in Africa professional social work practice came about as a result of, among other things, the arrival of missionaries and colonisers although it can be associated with the existence of indigenous African mutual aid societies.[11] The missionaries arrived in Lesotho from France in 1833 and served more as informal social workers.[12] Although they were primarily focusing on responding to the religious and spiritual needs of Africans, the missionaries established vocational schools, institutions and homes to administer services, mainly targeting the poor, children, people with disabilities and older persons. Thus, they followed an approach referred to as 'social philanthropy'. The kind of social work-oriented services they offered advocated for almsgiving, charitable giving, altruism and benevolence.[13]

Christian philanthropy and charitable giving characterised the era of the missionaries' arrival in Lesotho. For some philanthropic organisations, legibility to social welfare services was mostly determined by religious affiliation or the notion of 'the worthy poor'. However, Patel (2005) contends that although this philanthropic approach to social provision was of humanitarian value, it undermined indigenous and traditional systems of giving and the provision of social support.[14]

---

10    Manyeli, 2007:24.
11    Chitereka, 2009:145; Mhiribidi, 2010:122.
12    Darkwa, 2007:38; Patel et al., 2012:13; Chitereka, 2009:145.
13    Chitereka, 2009:145; Mupedziswa, 2005:276; Mwansa, 2011:6.
14    Patel, 2005.

The arrival of the first French missionaries characterised Lesotho in the 1830s. King Moshoeshoe I invited them mainly as agents of peace in the then warring country. They contributed significantly towards nation building by establishing schools to promote literacy and farming technology, and to introduce formal Western education. The schools focused more on providing basic literacy at an elementary level and teaching simple vocational skills for boys and housecraft for girls. Constant Gosselin of the Paris Evangelical Missionary Society started the first formal school in 1833. He opened an infants' school and an adult centre that taught 200 Basotho how to read and write.[15] Later, in 1846 and 1875, the Roman Catholic and Anglican missionaries respectively arrived and opened their missions in the kingdom.[16] In 1862, the Roman Catholics opened more schools, and by 1909 nine elementary schools were educating 12 000 children. Kelleher (2011) further indicates that the first four secondary schools were established in 1948, with only one offering senior classes.[17] Missionaries provided financial support to those members of their church who could not afford to pay their school fees and medical bills. Most of the Catholic and Anglican missionary schools enrolled needy children at no cost and continued to finance their studies up to tertiary level.

Generally, missionaries offered charity services to the destitute in the form of financial assistance, temporary accommodation, and food aid. The schools were mainly used for recruiting converts into various church denominations. Missionary schools indoctrinated children in their charge into Christianity and converts were not allowed to enrol in any other school except that of their denomination. According to Kelleher (2011) in the process of helping Moshoeshoe I to retain his sovereign power, the missionaries were working hard to convert the Basotho nation into Christianity by spreading the gospel.[18] In doing so, they were not only imposing their Christian beliefs but also strived to impose their cultural, political and commercial values. Efforts to convert the Basotho into Christians were met with much resistance.

According to Eldredge (1993), when the first European missionaries arrived, they found a nation at peace and on the threshold of prosperity.[19] However, during the time of war, the

---

15    Kelleher, 2011:58.
16    Wingate, 1998:1.
17    Kelleher, 2011:58.
18    Ibid:56.
19    Eldredge, 1993:147.

Boers destroyed most of the missions. Together with land disputes, missionaries were forced into political roles they had tried to avoid. Thus, the missionaries played a major role in helping Moshoeshoe I retain his land by facilitating a signed treaty between him and the Cape governor. In 1843 Moshoeshoe I, with the missionaries' advice, sought British protection from the Queen of England and in 1868 the then Basutoland became a British protectorate. During that time, Lesotho became the main supplier of surplus food grains to neighbouring communities of both Africans and Europeans. However, British and Dutch settlers attempted from 1856 to defeat the Basotho and King Moshoeshoe I's flourishing economy. Lesotho suffered a great deal as it lost most of its fertile land and minerals, ultimately falling under British influence in 1868.

Due to this unpleasant turn of events, most of the men trekked to the South African mines as labourers, generating a huge impact on the agricultural economy as families became disintegrated and social problems mounted at an alarming rate.[20] The indigenous practices of giving and helping one another faded slowly and the Basotho's poor adopted other informal survival strategies which may be termed as the 'informal social security system'; mutual aid societies made up of *stokvels*, burial schemes, savings clubs and others. Triegaardt (2005) observes that these arrangements are oriented towards meeting the immediate and future needs of both men and women.[21] As McPherson and Midgely (1987) point out, colonialism disrupted and disintegrated most traditional forms of social welfare.[22]

Similarly, in Lesotho, organised social welfare services emerged with the destruction of indigenous forms of welfare provision. The formal education system continued to be improved, and in 1938 the first university, the PIUS XII Catholic University College, was opened. It became an independent and non-denominational university and was formally inaugurated as the University of Basutoland, Bechuanaland and Swaziland in 1964. Then in 1966, when the three sister countries gained their Independence, it became the University of Botswana, Lesotho and Swaziland. In 1975, the three countries officially separated and the university became the National University of Lesotho.

---

20    Manyeli, 2007:23.

21    Triegaardt, 2005:8.

22    McPherson & Midgely, 1987:28.

## Social Welfare and Social Work in the Post-Colonial Era

According to Kelleher (2011) after gaining Independence, education from primary school level to tertiary level remained the responsibility of the missionaries except with the National University of Lesotho.[23] The education system of Lesotho has been steadily growing over the years. It is now even expanding extensively because of the Free Primary Education system, introduced in 2000. According to Kelleher (2011) out of 1 476 primary schools, 512 (34 per cent) are owned by the Roman Catholic Church, 484 (33 per cent) belong to the Lesotho Evangelical Church, the Government of Lesotho own 164 (11 per cent), and the rest belongs to the African Methodist Episcopal and Anglican Church of Lesotho.[24] The remaining few are private schools.

Social work is a relatively new profession in Lesotho. A decade after attaining Independence, in 1976, Lesotho established the Department of Social Welfare (DSW). Nyanguru (2003) postulates that in Lesotho, social welfare services were offered in such specialised areas as psychiatry and health sectors and focused more on micro-social work interventions, mainly remedial and not addressing the causes of social problems. In Lesotho, as in most African countries, social welfare services were introduced primarily as a response to destitution, poverty-related problems as well as the effects of the declining economic conditions.[25] As Chitereka (2009), Mwansa (2011) and Darkwa (2007) state, none of the colonisers introduced social welfare approaches that emphasised prevention or development.[26] According to Asamoah, cited in Watts, Elliott & Mayadas (1995), services were more rehabilitative and geared towards addressing the plight of vulnerable children; women; persons with disabilities; the unemployed; physically and mentally ill persons; and youth in conflict with the law. Interventions were curative, and a developmental focus was virtually non-existent. Voluntary, charity, religious and philanthropic organisations contributed immensely towards the introduction of the present social welfare system.

---

23    Kelleher, 2011:58.
24    Ibid:57.
25    Patel et al., 2012:28; Mwansa, 2011:5; Laird, 2006:135.
26    Chitereka, 2009:150; Mwansa, 2011:5; Darkwa, 2007:38.

Massive retrenchments of migrant labourers from the mines in South Africa, exacerbating the situation of poverty in the country, characterised the beginning of the 1980s.[27] With time, other social problems emerged and added more strain to the general economy of the country, including HIV/Aids as well as related problems like child vulnerability and orphan-hood; gender-based violence; human trafficking; prostitution; crime; problems of older persons; and disability.[28] Despite many challenges, the DSW's capacity and response was quite minimal and made little, if any, impact on the clients' general wellbeing.

With a population of 1.8 million served by 15 social workers using a residual approach and most primarily casework, service delivery was quite appalling. Most people who needed services, especially those who lived in rural areas, could not be reached.[29] Furthermore, following the residual approach, during times of need, the family and community structures were arguably supposed to be the first lines of intervention before the DSW could come in. However, most of the poor, who constituted more than 90 per cent of the DSW's clientele was still left out and not deemed eligible because of the selective nature of the approach. The DSW mainly provided public assistance in the form of social grants and in-kind assistance such as clothes and food parcels for orphaned and vulnerable children (OVC); the poor; world war veterans grant; and social relief for those in emergencies.[30] Social welfare services were generally remedial and focused only on the prevailing situation without studying the underlying causes of the problems. In the same vein, the interventions were offered as short-term relief but proved to be costlier and had little impact on the clients' lives. Social welfare services were fragmented due to lack of coordination and inadequate allocation of resources, consequently leading to duplication of services in some cases.[31] Centralised services were still rendered from the capital city of Maseru until the late 1990s, adversely impacting on the quality of social welfare services offered in the rest of the country. Mounting social ills, coupled with the need to introduce new measures of intervention, stimulated the transformation of the social welfare system in Lesotho.

---

27    Government of the Kingdom of Lesotho, 2012:35; Kaseke, 2004:43; Olivier, 2013:100.

28    Government of the Kingdom of Lesotho, 2013:4; Olivier, 2013:99; Manyeli, 2007:28.

29    Manyeli, 2007:3; Government of the Kingdom of Lesotho, 2013:17.

30    Government of the Kingdom of Lesotho, 2013:4,35; Olivier, 2013:99.

31    Kingdom of Lesotho, 2003: 11.

However, poverty reduction efforts' impact was invisible, mostly because of the positioning of the DSW within the Ministry of Health and Social Welfare. The government's attention was mainly directed towards health issues rather than social welfare-related ones, and as a result, more resources were directed towards the health sector.[32] The department moved from one ministry to another, due to a lack of understanding of the social work profession.[33] As Gray and Lombard (2008) contend, social work struggles with a deep and complex issue for professional identity.[34] Additionally, as a result of the small size of the DSW, which had trained a few social workers, it became difficult to function effectively and, in turn, received little recognition. From 1976 to the early 1990s, the country depended on other countries like South Africa, Tanzania and Zimbabwe for the training of local social workers. Hence, only a few social workers could be trained, with the highest qualification being an Advanced Diploma in Social work. This level of training, in turn, influenced the kind and quality of services offered. The fact that training was obtained outside the country meant that in some cases, it would not be relevant to the needs and problems of the country, a situation seriously impacting the quality of social work service delivery. Given the high costs of training social workers outside the country, the Government of Lesotho could not afford to send the required number of people to be trained.

As a result of this shortage of professionals, social work services were only being offered from Maseru. The rest of the country struggled until 1995 when the government gradually attempted to decentralise services to the districts. Therefore, in response to the then glaring shortage of qualified social workers in Lesotho, the Government of Lesotho and the National University of Lesotho introduced the Master of Social Work programme (MSW) in 1990 in the then Department of Social Anthropology and Sociology. However, the need for a fully-fledged undergraduate bachelor degree in Social Work was still noted and introduced in 2000. The social work curriculum was a total replica of that of the University of Zimbabwe, and as a result, was aligned with the Zimbabwean social welfare model. To date, the National University of Lesotho remains the only institution in the country offering social work training at degree level. In 2010 a new programme was mounted to offer a one-year certificate training in social work after noting the increasing

---

32    Manyeli, 2007:25.

33    Government of the Kingdom of Lesotho, 2013c:6.

34    Gray & Lombard, 2008:129.

need for social work services at the community level. The National Health Training College introduced the programme because the DSW fell under the Ministry of Health and Social Welfare. This one-year certificate was for a new cadre of social workers, namely, the auxiliary social workers since introduced in most of the community councils.

The major employer of social workers in Lesotho has always been the Ministry of Social Development. However, some social workers are employed in other government ministries and departments including the Ministry of Gender, Sports and Recreation; Ministry of Justice and Correctional Services; Ministry of Law and Constitutional Affairs; and the Ministry of Health. They are employed in local, regional and international non-governmental organisations (NGOs) as well as faith-based organisations and other organisations such as the United Nations Children's Fund; SOS Children's Villages; Elizabeth Glaser Paediatric Aids Foundation; Population Services International; and the Catholic Relief Services. Complementarily, other organisations, offering charitable service, mostly owned and run by churches, have employed social workers to ensure the provision of effective service delivery. Some have established residential homes and vocational rehabilitation schools. Except for just one, a government-owned vocational rehabilitation centre for people with disabilities, the rest the Catholic Church or NGOs own, and they mainly target children, people with disabilities and older persons. Notably, these were all opened way after gaining Independence. In as much as residential care is still considered the last resort, upon realising that older persons needed proper care and protection, the Catholic Church opened two old-age homes in the Leribe and Maseru districts. Since attaining Independence, Lesotho has had about 12 children's homes, and all have been under private ownership. Ironically, most of these centres do not have professional social workers in their employ, primarily due to financial limitations and as a result, depend on government support for any social work services and support.

In 2000, the first National Social Welfare Policy and Strategy was developed. The policy's major focus was on poverty reduction through the empowerment of communities and disadvantaged groups. However, service delivery has not visibly changed, most probably because the DSW fell under the Ministry of Health and Social Welfare. However, in 2012, with the introduction of the first Coalition Government, the DSW graduated into the Ministry of Social Development. An effort of developing new policies, programmes and delivery systems that ensure basic welfare rights to all citizens commenced, culminating in the formulation of the *National Social Development Policy of 2014*, a framework for developmentally and holistically addressing human needs.

The Ministry of Social Development formed four main programmes: children services, elderly-care services, disability services and community development. Services have been decentralised to ten districts headed by a District Senior Child Welfare Officer/ Social Worker, to strengthen the programmes. At the community level, there is also a new cadre of auxiliary SWOs focussing on early identification of clients' problems, basic services provision and referrals to the next level.[35] All services offered to these vulnerable groups in Lesotho are guided by national laws and policies, and the Ministry of Social Development in collaboration with others enforce them. Lesotho has ratified and adopted international conventions and charters which protect the welfare and rights of people with disability and children. These include the United Nations Conventions on the Rights of People with Disabilities; United Nations conventions on the child rights and the African Charter on the Rights and Welfare of Children.[36]

## Social Work and Social Welfare in Lesotho

The formulation of the National Social Development Policy indicated the government's general shift towards developmental social work services. The policy, considered as overarching, underpins other social policies and provides a framework for developmentally and holistically addressing human needs to improve the quality of life of all Basotho.[37] However, this policy does not provide direction on how these specialised areas and/or departments will adopt the proposed developmental processes. Instead, it states that the biggest challenge is the initialisation of the social development concept, given its broader meaning.[38] For the policy to be effectively implemented, there has to be a common understanding of the social development concept by everyone involved in undertaking developmental social work, namely social workers, rehabilitation officers and auxiliary social workers.

---

35    Government of the Kingdom of Lesotho, 2012.

36    UN, 2006; UN, 1989; African Union, 1989.

37    Government of the Kingdom, 2013:18.

38    Government of the Kingdom of Lesotho, 2013:5.

Recent research has observed a gap between policy and practice regarding the State's involvement in the implementation of the developmental social welfare services in most African countries.[39] Notably, this is the case in Lesotho as there have not been any changes in social work practice and service delivery since the introduction of the new policy. Another prerequisite of the emerging developmental social work paradigm is not only a rigorous knowledge base; it requires social and institutional support for the approach's values; a set of defined issues, interests, practices, and institutional arrangements. According to Gaba (2014), being forced to adopt the State's welfare policy, social work has shown profound and important transformations.[40] For transformation in social work services in Lesotho to take effect, the National Social Development policy should indicate how policies and services for older persons, people with disabilities, and children, will become developmental. In the absence of clear plans and guidelines on processes and methods of transforming services using a developmental approach, there will be no changes in the living conditions of the most vulnerable. The newly established departments and policies require accompanying resources for them to be responsive and functional.

The Government of Lesotho still strives for change from a welfare-oriented approach to a developmental one, but there are still several challenges, including the problem of lack of recognition from other professions. Although there is a non-functional registered association of social workers in Lesotho, the absence of a council of social workers makes it difficult to draw the expected recognition.

## Conclusion

This chapter discussed the transition of social welfare and social work in Lesotho from the pre-colonial times to date. As highlighted in this chapter, the indigenous social welfare system in Lesotho undoubtedly had a significant contribution towards improving the wellbeing of the most vulnerable. Although the Western system of social welfare largely influenced most of the practices, it can still fit the current context if resuscitated. In line with what the indigenisation discourse advocates, social work practice and education in

---

39    Bak, 2004:94.
40    Gaba, 2014:66.

Lesotho should consider other salient aspects like the historical practices, the vulnerable people's needs alongside their culture and issues of social change when designing curricula, policies, laws and interventions.

# References

Abdi, A.A. 2013. Decolonising education and social development platforms in Africa. *African and Asian Studies*, 12:64-82.

Bak, M. 2004. Can developmental social welfare change an unfair world? The South African Experience. *International Social Work*, 47(1):81-94.

Bettman, E.J., Osei- Hwedie, K., Mmatli, T., Jacques, G., Jasperson, R.A., Rankopo, M.J. & Maundeni, T. 2009. 'Building Jerusalem': Cultural Relevance of Social Work Education and Practice in Botswana. *Social development issues*, 31(1):86-101.

Chitereka, C. 2009. Social Work Practice in a Developing Continent: The Case of Africa. *Advances in Social Work*, 10(2):144-156.

Darkwa, O.K. 2007. Continuing social work education in an electronic age: The opportunities and challenges facing social work educators in Ghana. *Professional Development*, 2(1):38-43.

Eldredge, E. 1993. *A South African Kingdom: The pursuit of security in 19ᵗʰ century Lesotho*. Cambridge: Cambridge University Press.

Gaba, D. 2014. Recent developments in social work in the context of development paradigms: Untangling the link between social work and development. *Social Work Review / Revista de Asistenta Sociala*, 13(4):57-71.

Government of the Kingdom of Lesotho. Ministry of Development Planning. 2012. *National Strategic Development Plan 2012/13–2016/17: Growth and Development Strategic Framework*. Maseru: Government Printing Works. [https://bit.ly/3ilMKSJ].

Government of the Kingdom of Lesotho. 2013. *National Policy on Social Development 2014/2015-2024/2025*. Maseru: Government Printing Works.

Gray, L. & Lombard, A. 2008. The post-1994 transformation of social work in South Africa. *International Journal of Social Welfare*, 17(2):132-145.

Kaseke, E. (ed). 1998. *Social Security Systems in Rural Zimbabwe*. Harare: Weaver Press.

Kaseke, E. 1999. Social Security and the elderly: The African Experience. *The ACP-EU Courier*, 1976:50-52.

Kelleher, F. 2011. *Women and the teaching profession. Exploring the feminisation debate*. London: Charlesworth Press.

Kingdom of Lesotho. 2003. *National Health and Social Welfare Policy*. Maseru: Government Printing Works.

Laird, S.E. 2006. Social work practice to support survival strategies in Sub-Saharan Africa. *British Journal of Social Work*, 38(1):135-151.

Manyeli, T.F. 2007. The evolution of social welfare in Lesotho. *Lesotho Social Sciences Review*, 11(1&2): 21-33.

McPherson, S. & Midgely, J. 1987. *Comparative Social Policy and the Third World*. Brighton: Wheatsheaf.

Mhiribidi, S.T.W. 2010. Promoting the developmental social welfare approach in Zimbabwe: Challenges and prospects. *Journal of Social Development*, 25(2):121-147.

Midgley, J. & Conley, A. 2010. *Social Work and Social Development: Theories and Skills for Developmental Social Work*. Oxford: Oxford University Press.

Mupedziswa, R. 2005. Challenges and prospects of social work services in Africa. In: J.C. Okeibunor & E.E. Anugwom (eds). *The Social Sciences and Socioeconomic Transformation in Africa: Essays in Honour of Professor D.S. Obikeze*. Nsukka: Great AP Express Publishers. pp.271-283.

Mwansa, L-K. 2011. Social Work Education in Africa: Whence and Whither. *Social Work Education*, 30(1):4-16.

Olivier, M. 2013. *Acceptance of social security in Africa*. A paper presented at the International Social Security Association Regional Conference for Africa, Lusaka, Zambia, 9-12 August.

Patel, L. 2005. *Social welfare and social development in South Africa*. Cape Town: Oxford University Press.

Patel, L. & Hochfeld, T. 2012. Developmental social work in South Africa: Translating policy into practice. *International Social Work*, 56(5):690-704.

Patel, L., Kaseke, E. & Midgley, J. 2012. Indigenous welfare and community-based social development: Lessons from African innovations. *Journal of Community Practice*, 20(1):12-31.

Republic of Ghana. Ministry of Gender, Children and Social Protection. 2020. *Department of Social Welfare*. [https://bit.ly/33cnv0E]. (Accessed 23 June 2020).

Triegaardt, J.D. 2005. *Transformation of Social Security in South Africa: Accomplishments and challenges for partnerships in development*. Pretoria: Development Bank of Southern Africa. [https://bit.ly/2S5Nj8i]. (Accessed 20 June 2017).

UNICEF (United Nations International Children's Fund). 2008. Social protection in Eastern and Southern Africa: A framework and strategy for UNICEF. Nairobi: UNICEF ESARO.

Wingate, A. 1998. *Anglicanism: A global communion*. London: Church Publishing.

Zastrow, C. 2014. *Introduction to social work and social welfare: Empowering people*. 8th Edition. Belmont, CA: Thomsons/Cole.

# 05

# EVOLUTION OF SOCIAL WELFARE AND SOCIAL WORK IN MALAWI

*Loveness Mwayi Imaan, Agness Wizi, Daniel Kabunduli Nkhata, Vilanti Tambulasi, Delipher Magola, and Blessings Msowoya*

## Introduction

This chapter examines the historical evolution of the social welfare system and social work profession in Malawi. It locates the background of social welfare initiatives and the evolution of social work as a profession in different historical eras of the country. It then concludes with the challenges and opportunities of the social work profession in Malawi by looking at five distinctive political dispensations of the country: the pre-colonial era (1891-1964); the colonial era and just before Independence (1950-1964); independent one-party state under President Kamuzu Banda (1964-1994) and the multi-party state era from 1994 to the present. The chapter reviews different historical papers and draws heavily on archival data to specifically address colonial policies that precipitated poor living standards, family disintegration, structural leakage and several other social malaises that accumulated in the country. The chapter discusses the changing and unchanging patterns of social welfare practices in the transition period of Malawi's colonial state to its Independence in 1964. The chapter also acknowledges the lack of an identifiable well organised welfare system in Malawi throughout the years. The central theme of this chapter's thrust is on what Chitereka (2009) postulated, that the development of social welfare systems and social work practice must be understood within the historical context of each country's pre-colonial and post-colonial experience. The chapter finds that the origin of the social welfare system in Malawi has evolved along with the political structures while acknowledging that social welfare has always been the responsibility of the community and family institution. Later, during the Independence era, when the social welfare system was institutionalised, the government took over the provision of social welfare services and this required effort of social work professionals.

Africa has a universal history of the pre-colonial era related to how the welfare of communities and individuals was organised, as illustrated by Noyoo (2015).[1] It is a universal fact that almost all societies had created mechanisms, over the centuries, to safeguard people's wellbeing. Thus, in the pre-industrial age where communal existence defined social interaction, informal systems that responded to human needs predominated. All societies at the time had indigenous modalities of looking after the disadvantaged and vulnerable, the case in pre-colonial Africa, where the extended family system met the needs of individuals through strong bonds of solidarity and networks of reciprocity is exemplary. The caring of the old, infirm, and at times, people with disabilities was a core function of the family in pre-colonial Africa. In this context, family ties were based on the kinship system, and each family member had a specific role to play in maintaining the overall wellbeing of the community. Like in other parts of the world at the time, the family was the pillar of pre-colonial societies. The mutual-aid system, underpinned by bonds of reciprocity and solidarity, held families, organised as clans, together.[2]

Established kingdoms that varied in structure and size held the social, political, and economic fabric of pre-colonial Africa together. Before European colonisation, Malawi had a long history of decentralised or stateless state-building and socio-political formations, usually in the form of kingdoms. The Amaravi kingdom, with smaller chiefdoms under it, was the most prominent. A significant part of the Amaravi people lived in small-scale, egalitarian societies in which government was more a matter of consensus among the entire adult population than rule by an elite few. Social order in most polities of the Amaravi kingdom emerged from normative and cultural consensus whose custodians were chiefs, kings, spirit mediums and elders of the community. The kingdom heavily

---

1    Noyoo, 2015:170.
2    Noyoo, 2015:170.

relied on an emerging salt industry and productions of a popular cloth called *machira*, traded in the region. Salt-making and cloth-making were businesses for women who contributed a portion of spoils as a homage to the chief's court for redistribution.[3] This redistributive account of spoils from the salt and clothes industry reflects a welfare system that was dependent on contributions from women to the chiefdom. At the top of this society was an organised kingdom whose mandate extended to political (usually military) and economic control of its geographical boundaries.

Malawi's colonial history dates to around 1859 when David Livingstone arrived in the land and called it Nyasaland. Three economies emerged with the coming of the British, who declared it a protectorate in 1891: the plantation economy, the peasant cash-cropping economy and the labour-reserve economy, all functioning simultaneously in the now monetary based economic system.[4] Just before the First World War, a two-tier agricultural system emerged with white settlers participating in cash-cropping of coffee, tobacco and tea, and a small-scale Malawian subsistence farming system growing tobacco and tea for export. The second tier (Malawian subsistence farming) served as a labour reserve for the profit-making first-tier run by white settlers. Arguably, this was the beginning of poverty and inequality in Nyasaland. It is important to note that over time, the protectorate legislated discriminatory laws that were a precursor to several other socioeconomic malaises in Nyasaland. The major issues that created and directly contributed to this inequality were labour policies for the natives. The growing first-tier cash-cropping economy was hungry for more labour from a limited native labour reserve; consequently, the hut tax, tenant and then *thangata* systems were legislated to manage this labour shortage.

The colonial government introduced the hut tax, charged on everyone who owned a hut, to increase its revenues. This practice presented households with two options, either to desert their huts and live a homeless life or work on white-owned estates to afford to pay the tax.[5] Defaulters were caught and forced to work for free on these farms during the growing season and consequently pushing them into a poverty food-insecure trap. The *thangata* system, whereby land was exchanged for labour, came into operation in

---

3    Sindima, 2002; Kwengwere, 2011.
4    Sindima, 2002; Kwengwere, 2011.
5    Kwengwere, 2011.

1904.[6] Workers were given land for cultivation just like in a feudal system, and rent on this land was one month's labour per year.[7] This exploitation continued for years, and the government had little control over it as the agreement between the estate owners and indigenous workers, was usually verbal and informal. The tenant system, to date, is still in existence in modern civilised Malawi. This system functions as a share-cropping arrangement where immigrating tenants grow burley tobacco for four to six months and sell it to the landowner before returning to their homes. The tenants work for accommodation and their families' welfare; all calculated within the final payment for cost recovery. However, these three forceful oppressive policies met resistance from the male Malawians who opted to emigrate to South Africa, Northern Rhodesia (Zambia) and Southern Rhodesia (Zimbabwe) to work in the mines. These labour policies had a multiplier effect on several other social arrangements in the system, as argued by Mhone (2002). The British estate owners' wage economy was the beginning of the erosion of mutual support systems in communities and a culmination in individualism as the family structure began to be eroded. The concept of single mothers emerged, and the extended family started to lose its shape. Hence in the absence of fathers, most youth became disruptive, while strange diseases were brought into the families by men returning from the mines. Also, social stratification, based on money, became apparent, and this demanded the attention of its creator, the colonial system.[8]

The colonial period reflected a dual-tier model of social welfare. Community welfare, organised by kinship, village and geographical ties, took care of orphans in the extended family and catered for the elderly and those without close kinsmen through voluntary and mutual community house repairs, tilling and harvesting. The elderly within kinship ties functioned as the repository of knowledge of the community for religion; medicine; conflict management; marriage ritual custodianship; and weather and climate advisors. They served as child educators through the telling of *nthano* or folktales.[9] This function positioned the elderly in one of the most revered social statuses of the time. The family and the community remained the thrust of safety nets to a variety of individuals with

---

6    Ibid.
7    Pryor, 1990.
8    Mhone, 2002.
9    Phulusa, 1988.

conditions deemed as 'misfortunes' like disability, mental illness and chronic sickness, within their contexts.[10]

The second tier of the welfare system was developed in the pre-Independence era between 1950-1964 when Nyasaland became part of the Federation of Rhodesia and Nyasaland, a period of the united settler administration under three countries (Zimbabwe, Malawi and Zambia). The formation of a Federation of Rhodesia and Nyasaland accelerated several social problems communities in the federation were experiencing, leading to indigenous people in Nyasaland to trek to Zimbabwe, Zambia and South Africa to seek greener pastures as the labour policies grew tougher in their homeland. In 1954, the united federation administration met for the first time to discuss the need for social welfare programmes, especially for Nyasaland. At this landmark gathering on 24 October 1954 in Mandala, Blantyre, Nyasaland, several issues were discussed, and a memorandum was drafted to advise the federation administrators. One of the key issues emanating from this meeting was the need for social welfare in the colony. Even Europeans recognised that the introduction of the wage economy created a lot of social problems in the African sections of the colony. The problems were, among others, destitution, child vagrancy, prostitution, housing shortage and juvenile delinquency.

## Post-Independence Social Welfare (1964-1994): Age of Welfare Darkness and Policy Confusion

The transitory period of power – from the colonial government to an independent Malawi – saw indigenous leaders like Banda assume high government positions from 1958-1964. Still, little social welfare work was done to address the emerging social problems the colonial order created. The pre-Independence government was preoccupied with political mileage, neglecting the united federation administration-drafted Mandala Kabula agreement of 1954 to achieve the coordination of social welfare activities in the country. Malawi got Independence on 6 July 1964, and the people of Malawi had expected quick solutions to their former and emerging social and economic challenges. Suffice to say, the expectations of the populace never materialised as the Banda administration inherited several structural challenges addressed by wrong prescriptions.[11] During the Federation of Rhodesia and Nyasaland, Malawi had increased its public services, and

---

10    Muzaale, 1987.
11    Morton, 1975; Williams, 1978.

it was possible to finance this through the periodic funding from the Federal Office in Zimbabwe.[12] The dissolution of the federation meant that the government had to finance a huge public service that surpassed its capacity. Prior (1990), acknowledges that: "[the] dissolution of the federation brought some serious economic problems to Malawi, not the least of which was the loss of this fiscal subsidy."[13] This challenge affected a decline in primary school enrolment while the population increased three times.[14] This scenario had a serious negative impact on the availability of skilled human power in the country. Morton (1975) observes that "… in 1963 there were only about 3 000 pupils at secondary school and less than 400 candidates for the School Certificate … at independence, few Malawians had technical and professional skills."[15]

Following Independence in 1964, communal civic action, whereby local chiefs mobilised their people to participate in development work, became increasingly institutionalised. Local self-help projects, using voluntary contributions of time, resources and labour, were selected, planned and overseen by district development committees, albeit under scrutiny by political leaders and party members.[16] Banda, the leader of the newly-independent Republic of Malawi, was made president for life in 1971, and quickly established a national youth service – the Malawi Young Pioneers – seen as central to his vision of nation-building. As with many government-sponsored national service programmes, this was primarily concerned with promoting unity and patriotism, as well as producing disciplined and productive citizens.[17]

It is imperative to note that the newly established Banda Government understood community development as the best approach to improving people's livelihoods at the time of Independence, given that most Malawians lived and still live in rural areas. Thus, the Department of Community Development was established in the Office of the President to address social development and focussed mainly on social welfare, sports, community centres, women's and youth clubs. This focus was justified as a way of ensuring the desire for social and economic improvement of the people who were empowered

---

12    Williams, 1978:156.

13    Pryor, 1990:47.

14    Williams, 1978:159-60.

15    Morton, 1975:14.

16    CSC, 1979.

17    Patel, 2005.

and self-confident. At this point, community development, encompassing social welfare, sanctioned processes to unite the efforts of the people and governmental authorities:

➢ The improvement of the economic, social, and cultural conditions of communities;

➢ The integration of these communities into the life of the nation;

➢ The enablement to contribute fully to national progress.

Essentially, social welfare in this regard was inclined:

➢ To help people free themselves from traditional restraints that hindered enterprise and innovation, hence fostering a sense of responsibility for the whole community's welfare.

➢ To assist people in understanding the material and social needs of their families and households and making use of their human and material resources for raising domestic living standards.

➢ To help recognise community needs and to form groups that could plan and carry out joint projects of communal interest using local resources and services, particularly helping leaders to accept new responsibilities in working with the communities' ideas on welfare and development.

➢ To prepare people for increased responsibility within the local government structure.

➢ To promote a greater sense of national consciousness by helping communities to see their place in national development and to draw on national resources to meet local needs.

At this point, as reflected above, the Government of Malawi took a developmental approach to welfare within the confines of community development. Communities' welfare was viewed within the spectrum of the 'trickledown' of development benefits to individuals and society, obvious for an infant state pursuing the agenda of development and national unity after leaving the wallops of colonialism. Mechanisms for the delivery of community development were put in place, and the government established the Magomero School of Social Development, to train community development workers functioning as SWOs on the ground in the early years of Independence. The same decade realised the development of several structures that would enhance and define the course of community development and social welfare in Malawi. Some notable innovations were community development assistants, district development committees and village development committees, responsible for rural infrastructure development, as well as coordination and encouraging, promoting and fostering the self-help spirit. The system introduced the area action groups that the Traditional Authorities overseeing the activities in their respective jurisdictions chaired. Such government initiated structures were an indication that the government recognised that welfare and development were utmost effective when the grassroots were in control. In retrospect, the government only formalised and institutionalised activities already under the control of local communities before and after colonisation. However, it is imperative to note that the Banda regime fused party structures in the social welfare system as 'surveillance cameras'.[18]

Community development and social welfare quickly took a top-down approach implemented through highly centralised and coercive party structures. Stakeholders argued that this was inevitable because of an authoritarian political system that emerged following the 1964 Cabinet Crisis. The local government, almost approaching the democratic ideal, was swiftly weakened. All state and local government structures were constitutionally subordinated to the party heading the Government of Malawi, consequently leaving the central government as the sole driver of community development processes. The Malawi Congress Party (MCP) was the only institution with proper structures down to grassroots level; hence the government tended to co-opt party officials, especially Malawi Young Pioneers, in trying to mobilise communities. The community development assistants, as well as other extension workers, worked with party officials and chiefs to the extent that no meaningful bottom-up approach was evident. The State used force, where necessary, to initiate community participation. An example often cited was the use of the youth week during which community members were expected to offer their labour to any community cause of their choice.

Social welfare in this regard became an over appeasement system for political benefactors at the grassroots level.[19] In 1965, the independent government drafted the first National Development Plan of 1965-69, emphasising four major areas:

---

18    Hodza, 1996:39.

19    Kwezeyani, 1996:44.

▷  The expansion of agricultural production;

▷  The provision of greatly improved internal communication;

▷  The great expansion of facilities for secondary and post-secondary education; and

▷  The stimulation of the economy's private sector.

The plan highlighted in passing some specific areas under social welfare mentioned as rehabilitation of the disabled, family and child welfare, probation and after-care services, and assistance to the destitute. The main areas of focus included the following:

> ... expansion of productive self-help community projects and improve the efficiency, with which they are related, designed and executed; the enhancement of the teaching of a range of basic and technical skills to community members to stimulate their further involvement in the development process; the improvement of communication between the authorities and communities on the policies of the former and the needs of the latter.[20]

Without a gender policy in place, this era used the presidential symbol of power to protect and promote women. Banda called women *mbumba za A Ngwazi*, translated as 'women of the president' or the 'president's women', generating respect for women in communities but at a price. Women were used politically at three levels in the Banda period. They gave public expression to the personal aggrandizement of the president by the composition and public performance of praise-songs and dances. Every woman was compelled to participate as a sign of loyalty and had to put on wrappers and dresses with the president's face. Through the Women's League, they served as informers for the party at the community (and sometimes family) levels. They were pressured into providing sexual favours to party leaders and functionaries, particularly when they were centrally encamped for days during party functions. The welfare of women was intrinsically connected to their participation in promoting the persona of Banda to communities, without which they would not be safe. From 1986, for another ten years, there was a hiatus in producing long term or medium-term plans. In the early 1980s, the Women in Development movement started to influence the research and planning of extension in the Ministry of Agriculture. The extension programmes moved beyond reaching women with practical homemaking skills to empowering them with access to strategic resources and skills, leading to activities to reach women farmers with credit and inputs. After the

---

20    Republic of Malawi, 1987:125.

Nairobi United Nations Women's Conference in 1985, the Malawi Government formed the National Commission for Women that spearheaded new programmes. The most successful of these was the Girls Attainment in Basic Literacy and Education.

The Banda administration used the kiosk system to provide safe drinking water to the underprivileged population. The system was introduced to ensure regular and affordable supply in traditional housing areas and squatter settlements when the government launched the Urban Communal Water Point Project in 1981, with financial and technical assistance from the United Nations Capital Development Fund (UNCDF) and the World Health Organisation (WHO). The objective of this initial project was to construct 600 communal water points in 50 urban settlements in Malawi, to provide affordable and safe drinking water to over 24 000 poor urban families, indicating how the government perceived the welfare of the urban poor. It is important to note that these programmes were not running under an organised social welfare system. The government was using a piecemeal approach as a safety net to the needs of an increasing population.

It is imperative to understand that 1964-1994 was a dark period of political repression for Malawi and also in terms of social welfare policy and programmes. The levels of poverty continued to soar regardless of the development plans in place. The economy was able to achieve impressive growth during the first 15 years after Independence in 1964, with an average annual growth in Gross Domestic Product (GDP) of about 4.9 per cent in the 1960s, accelerating to 6.3 per cent in the 1970s. Regardless of this growth, poverty levels did not significantly change.[21] In the late 1970s and early-1980s, Malawi's economy experienced oil crisis shocks; accumulatively impacting the populace's poverty levels. The government acknowledged the depreciating conditions of its people by implementing the Structural Adjustment Programme (SAP) that the International Monetary Fund (IMF) and World Bank prescribed, even though the intention was to rescue the economy. The adjustment hurt the poorest and most vulnerable sections of the country's population. Particularly, the SAP caused a downfall in the agricultural sector's performance in a country where 80 per cent of the population depends on the land. The health sector was affected by an attendant staff turnover as wages dropped. More significantly was the food insecurity that engulfed the country soon after the SAP was operational.[22] The most

---

21    Ngo'ng'ola, 2004.
22    Mkandawire & Bourenane, 1987.

tragic element of the Banda era towards social welfare of the people was not the lack of a coordinated system of welfare in legislation, policies and programmes. Rather, it was the State's unwillingness under the one-party system to open up the welfare sector to allow other players' participation, and the flagrant picture the State projected to the outside world, "that things are in shape".

## Multi-Party Democracy Era: Age of Liberalism in Social Welfare

Malawi was ushered into a multi-party democracy in 1994 when Bakili Muluzi was elected president. This period became significantly different from the system that was in place during Banda's administration. From the onset, the new Republican Constitution demanded a different way of doing things: built on the spirit of 'protection and promotion of human rights', and social welfare became an integral part of that spirit in the country. The transition from a single party to the multi-party system of governance was taking place simultaneously with the implementation of the SAP. At this point, the population was already immersed in poverty and other social problems.[23] Multiparty democracy was meant to liberate people from poverty, injustice, oppression, and discrimination. It meant to most Malawians a new era of prosperity. To the contrary, despite few notable changes in freedoms enjoyed by people, poverty was accompanied by new social problems like the devastating HIV/Aids problem; the growing population of orphans and street children; prostitution; violence against women; child abuse; and institutionalised corruption. The new multi-party government needed a plan to tackle 'the old and the new' social problems. The capacity of government to formulate, articulate and implement concrete policy interventions has been an issue of tremendous concern in recent years. The transition from authoritarian one-party rule to multiparty democracy is oddly considered as the tipping point in the versatility of the country's policy-making processes.[24]

The multi-party government quickly engaged in a formative decentralisation policy reform that sought to redefine, decentralise, and empower local communities in the approach to social welfare. The primary objective of the United Nations Development Programme (UNDP) funded district policy focus initiative under the auspices of the fifth country programme was to overhaul the delivery mechanisms for community

---

23    Chipeta, 1993; Chirwa, Mvula, Kadzamira & Horea, 2003.
24    Rakner, Mukubvu, Ngwira, Smiddy & Schneider, 2004.

development to make them responsive to and driven by genuine community needs. The idea was to empower communities so that they became subjects and not objects of development. Chinsinga (2007) alludes to the fact that the worsening impact of SAPs eventually led to the advent of the Social Dimension of Adjustment (SDA) initiatives at the beginning of the 1990s. The main objective of SAP was to do away with input and output price-controls as well as phasing out universal subsidies. The worsening impact of the SAP eventually led to the SDA initiatives' start at the beginning of the 1990s. According to Tsoka and Slater (2007), targeted nutrition programmes (therapeutic and supplementary feeding) for children and pregnant or lactating mothers became the sole intervention geared at protecting the vulnerable segments of society during this period, ultimately leading to the conception of the SDA under the auspices of the 1994 Poverty Alleviation Programme. As already alluded to, this not only opened the political space but provided an institutional framework for safety net programmes among NGOs, community-based organisations and even faith-based organisations. At this point, the Malawi Social Action Fund started to define once again the overarching meaning and dimension of social welfare in the new Malawi.[25] The main aim of the programme was to develop the institutional capacity of the government in partnership with civil society to integrate social and poverty concerns in the development process meaningfully.

In policy arrangement, the multiparty era posed one dynamic state of policy formulation and documentation to reflect the spirit of the new Constitution. Several development policies were developed, including the Poverty Alleviation Programme in 1994; the Vision 2020 (1998); the Malawi Poverty Reduction Strategy; the One Village One Product; and the Malawi Growth and Development Strategy.[26] Despite this turn around in policy, Malawi remained one of the poorest countries in the world despite undergoing significant economic and political reforms. The country's performance regarding the Human Development Index was still damming. Malawi dropped from position 138 in 1990 to position 166 in 2006 out of 178 countries. Consequently, this underlined a steady decline in healthcare delivery, education, economic growth, and general living standards.

In the late 1990s, Malawi realised that the popular 'adjustment with a human face' social protection vehicle in the Malawi Social Action Fund had made a little impact. Safety

---

25    Chilowa, Milner, Chinsinga & Mangani, 2000.

26    Ngwira, Chiweza & Binauli, 2001; Republic of Malawi, 2006.

nets interventions had limited impact because they were short-term, ad hoc, patchy and uncoordinated, necessitating the development of a National Safety Nets Strategy in 2000. There was also the development of the Malawi Poverty Reduction Strategy in 2001, with a specific pillar to improve the quality of life of the most vulnerable. It provided for four main safety nets interventions:

▷ The Public Works Programmes;

▷ The targeted nutrition programmes;

▷ The targeted input-subsidies (input transfers, food transfers); and

▷ The direct welfare transfers; food-aid support to secondary school-going orphans and vulnerable children (OVC).

These four safety nets directed and influenced the policy, programming and practice of social welfare in early 2000. The system used small-medium enterprise credit schemes as part of an 'almost' organised welfare system.

## Social Welfare Policies and Legislation in the Multiparty Era

By 2006, the Government of Malawi established a parent Ministry of Gender and Social Welfare, although it kept on changing names and direction in several government ministry restructurings. Interestingly, several government ministries such as the Ministry of Finance and Economic Planning; the Ministry of Gender, Disability, Children and Social Welfare; the Ministry of Agriculture; and the Ministry of Education, Science and Technology; continued to champion the social welfare system in Malawi as policy and programming dictated. The Ministry of Gender, Children and Community Development coordinates implementation of social welfare services in the country. The professional staff at the Ministry headquarters in Lilongwe and 28 district social welfare offices carry out the coordination of activities. In 2003, the Government of Malawi developed an OVC policy and launched the National Plan of Action for Orphans and Other Vulnerable Children in 2005. The overarching objective of this strategic document is to strengthen the capacity of families, communities, and government to scale up efforts ensuring the survival, growth, protection, and development of the OVC. The national action plan calls for the involvement of a multisector set of actors and stakeholders in the OVC response. Furthermore, Malawi enacted the Child Care, Protection and Justice Act in 2010 to be the overarching law for the welfare of children. Currently, the country is in the process of developing and operationalising the National Child Protection System for a coordinated, harmonised, and systematic approach to protect children from violence, abuse, exploitation, neglect and HIV/Aids.

In 2012, the Government of Malawi enacted the Disability Act to govern the protection and promotion of people with disabilities in the country, directly feeding into the national social welfare system guiding support towards people with disabilities. The government developed the following policies to operate in the social welfare system:

- National Health Policy and Health Sector Strategic Plan.
- National Nutrition Policy and Strategic Plan.
- National Social Support Policy.
- National Education Sector Policy.
- National Policy for Older Persons.
- Draft National Gender Policy.
- National Population Policy.
- Prevention of Domestic Violence Act.
- National Sports and Youth Development Policy.
- Decentralisation Policy.
- National Sexual and Reproductive Health and Rights Policy.
- National Social Protection Policy.

## Development of Social Work, Social Work Education and the Establishment of the National Association of Social Workers in Malawi

Social work education has easily traceable roots in Malawi. Before Independence, there was no formal social work education, and only missionaries drove social work activities in the colonial era. The Government of Malawi first established the Magomero

Community Development College after Independence in the 1960s to be the frontline training institution for community development workers, and they graduated with a Certificate in Social Work. Malawi, like many other sub-Saharan African countries, is facing a shortage of skilled frontline social work professionals, particularly at the district level. Additionally, many existing social workers that the Ministry of Gender, Child, and Community Development employ, do not possess the minimum education requirements due to the limited range of professional qualifications and training opportunities available in the country. While a degree-level education is required to qualify as a social worker in Malawi, most frontline social workers only possess a certificate-level training qualification.[27] In 2006, the Catholic University of Malawi was established and became the first tertiary institution in the country to offer a degree in social work. This ground-breaking work saw other tertiary institutions establishing schools of social work, but they were still few.

Four universities currently offer degrees in the social work field: the Catholic University of Malawi; the Chancellor College (a constituent college of the University of Malawi); the Blantyre International University; and the St John the Baptist University.[28] These colleges have been operating within policy frameworks that govern higher education in Malawi but not social work education. In 2013 and 2015, the United Nations Children's Fund funded preliminary forums for the colleges to meet with the Ministry of Gender and Social Welfare to plan towards the establishment of the Social Work Education Council of Malawi and the National Social Workers Association of Malawi. In August 2016, the three colleges recruited and trained social work educators to supervise social work interns from college.

## Challenges for Social Work as a Profession in Malawi

The prevailing socio-economic situation in Africa let alone in Malawi, presents several challenges for social welfare delivery, social work practice and social work education. Social workers are faced with socio-economic and cultural challenges that require a great deal of innovation. Social work remains a frontline profession and continues to play a critical role in increasingly complex social problems in the country as well as on

27    Guyer, Singleton & Linsk, 2012.

28    MNCHE, 2015.

the whole continent.[29] Malawi lacks a board to license social work practitioners as there is no accrediting body. Licensing is a process by which a government agency or other jurisdiction acting on legislative mandate grants permission to individuals to engage in the practice of a profession. By ensuring a level of safe practice and self-evaluation (through professional education and experience), the licensure process protects the public.[30] There is no such board in Malawi currently, and anybody can claim to be a social worker, hampering, in no small way, the development of the social work profession in Malawi. The country is in the process of forming a board as it will help the social workers to be accountable to their profession and to follow the code of conducts of being a social worker.

Another significant challenge is the concept of doing more work with fewer resources. The range of responsibilities for social workers continues to grow exponentially. Since the profession is new in the country, the number of professional social workers is yet to grow. Currently, each social worker has to be both a micro and a macro practitioner. As the needs of our environments pull and stretch the resources, coupled with natural disasters like floods, it is becoming more and more difficult for social workers to find mentors. Sometimes the social workers are just thrust into the environment without much support.[31] The work that social workers do is hard work because they interact with so much pain. Whatever realm the social worker is in, he/she ends up connecting with a lot of difficult experiences. To keep people fresh and vibrant in this work, they need time to take care of themselves; they need time to talk to others about what they are experiencing to avoid work-related stress.[32]

The social work degree is versatile; therefore, the schools and, the academic institutions, are being challenged more and more. They need to adequately prepare the students for an ever-changing environment because there are all types of demands being placed on social workers; reasonable time of working with the client's needs to be more.[33] Most times, social workers have really hard times with clients, and it affects them in that some Malawians face many challenges and cannot be helped in a short time. A concerted

---

29    Darkwa, 2007.
30    Morales & Sheafor, 2004.
31    Ibid.
32    Gray, Coates, & Bird, 2005.
33    Zastrow, 2004.

approach is needed to raise the standards of social work, and yet it is quite hard in the current system without a mother body for social workers. Another critical challenge for social workers in the country is the recognition of their role in society as many people do not understand what social work is. So, there is a need to demonstrate competence in implementing social work practices.

The Malawian experience indicates that a lack of clarity on what social work entails has a major impact on the progress of social work in the country. For social work to succeed, the Malawian experience demonstrates the critical role of partnerships between institutions, government and NGOs.[34] In social work, service beneficiaries should be central to all development and partnership initiatives. NGOs are well-positioned to render services at the grassroots level and have a responsibility to include the poor and the voices of the marginalised. Given its overall responsibility for the wellbeing of civil society, the government should create an enabling environment, if the development of social work is to achieve its goals, including a clear mandate and direction on social work roles in the country.[35] The government plays an important role in facilitating an enabling environment to regulate the profession, determine standards for training and attract people to the social work profession. The experience in Malawi shows the importance of a human resource strategy for all the role players in the social welfare sector. It is, therefore, critical that social work has a well-defined scope of practice for it to develop.[36]

## Opportunities and Prospects

Despite the problems discussed above, there are several opportunities available for the social work profession in Malawi. Midgley (1997) asserts that social problems the global south continues to face open a door for indigenisation of social work practice, where specifically social workers would be involved in rural development, social and family planning, social action and overcoming the problems of modernisation. Therefore, Malawi is not an exception even if it is one of the least developed countries in the world. It thus offers an attractive opportunity for social workers to grow in their professional career of developing rural communities.

---

34    Patel, 2005.

35    Ekpe & Mamah, 1997.

36    Asamoah, 1995.

## Conclusion

The Malawian experience shows that for the social work profession to flourish, it should be recognised as a profession and hence regulated to position itself as a role player in social work's development. This recognition should be supported by a political mandate and directed by a specific social work and social welfare policy embedded in a developmental approach. The political mandate must be drawn from broad national policies and legislation as well as specific legislation regulating the profession. Regulation of social work by law implies that the government has a statutory obligation to develop social work and would, therefore, be more committed to developing the profession in the country. It is necessary to establish curricula and practice methods that embrace the local context. Social work educators and practitioners in the country need to find paradigms that address social issues built on the socio-cultural, economic, political, and environmental conditions of the communities. Social work practitioners should be well versed in the diversified cultural knowledge of people's needs if the profession is to influence their lives positively and make a meaningful contribution to social development.

# References

Anders, G. 2002. Freedom and Insecurity: Civil Servants between Support Networks, the Free Market and the Civil Service Reform. In: H. Englund (ed). *A Democracy of Chameleons. Politics and Culture in the New Malawi.* Uppsala: Scandinavian African Institute. pp.287-326.

Apte, N. & Grieco, M. 1994. Urbanisation, caring for the elderly people and the changing African family: The challenge to social policy. *International Security Review,* 47(3-4):111-121.

Asamoah, Y.W. 1995. Africa. In: T.D. Watts, D. Elliott & N.S. Mayadas (eds). *International handbook on social work education.* Westport, CT: Greenwood Press. pp.223-239.

Booth, D., Cammack, D., Harrigan, J., Kanyongolo, E., Mataure, M. & Ngwira, N. 2005. *Drivers of change and development in Malawi.* Revised and Corrected Version. London: Overseas Development Institute.

Cammack, D. 2001. *Malawi at the Threshold: Resources, Conflict and Ingenuity in a Newly Democratic State.* Cambridge, MA: American Academy of Arts and Sciences, Committee on International Security Studies.

Chilowa, W., Milner, J., Chinsinga, B. & Mangani, R. 2000. *Social policy in the context of economic reforms: A benchmark survey report.* Harare: Southern African Regional Institute for Policy Studies.

Chinsinga, B. 2002. The Politics of Poverty Alleviation in Malawi: A Critical Review. In: H. England (ed). *A Democracy of Chameleons: Politics and Culture in New Malawi.* Uppsala: Nordic Africa Institute.

Chipeta, C. 1993. Malawi. In: *The Impact of Structural Adjustment on the Population of Africa, United Nations Population Fund.* New Hampshire: Heinemann. pp.105-118.

Chirwa, E.W., Mvula, P.M., Kadzamira, J. & Horea, L. 2003. *Community-Based Rural Development Project: Baseline Socio-economic Study.* Lilongwe: Wadonda Consult/Malawian Ministry of Lands, Physical Planning and Surveys.

Chitereka, C. 2005. The impact of HIV/AIDS on development and the role of social workers: The case Lesotho. In: G. Jacques & G.N. Lesetedi (eds). *The new partnership for Africa's development: Debates, opportunities and challenges.* Pretoria: Africa Institute of South Africa. pp.384-398.

CSC (Christian Services Committee). 1979. *Annual report on Christian Service Committee of the churches in Malawi.* Blantyre: Mandala.

Darkwa, O.K. 2007. Continuing social work education in an electronic age: The opportunities and challenges facing social work educators in Ghana. *Professional Development,* 2(1):38-43.

Deutsch, M. 1975. Equity, Equality and Need: What determines which value will be used as the basis of distributive justice? *Journal of Social Issues,* 31(3):137-149.

Ekpe, C.P. & Mamah, S.C. 1997. *Social Work in Nigeria: A Colonial Heritage.* Enugu: Unit Oriental Press.

Gray, M. & Fook, J. 2004. The quest for a universal social work: Some issues and implications. *Social Work Education,* 23(5):625-644.

Gray, M., Coates, J. & Bird, M.Y. (eds). 2005. *Indigenous social work around the world.* Cornwall: Ashgate.

Gutierrez, E. 2007. Delivering pro-poor water and sanitation services: The technical and political challenges in Malawi and Zambia. *Geoforum,* 38(5):886-900.

Harrigan, J. 1991. Malawi. In: P. Mosley, J. Harrigan & J. Toye (eds). *Aid and Power: The World Bank and Policy-Based Lending,* 2. London: Routledge. pp.195-218.

Harrigan, J. 2001. *From Dictatorship to Democracy: Economic Policy in Malawi 1964-2000.* Aldershot, UK: Ashgate Publishing.

Hillbrunner, C. 2007. *Integration of water, sanitation and hygiene into HIV/AIDS home-based care strategies.* Paper presented at the Integration of Water, Sanitation and Hygiene into HIV/AIDS Home-Based Care Workshop, Lilongwe, Malawi, 29 October - 1 November.

Hofstede, G. 1991. *Culture and Organization: Intercultural Cooperation and its Importance for Survival.* New York: Harper Collins.

Jere, P. 2006. *A Desk Study on the Underlying Causes of the 2005/2006 Food Crisis in Malawi.* Unpublished.

Kainga, O.J.M. 1979. Trade, the Kyungus, and the Emergence of the Ngonde Kingdom of Malawi. *International Journal of African Historical Studies,* 12(1):17-39.

Kwengwere, P. 2011. Inequality in Malawi. In: H. Jauch & D. Muchena (eds.). *Tearing us apart: inequalities in Southern Africa.* Johannesburg: Open Society for Southern Africa.

Kwezeyani, A. 1996. Linking Livelihood Strategies to Development: Experiences from Malawi. *Community Development Journal,* 36(1):42-52.

Malawi National Aids Commission. 2011. *Malawi National HIV and AIDS strategic plan and policy 2011-2016.* Lilongwe: NAC.

Malawi National Economic Council. 1998. *Reaching the Vision: Analysis of Possible Options.* Lilongwe: Government Printing Works.

McMullin, P., Antoniou, N. & O'Leary, M. 2003. *Mid-term Evaluation of the European Commission Food Security Programme 2001-2004 in Malawi.* Lilongwe: Transtec.

Mhone, G.Z. 2002. *Enclavity and Constrained Labour Absorptive Capacity in Southern African Economies.* Geneva, Switzerland: United Nations Research Institute for Social Development.

Midgley J. 1995. *Social Development: The Developmental Perspective in Social Welfare.* London: Sage.

Mkandawire, T. & Bourenane, N. (eds). 1987. *The State and Agriculture in Africa*. Dakar: Council for the Development of Social Science Research in Africa.

MNCHE (Malawi National Council for Higher Education). 2015. *Annual Report of the Council for Higher Education*. Lilongwe: MNCHE.

Morales, A.T. & Sheafor, B.W. 2004. *Social Work: A Profession of Many Places*. Boston, MA: Pearson Education.

Muchena, D. & Jauch, H. 2011. *Tearing Us Apart: Inequalities in Southern Africa*. Rosebank: Open Society Initiative for Southern Africa.

Munthali, W. 2004. *Kamuzu Banda of Malawi: A study in promise power and paralysis*. Glasgow: Dudu Nsomba Publications.

Mupedziswa, R. 2005. Challenges and prospects of social work services in Africa. In: J.C. Okeibunor & E.E. Anugwom (eds). *The social sciences and socio-economic transformation in Africa*. Nsukka: Great AP Express Publishing. pp.271-317.

Muzaale, P.J. 1987. Rural Poverty, Social Development and their implications for fieldwork practice. *Journal of Social Development in Africa*, 2(1):75-85.

Ng'ong'ola, F. 2004. Malawi and social development policies: a critical historical review. *International Labour Review*, 107(2):103-15.

Ngwira, N., Chiweza, A. & Binauli, A. 2002. Engendering the Malawi Poverty Reduction Strategy Paper: Lesson from failure. In: M. Mullinge & P. Mufune (eds). *Debt Relief Initiatives and Poverty Alleviation: Lessons from Africa*. Pretoria: The African Institute of South Africa. pp.275-302.

Noyoo, N. 2015. Social Development in Southern Africa. In: L. Calvelo, R. Lutz & F. Ross (eds). *Development and Social Work: Social Work of the South*, 6. Oldenburg: Paulo Freire Verlag. pp.167-185.

Okeibunor, J.C. & Anugwom, E.E. (eds) (2014). *The social sciences and socio-economic transformation in Africa*. Nsukka, Nigeria: Great AP Express Publishers. pp.271-317.

Osei-Hwedie, K. & Rankopo, M. 2008. Developing culturally relevant social work education in Africa: The Case of Botswana. In: M. Gray, J. Coates & M.Y. Bird (eds). *Indigenous Social Work around the world*. Cornwall: Ashgate. pp.203-219.

Patel, L. 2005. *Social Welfare & Social Development*. Cape Town: Oxford University Press Southern Africa.

Pryor, F. 1990. *The Political Economy of Poverty, Equity and Growth: Malawi and Madagascar*. A World Bank Comparative Study. Oxford: Oxford Press.

Rakner, L., Mukubvu, L., Ngwira, N., Smiddy, K. & Schneider, A. 2004. *The budget as theatre – the formal and informal institutional makings of the budget process in Malawi*. Bergen: Chr. Michelsen Institute.

Republic of Malawi. 1987. *Report on Decent Work Country Programme*. Lilongwe: Government Printing Works.

Republic of Malawi. 2006. *Malawi Growth and Development Strategy: From Poverty to Prosperity 2006-2011*. Lilongwe: Government Printing Works.

Republic of Malawi. Ministry of Gender, Children and Community Development. 2008. *The National Gender Policy*. Lilongwe: Government Printing Works.

Republic of Malawi. Ministry of Gender, Children and Community Development & National Statistical Office. 2010. *The Gender and Development Index*. Lilongwe: Government Printing Works.

Sindima, H. 2002. *Malawi's First Republic: An Economic and Political Analysis*. Lanham, MD: University Press of America.

Williams, L. 1978. *Casting curved shadows on curved surfaces*. New York: New York Institute of Technology.

Zastrow, C. 2004. *Introduction to Social Work and Social Welfare*. Belmont, CA: Brooks/Cole – Thomson Learning.

# 06

# HISTORY OF SOCIAL WELFARE AND SOCIAL WORK IN MAURITIUS

*Asrani Gopaul, Corine Saupin and Fabiola Ramsamy*

## Introduction

Mauritius reckons to have one of the most comprehensive systems of welfare provisions in Africa. However, its evolution from being a colonial slavery island to becoming an upper-middle-income country, enjoying a system of welfare pluralism, with a universal provision, shows that the former has not always been a right. Despite French and British colonial history; attaining Independence; inheriting a fragile, mono-crop economy; and undergoing further structural adjustment experiences; Mauritians today enjoy universal retirement pensions; cash transfers; in-kind transfers; free universal healthcare; corporate social responsibility; free education from pre-primary to tertiary levels; and a vast array of social services. Also worth mentioning is the welfare system's development leading to the incalculable need for social services' professional development through education and training of human resources. Despite the country's quite limited natural resources as it is an island – except for its reserve of human resources and a blue ocean, which the government is adamant about converting into a blue economy – the social welfare system has over time, been maintained consistently.

Many people have questioned the sustainability of the present social welfare system and asking whether there was a need for reform. However, Mauritian scholars argue that the debate is more political than socio-economic and that no political party would take the risk of engaging in the dismantling of the present system. Indeed, this could be equal to political suicide. This chapter traces the milestones of the welfare system in Mauritius, the resulting development of its social work profession, and paints a picture of the current state of the art in this era of a neo-liberal led globalisation. The colonial era, post-Independence and contemporary times are discussed below to highlight some of the major achievements in social welfare and social work in Mauritius. Though comprehensive, it should be specified that the information provided in this chapter is by no means exhaustive.

## In the Beginning: Louis XIV's *Code Noire*

Mauritius got to be placed on the world map through its history of colonisation and by becoming central to the world's race for international maritime business during the sixteenth century. The island has a long history of Portuguese landings; the Dutch's attempt at settlements in the sixteenth century; French colonisation in the seventeenth century; British settlement in the latter part of the same century; and then it became independent in 1968 and a republic in 1992.[1] After the departure of the Dutch, the French settlers brought slaves from Africa and Asia to work on the sugar cane fields. The history of social welfare on the island started on the sugar cane plantations during this period. French settlers owed their sugar productions to the slaves who were brought from Africa and India. The *Code Noire* ('black code'), a written decree by Louis XIV in 1697, administered and guided the lives of the slaves, who had virtually no rights and were provided meagre welfare through the Code.[2] According to Lingayah (2015), the French established a system of public administration on the island that was to become the precursor of the Mauritian Welfare system. Later, under the British rule and in the wake of the Fabian movement, a new approach to people's distress and needs would be adopted as socialist philosophies were being increasingly embraced in the last quarter of the nineteenth century. This approach was the first step towards the setting up of the Mauritian social welfare system, arguably the most comprehensive on the African

---

1    Dommen & Dommen, 1999.
2    UQAC, 2007.

continent with an influence of British social policy. Napoleon, in 1803, reinstated another set of laws in place of the *Code Noire*, where it was mentioned that only people of French origin were equal and free.

## Colonisation Years: From Code Noire to British Poor Ordinance

The Dutch settlers' attempt to establish a transit place for Dutch boats on the island, marked the colonisation period of Mauritius, named after the Dutch Prince Mauritze De Nassau and under the governance of the Dutch's East India Company, 1638-1710. The Dutch brought some slaves from Africa, but it is difficult to trace back any formal form of social welfare that may have existed on the island during this period. The Dutch, however, started the first economic activity on the island – the plantation of sugar cane.[3] Mauritius, at that time known as Ile de France, became a major destination on the British dominated spice route round the Cape towards the Indian Ocean.[4] The aftermath of the French Revolution later resulted in the abolition of slavery in 1835.[5] During the French slavery period in Mauritius, the *Code Noire* determined the life of the slaves. According to the *Code Noire*, slaves had no right and freedom and Articles 2 and 3 state that Christianity was to be the only religion authorised on the island, seemingly the first sign of ill fare during the French period.[6] In Article 6, the right of slaves to work only until noon on Sundays are mentioned. However, this was not observed on every sugar cane plantation.[7] The welfare of the slaves was only mentioned in two sentences in Article 22 of the *Code Noire* and read as follows:

> Slave owners have to provide every week to all slaves aged ten or above for their food two and a half pot of Tapioca Flour or at least three arrowroots of two and a half-pound each, ten pounds of salted beef or three pounds of fish. To children of age ten or less half of what has been mentioned above.[8]

It was further recommended that slave owners had the responsibility of providing two full sets of clothes or three measures of clothes to slaves. Article 27 mentions the fact that

---

3    Bunwaree, 1994.
4    Ibid.
5    Mathur, 1991.
6    Colbert, 1684.
7    Mathur, 1991.
8    Code Noire, 1684:3-4.

slaves' owners were responsible for fair treatment and even hospitalisation of the slaves in case of injury or illness. However, this was not always respected. The different articles treated slaves as merely goods rather than human beings. Following the colonisers' refusal to free slaves, the French crown sent two emissaries to the island to inquire into the welfare of the slaves. The local French sugar oligarch expelled the emissaries and thus rebelled against the French authorities. The French crown re-established the order in 1803.[9] Decaen was sent to Mauritius to establish the Napoleon Code to replace the *Code Noire*. The slave masters determined slaves' lives and welfare until the arrival of the British in 1810 when Mauritius became a crown colony. After this, as mentioned earlier, slavery was abolished in 1835, although the slave trade became illegal in British colonies by 1808.

## Components of the Welfare System from Inception

### Education System

The first central school was set up by Decaen in 1799 and parallel to the basic schooling, the church already offered. This was the beginning of a long history of a central provision of education in Mauritius. Mahe de Labourdonais attempted to set up a good education system in 1735; however, it was only in 1789 that the authorities expressed interest in education, according to Bunwaree (1991). In fact, during the French period, the church had been deeply involved in education. After the British took possession of the island in 1810, they brought in major changes. Education became the main concern of the British Central Government on the island. Reverend Lebrun, in the early 1900s, according to Bunwaree (1995), set up the first free day-school for all Mauritians. Thus, a first step was made to provide free education as part of welfare, from private sources to students.

### Healthcare System

According to the White Paper on Healthcare (2002):

> ... the general state of health of the population of Mauritius is good and has been improving steadily over the past decades. People are living longer, and fewer children die in their first year. In the last 30 years, in Mauritius, expectation of life

---

9    Mathur, 1991.

has increased from 63 years to 71 years and infant mortality has fallen from 64 to 14 deaths in the first year of life for every 1 000 live born babies.[10]

The healthcare system during the slave period was, as mentioned in the *Code Noire* (1684), the responsibility of the slave owners. Vaughan (2000) mentions that during the French period healthcare was only used to keep slaves fit for daily work to be performed on the sugar cane plantations, and Mauritius never had a suitable healthcare system. Adjacent to what the French offered; the Church helped the poor at that time. The first 40-bed hospital on the island was built in 1733 in Port Louis. Mahe de Labourdonnais, Governor of Mauritius, constructed the first 240-bed hospital in Port Louis in 1740. According to Parahoo (1986), during the British era, it was common to have outbreaks of epidemics in Mauritius, mainly imported from India. The revolution in healthcare came during the British period with the construction of large hospitals. Private medical institutions exist on the island, and Mauritians have a choice between public and fee-paying services and can enjoy private medical health insurance. Social work in the medical setting was introduced later, as the healthcare field evolved further, in the 1980s, to support the medical and paramedical staffs in their daily work.

## Foundations of Mauritius' Modern Welfare System

The contribution of great welfare scholars of the 1950s and 1960s such as Sir William Beveridge shaped the contemporary welfare system. The British Government requested Beveridge to survey the British Social Services structure and devise a system of social security, to guarantee a basic level of income for all citizens. Beveridge's report (1942) became the foundation of the modern social welfare legislation of Great Britain, as well as a model for other countries, namely the various British colonies, among them, Mauritius. Additionally, the Mauritian Government appointed Sir Richard Titmuss in 1957 to investigate welfare issues and propose a welfare state plan for the island. Titmuss visited the island accompanied by Brian Abel Smith. His report on social policy and population growth on the island was the major precursor to the development of a sound welfare state in Mauritius. Professor James Meade's visit followed that of Titmuss and Abel Smith, and he came to Mauritius to advise the government on economic reforms in the early 1960s.[11]

---

10   Republic of Mauritius. Ministry of Health & Quality of Life, 2002:3.

11   Dommen & Dommen, 1999.

## Early Social Security System

The most impressive chapter in the history of the Mauritian welfare system is perhaps the social security system. Despite the island having limited resources, its social security happens to be one of the most effective publicly financed and comprehensive systems of social protection in Africa. It nowadays accounts for nearly 11 per cent of the Gross Domestic Product (GDP) of the Country. The present system had been in place since 1950. Still, the first major piece of legislation on social protection was enacted in 1902 when the Poor Law Ordinance was passed. The law at that time, under the British system, provided for payment of social assistance to impoverished households. In 1951, the name 'poor law' was changed to 'public assistance', and in 1981 it was renamed 'social aid'. Under the *Social Aid Act of 1983*, until today, a wide range of social assistance is paid to heads of households or individuals whose resources are insufficient to meet their needs.[12] Initially, the system was covering the following categories of beneficiaries: heads of households or individuals who are unable to earn a living because of illness, disability; cases of abandonment of household; single women with children; poor families of prisoners; and heads of households who being poor cannot cater for the needs of one or more severely disabled children.

## Evolution of Pension Scheme

In 1950 Mauritius became a trendsetter in its approach to social protection and social security, when the old-age pension became payable on a means test basis, to all persons who had reached the age of 65 years. However, in 1953, the women's pension age was reduced to 60 years, and in 1967 that of men equally reduced to 60 years. In 1961 the Family Allowances Ordinance was introduced, and according to this ordinance, the law provided for the payment of a child's allowance to heads of households who had at least three children and whose earnings did not exceed a prescribed ceiling.[13] The National Pensions Scheme was introduced following the enactment of the National Pensions Act in 1976. This scheme represents around 13 per cent of the government's recurrent budget or nowadays around 3 per cent of GDP. The scheme is made up of three main components: payment of non-contributory universal pensions; payment of contributory pensions under a social insurance scheme; and payment of industrial

---

12     Ministry of Social Security and National solidarity (MSSNS) 2011.

13     Ibid.

injury benefits to insured persons suffering from work-related injuries or prescribed diseases.[14] In 1983, the Unemployment Hardship Relief Act was passed. It provided for the government to pay unemployment hardship relief to households' heads who were unemployed, actively seeking work and without adequate resources to cater for their families' needs. The scheme has never been comprehensive following the conditional ties of the Structural Adjustment Programme introduced under the watch of the World Bank and the International Monetary Fund (IMF) in the 1970s.

According to the MSSNS (2010), the pension system in Mauritius is a five-pillar model, with a strong poverty reduction thrust, consisting of:

➣ A universal non-contributory basic pension from government revenues;

➣ A contributory pension scheme for both the public sector and the private sector including a transitional unemployment benefit for redundant workers of the private sector;

➣ A provident fund called the National Savings Scheme for both the public sector and the private sector;

➣ A private occupational pension scheme on an optional basis for private-sector workers;

➣ Subsidies on rice, flour, cooking gas and other services; free education up to tertiary level, free healthcare, including tertiary healthcare and free transport for older persons, disabled persons and students; financial governmental support to several non-governmental organisations (NGOs) to perform some of the social tasks that only such organizations can carry out for the benefit of vulnerable groups.

Today the Mauritian welfare system is viewed as an exemplary one on the African continent. The fight for such rights was longstanding, but our forefathers were visionaries, and majorly contributed towards the building up of our country.

---

14    Ibid.

## Post-Independence Period

The British colony of Mauritius became an independent nation in 1968, and the post-Independence era witnessed the consistent development of the welfare state in Mauritius.[15] Indeed, as we stepped into the post-Independence period, several challenges cropped up politically, economically and socially. Earlier in 1960-1961, the release of Titmuss's and Meade's reports on the social and economic situation of the country respectively depicted a gloomy future for Mauritius. In discussing these two reports, Dommen and Dommen (1999) claim that the strategy of Meade's and the Titmuss's report was to propose ways of dealing with the overriding issue of population growth. The explosion of numbers struck the authors, especially alarmed by the growth of the under 15 age group, combined with what appeared to be declining work opportunities. For this reason, their strongest recommendation was for vigorous birth control measures to limit families to three children at most.

The fact of the matter is that the Mauritian society's awareness of ethnic differences had exacerbated several challenges. After being under British rule for more than a century since 1810, some ethnic groups' quest for power became a major issue, resulting in fragile ethnic relations and social fabric.[16] Over and above the steady population growth rate issue and ethnic tensions, Mauritius was classified as a poor country, with a high unemployment rate, giving rise to many social problems.[17] Phaahla (2014) accurately reiterates the economic challenges, existing then.[18] The Mauritian economy at the time of Independence was appalling. Exacerbating the problem was the population explosion that threatened to destabilise the country by increasing the numbers of the unemployed and discontented in society.

### Welfare in the 1970s

Meade's report additionally highlighted the weaknesses, potential failures, and the resulting negative impacts on the Mauritian economy and its prospects. In response

---

15   Phaahla, 2014: 3-4.

16   Addison & Hazareesingh, 1993:43; Phaahla, 2014:3; Betchoo, 2015.

17   Vandemoortele & Bird, 2010.

18   Phaahla, 2014: 3.

to this report, several measures were undertaken to diversify and boost the economy.[19] However, the initial poor economic conditions and social inequalities of the early 1970s favoured the rise of militancy and activism, as several workers' groups went on strike to demand better living conditions and rights for vulnerable groups. For example, the sugar sector's strike in 1971, the Dockers' strike (1972) and the students' strike (1975), respectively.[20] Other important landmarks of the 1970s are the drafting of the First and Second National Plans (1971-1975 and 1976-1980 respectively). The Ministry of Economic Planning and Development drew up these plans to propose solutions to the highlighted gaps in the economic system. For instance, a family planning programme was proposed and implemented to curb the population growth rate. By 1975, the growth rate was down to about 1.7 per cent. The government adopted a policy of encouraging emigration to control population growth.[21] Despite the economic crises experienced in the mid-1970s, the country had its first sugar boom, with more than a five-fold increase in exports between 1971-1974, as the price of sugar rose on the international market.[22] Betchoo (2015) explains:

> The Mauritian quota under the European Economic Community Sugar Protocol – former EU – increased from 380 000 tonnes to 505 000 tonnes at a guaranteed price of 260 pounds per tonne from the previous price of 57 dollars per tonne.

Following this, Mauritius signed an agreement under the Lome Convention in 1976, replacing the earlier agreement under the Yaounde Convention, to sustain the sugar industry further.[23] The sugar boom had several positive outcomes on the community's welfare – major infrastructural facilities such as roads, electricity supply and street-lighting connected to remote villages and to more developed areas were erected. Also, subsidies on staple foods could be maintained. More importantly, for the first time after Independence, salary compensations were paid universally, as well as end-of-year bonuses, improving the working class's standards of living.[24]

---

19    Addison & Hazareesingh, 1993: 98; Nowbutsing, 2013:31.
20    Gill, 2007; The Editorial Team, 2007; Betchoo, 2015.
21    Addison & Hazareesingh, 1993:99.
22    Betchoo, 2015.
23    Addison & Hazareesingh, 1993:100-101;104.
24    Betchoo, 2015.

On the other hand, the government in 1975 worked on a comprehensive National Pension Scheme to benefit the elderly.[25] In 1976-1977, basic widows, orphans and invalidity pensions were introduced.[26] Another key measure the government took was to subsidise the education sector fully, to make education available to all Mauritians. In 1976, education became free for primary-school children while in 1979, it became free for secondary students. Finally, in 1988, education was made freely accessible to university students. Similarly, the government improved upon health services, making these two major basic needs of the nation, accessible to all. These social policies majorly contributed positively to the country's overall wellbeing.[27]

Meanwhile, voluntary movements focusing on grassroots interventions among vulnerable groups, intervened, because they were keen to address the different social issues. With time, the Mauritius Council of Social Services, a social service coordinating body founded in 1965, started to support their work.[28] It is in the 1970s, while many social concerns were being highlighted, alongside the provision of welfare benefits, that decision-makers understood the growing need to ensure effective and efficient social service delivery by professionalising the country's social services. The University of Mauritius (UOM) thus became a privileged partner to help realise this goal. It offered its first part-time Diploma in Social Work in 1973, to enable students, already working in different social service sectors like the Ministry of Social Security or Probation and Aftercare, to take the course and become qualified social workers. The course was to be upgraded to a degree level, two decades later.

## Welfare in the 1980s

Due to major advances in the welfare field, through the universal provision of benefits like education, health, the Basic Retirement Pension and the strategic economic positioning of the country, the 1980s turned out to be Mauritius' golden years. The country experienced an economic boom, much against the expectations of Meade (1961), who, as explained earlier, had foretold an economic fiasco for Mauritius.[29] Nonetheless, the

25    Addison & Hazareesingh, 1993:105.
26    Yen, 2007.
27    Photius.com, 1994.
28    MACOSS, 2015.
29    Chapin Metz, 1994.

decision was made to maintain welfare provisions, especially universal provisions, at a time when the IMF was proposing debt relief against the conditional application of Structural Adjustment Programmes (SAPs); a bold proposal, given that the application of SAPs implied the liberalisation of markets and privatisation of services. Thomson (2010) explains that SAPs provided conditional lending to assist African development.[30] 'Conditional', in that governments receiving debt relief, were obliged to adjust their economic policy. In general, 'adjustment' meant liberalising and privatising.

Mauritius diversified its economy, proposing new sectors other than agriculture (the sole pillar of the economy till the 1970s), like the manufacturing sector, namely the textile industry, and tourism. These two sectors rapidly expanded during the 1980s to become solid pillars Mauritius relied upon to sustain itself. Hence, Mauritius became known as 'the tiger of the Indian Ocean' by the late 1980s.[31] Bunwaree (2002) states:

▷ The development strategies adopted in the post-Independence period provided windows of opportunity to various sections of society. The population experienced an improvement in their standard of living, and a middle class grew in the 1980s.[32]

▷ The government's publication issued on the 40th anniversary of Independence, surveying the country's journey between 1968-2008 supports this view.[33]

▷ The bold and decisive measures taken to steer the economy back on track were fruitful. The 1984-1988 period marked an important economic turnaround, with average real output growing by 7 per cent. The engine of growth started rapidly in the export-processing-zone sector after 1983 and shifted to the service-sector during the late 1980s.

In the same vein, the country experienced rampant social problems related to the widened gap between the wealthy and the poor, and resulting in social ills, like, substance abuse and criminality. Illicit drug consumption and trafficking, though already present for a while in the country, became infamously popular during the 1980s. The mediatised arrest of four members of the Mauritian parliament overseas in 1985, highlighted the

---

30    Thomson, 2010:197 in Logan, 2015.
31    Bunwaree, 2002.
32    Ibid:1.
33    Republic of Mauritius. Government Information Service, 2008.

growing concerns around illicit drug abuse in the country, leading to the birth of several anti-drug movements in 1986: the Groupe A de Cassis, active in primary prevention among the youth; the Dr Idryce Goomany Drug Rehabilitation Centre; the Solidarity Centre (*Centre de Solidarite*) in 1988; and several others.[34] These initiatives set the ball rolling. A diligent and longstanding battle, for the next three decades, would be waged against substance abuse. First, the Trust Fund for the Treatment and Rehabilitation of Drug Addicts was set up in 1986 to educate about and prevent the public from drug abuse, and rehabilitate substance abusers. Next, the National Agency for the Treatment and Rehabilitation of Substance Abusers (NATReSA), a parastatal body, was established in 1996 operating with the Ministry of Social Security, National Solidarity's and the Senior Citizens Welfare and Reform's backing. In 2016 however, the State decided to wind up the NATReSA, the only state agency responsible for the prevention, treatment and rehabilitation of substance abusers because it was using too many resources. Instead, the decision was made to redirect its services to the Ministry of Health.[35]

During this same time, the government set up for the first time, a Ministry of Women's and Family Affairs in 1982 to address the concerns of women and children, considered as a vulnerable group.[36] In 1988 SOS Femmes, an NGO was launched to address the many cases of domestic violence, mainly against women.[37] Many developments would be achieved during the next decade, in the area of women's empowerment, gender equality, and children's protection in the country as a result of these first steps, as discussed further down. The 1980s witnessed the proliferation of NGOs, with targeted action towards specific populations in need, including the Georges Charles Foundation (*Fondation Georges Charles*), welcoming children with either physical or mental disabilities; Lizie dan La main, taking care of children with visual impairment; and the ATD Fourth World (*ATD Quart Monde*), working with the materially most vulnerable groups of the country.[38]

Though services were offered with genuine concern, and a deep sense of voluntary engagement, they were still largely unprofessional, at least where social workers'

---

34    BBC, 2019; Groupe A of Cassis, 2020; UNODC, 2016; NATReSA, 2016.

35    NATRESA, 2016.

36    Republic of Mauritius. Ministry of Gender Equality, Child Development and Family Welfare. 2016.

37    SOS Femmes, 2010.

38    ACTogether, 2016; Lizie dan La Main, 2006; ATD Quart Monde, 2016.

inputs were concerned. It is important to reiterate that social actors and stakeholders were intervening in social issues out of on-field exposure and longstanding personal experience. Throughout the years it became obvious to the different voluntary organisations that service delivery should and could only improve by involving all the policy-makers, social actors, education partners and other stakeholders, who would contribute to the professionalisation of all social services.[39] It can be inferred that during the 1970s and 1980s, welfare and social work development were inevitably intertwined as more community needs were identified and advocated for. More decision-makers had to develop policy responses to them. Appropriate service delivery had to follow.[40] Consequently, employers encouraged and even sponsored civil servants from the Ministry of Social Security and Reformed Institutions, Youth, Women and others, who intervened directly with their respective targeted populations, to enrol in UOM' Social Work diploma course. They were to acquire the specific technical know-how, knowledge-based education and practical training, peculiar to the social work profession, to deliver efficient services to the population.

## Welfare of Women and Children

Indeed, the 1990s and 2000s onwards brought new dimensions to the welfare sphere. One such radical change happened on the women and children welfare fronts. Mauritius had acceded and ratified several conventions, compelling the setting up of national legal frameworks and relevant implementing mechanisms. Two conventions had a direct impact on the way social welfare and social work were carried out: Mauritius acceded to the Convention on the Elimination of All Forms of Discrimination Against Women in 1984, and the Convention on the Rights of the Child in 1990; thus it was compelled to introduce the Child Protection Act (1994) and the Protection from Domestic Violence Act (1997). One of the mechanisms the State put in place to enforce the Child Protection Act, was the Child Development Unit. Set-up in 1995, the unit aimed to ensure the upholding of the Mauritian child's welfare in line with the Child Protection Act and the Convention of the Rights of the Child. These State policies, programmes and actions consider the best interests of the child. Another landmark in the service delivery of family welfare has been the setting up of the Family Welfare and Protection Unit in 2003.

---

39    MACOSS, 2015.

40    Healy, 2008.

It was a merger of the Family Counselling Service, existing since 1986, and the Domestic Violence Intervention Unit, a mechanism the State put in place in 1997 to enforce the Domestic Violence Act. The Family Welfare and Protection Unit aims to implement family welfare policies and strategies and to adopt strategies and implement actions that address gender-based violence.[41]

## Welfare of Old People

Elderly welfare is another area experiencing several changes. The State has not shied away from the need to expand its welfare provision to old people despite concerns about a growing elderly population. People aged 60 and above are estimated to be around 15 per cent.[42] The figure is projected to rise to 30 per cent by 2050.[43] In 2001, Mauritius developed a national policy to address the welfare needs of the ageing population. One measure taken was the creation of elderly day-care centres to cater to the elderly living with their families or on their own, who required assistance during the day.

Moreover, social protection measures have been reviewed over the years. New protection measures have been added over and above the universal basic retirement pension and basic widows' pension. One such example is the carers' allowance. Indeed, carers' retirement pension beneficiaries, who are disabled to the extent of not less than 60 per cent and needing constant care and attention, can apply for an allowance. Another example is the introduction of a widowers' contributory pension to eliminate gender discrimination.[44]

Several facilities have been introduced recently. Besides free wheelchairs, eyeglasses, hearing aids, dentures, healthcare and medical visits for those above 90, they are also entitled to travel freely on public transport. The elderly and severely disabled people are now eligible for free medical home visits.[45] Growing concern about the ageing of Mauritian society prompted the State to introduce the Elderly Persons Act in 2005 to provide adequate protection against ill-treatment. Following the enactment of the law, the Welfare and Elderly Persons Protection Unit was set up in 2006 to take up reported

---

41    Republic of Mauritius. Ministry of Gender Equality, Child Development & Family Welfare, 2016.
42    Jeewa-Daureeawoo, 2016.
43    UN, 2015.
44    Jugnauth, 2016.
45    Ibid.

cases of abuse and neglect. However, while efforts to ensure the upholding of older persons' rights and welfare were made, Rosa Kornfeld-Matte, an independent expert on the elderly's enjoyment of human rights, observed in her report on Mauritius that the law is not enough. She recommended that the authorities make detection of elder abuse and law enforcement a priority.[46] Such a step would call for the speedy development of social work with a gerontological specialisation.

## Welfare Responses to Poverty and Social Exclusion

Although world commentators acclaim the economic miracle of Mauritius, a phenomenon branded as the 'malaise creole' marked the beginning of the 1990s. 'Malaise creole' is a term used to refer to the general feeling of dissatisfaction and frustration of the descendants of the former African and Malagasy slaves, towards situations of social exclusion they are confronted with, as compared to the rest of the population.[47] Indeed, although living standards had improved much across the country, several households were still living in poverty in the majority from the creole community, in particular, those of African and Malagasy ancestry. Roman Catholic Priest Roger Cerveaux voiced the 'lack of welfare' the creole community experienced in 1993, claiming that targeted intervention was required to improve their lot.[48] The 'malaise creole' was explained as being a direct consequence of the colonial past and trauma their enslaved ancestors experienced.[49] The descendants of former slaves were reportedly living on the margin of the socio-economic development of the 1980s. Invisible in the higher echelons of the civil service, business and decision-making, the creoles were disadvantaged in comparison to other ethnic groups.[50]

The blacks were economically, socially and politically marginalised and excluded. The growing perception of state officials functioning as gatekeepers to state resources led the creole people to distrust the government and distance themselves from state services.[51] The frustration and despair contributed to the brewing social malaise, climaxing with the

---

46    UN, 2015.
47    Eriksen, 2007; Bunwaree, 2002; Boswell, 2006.
48    Chan Low & Reddi, 2000.
49    Maurer, 2014.
50    Chan Low & Reddi, 2000.
51    Gill, 2010.

death of Louis Reginald Topize also known as Kaya, a famous reggae singer who died of skull fracture while in police custody in 1999. The singer's supporters accused the police of brutality against the creole community and directed their initial anger against the government whose workforce predominantly consisted of Hindus.[52] The protests took an ethnic dimension quickly leading to island-wide rioting in major parts of the island between the creoles at one end and Hindus and Muslims at the other.[53]

One of the State's immediate reactions to the riots was the setting up of government departments, to focus on stemming social exclusion. The Trust Fund for the Social Integration of Vulnerable Groups was thus set up in 1999 as a poverty alleviation programme with the Ministry of Finance's backing. The National Non-Government Organisation Trust Fund was another agency created in the same year parallel to the Ministry of Social Security, National Solidarity and Senior Citizens Welfare and Reform Institutions, to provide financial support to NGOs involved in community-based social projects. International donors, especially the United Nations Development Programme, the European Union (EU) and the International Fund for Agricultural Development, came up with similar programmes, running from 1999 until around 2004.[54] All programmes aimed to adopt a participatory approach in line with the Millennium Development Goals' initiative and the sustainable development goals' agenda of involving the community in all development initiatives. Civil society, particularly non-governmental and community-based organisations (CBOs), became important development actors and partners of the government. The poverty alleviation programmes recruited qualified social workers and other social science graduates to facilitate clients' access to the programmes' specific welfare provisions. The Trust Fund for the Social Integration of Vulnerable Groups funded community development projects; microcredit schemes; and loans to needy students. The EU-funded Anou Diboute Ensam ('let us stand together') programme (1999-2004) provided financial assistance for social infrastructure and income-generating as well as technical assistance projects in poverty-stricken areas of Mauritius.

All the poverty alleviation schemes highlighted lack of capacity of vulnerable groups to make judicious use of the available funds.[55] Civil society organisations, particularly

---

52    Dobson, 2005.
53    Bunwaree, 2005.
54    FAO, 2005.
55    Ibid.

NGOs and CBOs involved in poverty reduction projects, agreed that they were insufficiently equipped and lacked trained staff. They reckoned that the professional training of grassroots workers was an essential contributor to sustainable development. The 2001 National Action Plan for Poverty Alleviation stressed that for greater efficiency and empowerment of grassroots workers to reach the poorest of the poor, social and community work had to be professionalised and valued. The various stakeholders have time and again reemphasised the need to train voluntary social workers and build the capacity of the NGO sector for more effective service delivery.

The United Nations Development Programme's (UNDP) Non-State Actors Unit along with the EU-funded Decentralised Cooperation Programme, the NGO Trust Fund, the Mauritius Council of Social Services and the private sector's corporate social responsibility initiatives have been highly involved in the training of grassroots workers as part of their pro-poor actions and capacity building of civil society organisations. One of the latest additional actions has been the establishment of the UNDP's Social Register of Mauritius programme in 2008, aiming to improve the targeting efficiency of social programmes so that maximum programme resources reach the poor and hence to minimise leakage to non-poor; so that the poor are not minimally covered.[56]

## Social Housing

Social housing is a topic closely linked to poverty. Housing insecurity is known to be a common feature among the poorest. The social housing sector underwent an important change from 1990 onwards. In 1990, the Government of Mauritius introduced a new housing policy as a response to the housing needs of lower-income groups. The National Housing Company Ltd was set up in 1992 to implement the policy. The objective was to provide decent housing structures with water and electricity and other facilities included. Care was taken to avoid the creation of ghettoed housing estates as the aim was to alleviate poverty and fight social exclusion. Fostering community building for social inclusion was an important component of the housing projects. Low rise flats were thus built in several locations across the island. Low-income and middle-income earners were required to make a down-payment of 5 per cent and 10 per cent respectively to acquire a housing unit, and a progressive repayment mechanism was put in place to alleviate the

---

56    UNDP, 2015.

financial burden of the loan. Moreover, in 1997, low-income earners owning a plot of land and wishing to build a concrete house were granted funds for payment of roof slabs and building materials free of charge.[57]

In 2000, the State decided to provide timber and corrugated iron sheets along with other building materials to low-income households as part of the intervention strategy of the Trust Fund for the Social Integration of Vulnerable Groups. Furthermore, to discourage squatting, the State allocated building site leases for housing purposes. Some 2 700 squatters saw their settlements regularised under that scheme.[58] In 2009, integrated housing projects with a kindergarten, a community centre and recreational facilities were set up. Squatters were again targeted.[59] In 2011, housing ownership was estimated to have reached 90 per cent.[60]

## Conclusion

Mauritius has successfully transformed itself from a mono-crop economy into a diverse economy with a democratic political system and a strong safety net to become one of the most prosperous countries in Africa.[61] Welfare provisions and the social work profession have evolved alongside each other. However, important measures on the way welfare provision is distributed and delivered need to be taken. Alternatives are discussed hereafter.

Welfare spending in Mauritius has seen a consistent increase over the years. However, the evolution of the actual overall cost of the welfare budget is not known. The broad and complex welfare system makes data collection on actual welfare spending hard as statistics are scattered.[62] There is thus the need to devise a mechanism to account for actual total welfare spending by both the State and non-State actors. According to Basant Roi (2014), "… a very crude estimate of total welfare spending by the government gives a figure of around 27 per cent of GDP compared to around 25 per cent for most Welfare States." The

---

57    Autar, 2012; Chagny, 2013; Sewpal, 2013.
58    Sewpal, 2013.
59    Chagny, 2013.
60    Autar, 2012.
61    Zafar, 2011; Stiglitz, 2011.
62    Basant Roi, 2014.

three largest items of welfare expenditure, the comprehensive social security system; free education from primary to tertiary level; and free healthcare; are reported to have grown by an average of just over 10 per cent from 1999-2013.[63] The State's strong commitment to the welfare philosophy has paid off by contributing to make Mauritius stand out from its African counterparts, evident by the increased Human Development Index.[64] The figure rose from 0.619 in 1990 to 0.777 in 2014.[65]

Mauritius has until now been successful in striking a balance between its adherence to free-market principles and its commitment to social welfare philosophy. However, maintaining such a comprehensive welfare system in an ageing society will be challenging for the State. Soto, Thacoor and Petri (2015) assert that the weighing down of government finances caused by the ageing population make reforms 'unavoidable'. The political sensitivity of the issue makes it difficult for the government to take unpopular decisions as welfare allocations can influence voters' decisions. Thus, the State's attempt at replacing the universal retirement pension scheme with a targeted one has been subject to debates since 2005.

Similarly, the government's announcement of its plan to privatise the water sector has been facing many criticisms.[66] Hence, any attempt at diminishing welfare provision has to be dealt with gradually and cautiously. One such attempt has been the introduction of tax reliefs on premiums of private medical insurance schemes as an incentive for people to embark on such plans.

Another challenge would be the professionalisation of social work. Historically, trained social workers have been employed in the public sector. Social security officers; probation officers; medical social workers; family welfare officers; youth officers; community workers; and newly recruited educational, social workers, among others, are either a holder of UOM Social Work programme's diploma or the degree. While statistics on the employment of qualified social workers are not available, a new trend has been observed lately. Civil society organisations, namely NGOs and CBOs, have been recruiting trained social workers. Rigorous conditions that funders impose have catalysed the

---

63    Ibid.
64    Phaahla, 2014.
65    UNDP, 2015.
66    Boutia, 2016.

professionalisation of the NGO sector. There is thus need for specialised training of post-graduate students in social work. UOM was the sole provider of social work diploma education until recently. In 1994, UOM introduced a 4-year degree programme. It was offered to secondary school leavers for the first time. The need for an upgrading of skills and improved work status had prompted former diploma holders to lobby for the introduction of the degree programme. However, the minimum qualifications required for admission at UOM has been closing the door to several unqualified people involved in the field. As a response to that need, the Charles Telfair Institute has started recently to offer a certificate and a diploma programme in Community Services.

In 2015, the Mauritius Qualifications Authority embarked on a project for the Recognition of Prior Learning in social work for grassroots level social workers in NGO settings. A National Certificate in Social Work Practice was thus launched. However, there is a need to demystify the profession in Mauritius. Social work as a profession is highly misunderstood. There is a belief that social work is not rocket science and that anyone involved in some kindness or charity work, or in the organisation of religious or cultural activities, or involved in political activism is a social worker. The misunderstanding towards the profession has led to professionally qualified social workers directed and supervised by professionals from other professions. The time is, therefore, ripe for a regulatory body in Mauritius to set standards of practice; register social workers; protect them and their clients; deal with malpractices; and promote the profession, so that social work can get the formal recognition it deserves – as a profession in its own right.

# References

Abel-Smith, B. 1992. The Beveridge Report: its origins and outcomes. *International Social Security Review*, 45(1-2):5-16.

ACTogether. 2016. *Find an NGO: Professionals: Georges Charles Foundation.* [https://bit.ly/2G0uSzD]. (Accessed 5 October 2016).

Addison, J. & Hazareesingh, K. 1993. *A New History of Mauritius.* Beau Bassin-Rose Hill, Mauritius: Editions de l'Océan Indien.

Anonymous. 2016a. Personal phone interview with an ex-assistant programme officer, 8 October. Ministry of Health and Quality of Life: National Agency for the Treatment and Rehabilitation of Substance Abusers.

Anonymous. 2016b. Personal phone interview with a principal executive assistant, 7 October. University of Mauritius: Faculty of Social Sciences.

ATD Quart Monde. 2016. [https://bit.ly/349zETh]. (Accessed 6 October 2016).

Autar, A.B. 2012. S*ocial Housing in Mauritius Social Movement and Low-Income Housing in Mauritius.* Academia Education. [https://bit.ly/33aw77X]. (Accessed 8 October 2016).

Basant Roi, R. 2014. The Welfare State: Need for a Kiss of Change (Part VIII): Is the Welfare State Sustainable? *Le Mauricien*, 24 May. [https://bit.ly/3n9NRIP]. (Accessed 4 October 2016).

BBC. 2019. Mauritius profile – Timeline. *BBC News: World*. [https://bbc.in/33dUDVH]. (Accessed 6 October 2016).

Betchoo, N. 2015. King Sugar, The First Economic Boom of 1973. *Le Mauricien*, 17 October. [https://bit.ly/36gDqNf]. (Accessed 7 October 2016).

Beveridge, W. 1942. *Social Insurance and Allied Services.* London: His Majesty's Stationery Office.

Boswell, R. 2006. *Le Malaise Créole. Ethnic Identity in Mauritius.* New York-Oxford: Berghahn Books.

Boutia, M. 2016. Rhadakrishna Sadien, Syndicaliste: 'Privatiser la CWA sera catastrophique'. *Le Defi Media.* [https://bit.ly/3jdRfQv]. (Accessed 6 October 2016).

Bunwaree, S. 1994. *Mauritian Education in a Global Economy.* Beau Bassin-Rose Hill, Mauritius: Editions de l'Océan Indien.

Bunwaree, S. 2002. Economics, conflicts and interculturality in a small island state: The case of Mauritius. *Polis*, 9:1-19. [https://bit.ly/2SfTXZz]. (Accessed 7 October 2016).

Bunwaree, S. 2005. State-society relations: Re-engineering the Mauritian social contract (Draft Paper). Presented at the Eleventh Council for the Development of Social Science Research in Africa's General Assembly Conference, Maputo, Mozambique. 6-10 December.

Chagny, M. 2013. *Overview of Social Housing Programmes Effected in Mauritius since the 1960s by the Government, Private sector and NGOs*. Mauritius: United Nations Development Programme Mauritius Country Office.

Chan Low, J. & Reddi, S. 2000. Malaise Créole: towards a new ethnic identity. Towards the Making of a Multi-cultural Society. In: S. Nirsimloo-Gayan (ed). *Towards the making of a Multi-Cultural Society*. Moka, Mauritius: MGI Press. pp.228-237.

Chapin Metz, H. (ed). 1994. *Mauritius: A Country Study*. Washington, DC: US Government Publishing Office for the Library of Congress.

Colbert, J. 1684. *Code Noir: ou Recueil d'edits, déclarations et arrets concernant les Esclaves Nègres de l'Amérique*. France: n.p.

Diniejko, A. (ed) & Litt, D. 2013. *The Fabian Society in Late Victorian Britain*. The Victorian Web. [https://bit.ly/3jhCU5A]. (Accessed 14 October 2016).

Dobson, R. 2005. L'Affaire Kaya: creole malaise in Mauritius. Paper presented at the University of Western Sydney's College of Arts, Education and Social Sciences Research Conference, Bankstown Campus, 7-9 October.

Dommen, E. & Dommen, B. 1999. *Mauritius An Island of Success: A Retrospective Study 1960-1993*. Oxford. Pacific Press.

Eriksen, T.H. 2007. Creolization in anthropological theory and in Mauritius. In: C. Stewart (ed). *Creolization: History, Ethnography, Theory*. Didcot, United Kingdom: Taylor & Francis Group. pp.153-177.

FAO (United Nations Food and Agriculture Organisation). 2005. *Government of the Republic of Mauritius: Support to NEPAD-CAADP Implementation, TCP/MAR/2904 (I) (NEPAD Ref. 05/16 E)*, 7(3). [http://www.fao.org/3/a-ae957e.pdf]. (Accessed 15 September 2016).

Gill, G. 2010. *Understanding the Linkages between Poverty and Ethnicity in Mauritius*. A Presentation of Research Findings at the Ministry of Social Integration and Economic Empowerment.

Gill, M.S. 2007. *Trials That Changed History: From Socrates to Saddam Hussein*. New Delhi, Sarup & Sons.

Groupe A of Cassis. 2020. *Group A*. [https://bit.ly/2GfFHxo]. (Accessed 5 October 2016).

Healy, L.M. 2008. *International Social Work: Professional Action in an Interdependent World*. New York: Oxford University Press.

Jeewa-Daureeawoo, F. 2016. *Message on the occasion of the International Day of Older Person celebration*. Ministry of Social Integration, Social Security and National Solidarity. Mauritius.

Jugnauth, P. 2016. *Budget Speech 2016/17*. Port Louis: Republic of Mauritius. Ministry of Finance and Economic Development.

Lingayah, S. 2015. *The Prisoner of Migration, Reflection and Reviews of a Migration Enterprise.* Scotland: Diadem Books Publication.

Lizie dan La main. 2006. *About us. Lizie dan La main – Union of the blind people of Mauritius.* [http://www.ldlm.intnet.mu/index.html]. (Accessed 5 October 2016).

Logan, F. 2015. Did Structural Adjustment Programmes Assist African Development? *E-International Relations.* [https://bit.ly/3jknGwI]. (Accessed 7 October 2016).

MACOSS (Mauritius Council of Social Services). 2015. *Profile.* [https://bit.ly/3iesNNl]. (Accessed 5 October 2016).

Mathur, H. 1991. *Parliament in Mauritius.* Beau Bassin-Rose Hill, Mauritius: Editions de l'Océan Indien.

Maurer, S. 2014. Post-Colonialism: The So-Called Malaise Creole in Mauritius. *Antrocom Online Journal of Anthropology,* 10(1):1973-2880.

Meade, J.E. 1961. *The Economic and Social Structure of Mauritius: Report to the Governor of Mauritius and Others.* London: Methuen & Co.

NATReSA (National Agency for the Treatment & Rehabilitation of Substance Abusers). 2016. *Centre de Solidarite Pour Une Nouvelle Vie: Situation of drug and alcohol in Mauritius.* [https://bit.ly/2SbCEJq]. (Accessed 6 October 2016).

Neeliah, H. & Seetanah, B. 2016. Does human capital contribute to economic growth in Mauritius? *European Journal of Training and Development,* 40(4):248-261.

Nowbutsing, B. 2013. The Macroeconomic Framework of Mauritius – Lessons and Alternatives. Working Paper, ANSA Initiative. Mauritius Congress of Trade Unions.

Parahoo, K. 1986. Early Colonial Development of Health Care in Mauritius. *International Journal of Health Services,* 16(3):409-423.

Phaahla, E. 2014. The Welfare State of Mauritius: A Critical Appraisal. [https://bit.ly/2GcTHIq]. (Accessed 4 October 2016).

Photius.com. 1994. *Mauritius Society of Health and Welfare.* [https://bit.ly/3cKq5hI]. (Accessed 5 October 2016).

Republic of Mauritius. Ministry of Gender Equality, Child Development and Family Welfare. 2016. *Family Welfare and Protection Unit.* [https://bit.ly/3kXQFGV]. (Accessed 30 September 2016).

Republic of Mauritius. Ministry of Health & Quality of Life. 2002. White Paper on Health Care, 3. La Tour Koenig: Government Printing.

Republic of Mauritius. Government Information Service. 2008. *Mauritius 40 Years After: New Goals, New Challenges.* La Tour Koenig: Government Printing.

Republic of Mauritius. *Ministry of Social Security and National Solidarity*. 2020. [http://socialsecurity.govmu.org/English/Pages/default.aspx].

Republic of Mauritius. *Ministry of Social Security and National Solidarity*. 2011. [https://bit.ly/36klS2S]. (Accessed 6 October 2016).

Sewpal, S. 2018. Mauritian Housing: 1955 to the Present Day, *Le Mauricien*, 17 February. [https://bit.ly/33avICC] (Accessed 8 October 2016).

SOS Femmes. 2010. *Presentation of S.O.S Femmes*. [https://bit.ly/3ietyWH]. (Accessed 5 October 2016).

Soto, M., Thakoor, V. & Petri, M.M. 2015. *Pension Reforms in Mauritius: Fair and Fast - Balancing Social Protection and Fiscal Sustainability*. New York: International Monetary Fund.

Stiglitz, J. 2011. The Mauritius miracle, or how to make a big success of a small economy. *The Guardian*, 7 March. [https://bit.ly/33dXhe5]. (Accessed 10 August 2016).

The Editorial Team. 2007. A repeat of the 1975 student revolt: says who? *Le Express*, 8 March. [https://bit.ly/2S99tqf]. (Accessed 5 October 2016).

Thomson, A. 2010. *An Introduction to African Politics*. 3rd Edition. New York: Taylor & Francis Group.

UNDP Mauritius & Seychelles. 2016. *Streamlining Social Services Assistance with the UNDP 'Social Register of Mauritius (SRM)' project*.[ www.mu.undp.org] (Accessed 15 August 2016).

UNDP (United Nations Development Programme). 2015. *Human Development Report 2015: Work for Human Development*. [https://bit.ly/3la6KcP]. (Accessed 8 October 2016).

UNODC (United Nations Office on Drugs and Crime). 2016. *NGO Directory – Dr I Goomany Centre for Prevention & Treatment of Alcoholism & Drug Addiction*. [https://www.unodc.org/pdf/ngo_directory.pdf]. (Accessed 6 October 2016).

UN News. 2015. UN expert urges Mauritius to prioritize legal protections against abuse of older persons. *UN News*. [https://bit.ly/3mZnghj]. (Accessed 4 October 2016).

UOM (University of Mauritius). 2016. *History*. [https://bit.ly/2G86tba]. (Accessed 5 October 2016).

UQAC (University of Quebec at Chicoutimi). 2007. The Black Code. Edict of the King on the slaves of the islands of America. 1680. *Les Classiques des Sciences Sociales*. [https://bit.ly/36hem96] (Accessed 23 August 2016).

Vandemoortele, M. & Bird, K. 2010. *Mauritius' Story: Progress in economic conditions in Mauritius: Success against the odds*. London: Overseas Development Institute.

Vaughan, M. 2000. Slavery, smallpox, and revolution: 1792 in Île de France (Mauritius). *Social History of Medicine*, 13(3):411-428.

Yen, B. 2007. Pension Reform – Lessons from a Small African Country. Paper presented at 2nd Annual Eastern and Central Africa Pension Fund Conference, Hilton Hotel, Nairobi, Kenya, 7-9 May.

Zafar, A. 2011. Mauritius: An economic success story. In: P. Chuhan-Pole & S. Devarajan (eds). *Yes, Africa Can: Success Stories from a Dynamic Continent*. Washington, DC: World Bank. pp.91-106.

*07*

# SOCIAL PROTECTION IN MOZAMBIQUE: SOCIAL WELFARE AND SOCIAL WORK CONSIDERATIONS

*José Ivo Correia and Cheila Muthombene*

## Introduction

This chapter discusses social welfare and social-protection mechanisms in the light of experiences of colonialism and racism, Marxist - socialism, and neoliberal structural adjustment that Mozambique went through and their implied trade-offs. The chapter is divided into six sections. The issues discussed in the first section are expansion, inclusion and the traditional associations of social protection. In the second section, the welfare system and its relationship to social protection are discussed. In the third part, the social protection reforms underway in Mozambique, across the contributory and non-contributory systems in four historical periods (pre-colonial, colonial, post-Independence and neoliberal 1990s) are discussed. The fourth section highlights the relationship between the social protection system and developments in the labour market. In the fifth section, we discuss the future of social protection by looking at informality as the main feature of the labour market, and in the sixth part, we discuss the main issues at stake and conclude from the theoretical framework and the lessons of the Mozambican experience in the light of developments in Southern Africa.

## Pre-Colonial Era

Family, neighbours, friendly societies (associations and clubs) and charities have played a significant role in social welfare and social protection provision in Mozambique. Still, they were not the only alternatives to the welfare state and its agencies during the colonial and post-colonial era. Alternatively, citizens relied on mutual aid, helping people in need in several ways such as the provision of social solidarity, assistance, care and sound ethical values and principles. Most of their actions, experiences and lessons learnt have been largely informal and undocumented by social scientists and particularly historians and tended to be at the most, neglected and underestimated by mainstream state institutions.

At first, those associations were based on blood ties and place of birth. Later on, membership was expanded to neighbours and friends who met on special occasions: the birth of a child; sickness of a family member; the death of the breadwinner or a funeral. They met in common spaces and later on at church grounds, drinking spaces or the house of the elderly (*Mulumuzana or madodas*), making friends and socialising. Thus, the members contributed regularly in kind or with money, and this gave them an entitlement to a certain benefit. The accumulated surplus would be used for a feast or divided, usually at the end of the year. Most of those traditional African associations did not have any written rules, and each of them was autonomous from others. They had a self-governing system based on seniority and equality, attracting people to join them since members had a say and could have their needs met speedily and with tailor-made responses. Due to slavery and serfdom, wars and forced labour, most of those associations became weak and disgruntled, coupled with the colonial rule of divide and conquer, and the introduction of registration based on the capacity to read and write. They could not afford the wage system since they saw the slave trade and serfdom as going against their democratic and participative principles and practices.

Most of the early associations were organised around the same ethnicity and language, and the fact that differentiated them was race and availability of wages and salaries. Thus, each member had to pay an equal amount in-kind or in monetary terms. That contribution would go to a common pool of resources or fund whose benefits would be shared and then the surplus was divided among the memberships. They retained their relevance and utility up to the first years of colonialism. Still, weaknesses and disadvantages became pronounced in the colonial era due to a shortage of resources and cash, and the prevalence of endemic diseases and a lot of deaths among the membership. These weaknesses and disadvantages impeded them from creating bigger associations which could cover a wide range of issues and larger geography. These challenges were coupled with a lack of transport that could have enabled them access other remote areas. By the mid-nineteenth century, the evolution of local associations from local to district level with their direct democratic structures were constrained by regional events such as the *Mfecane*; the partition of Southern Africa among the colonial powers; and land disputes in Southern and Central Mozambique between the English and Portuguese crowns, and northern Mozambique involving the Germans from Tanzania and the Portuguese.

## Colonial Era

By the time the Portuguese colonial system and the Overseas Regulation for the Exchequer (*Regulamento Ultramarino da Fazenda*) in 1901 was established for the settlers at large and white public servants, in particular, coupled with forced labour in Mozambique, and neighbouring countries such as South Africa, Zimbabwe and Malawi, friendly societies that provided social security and protection to the indigenous people were displaced.[1] The friendly societies, commonly known as 'associations' grew after 1910 with the Republican coup in Portugal and the end of the First World War (1914-1918). Still, the rise of the Portuguese Dictator Oliveira Salazar (1927-1968) reversed the opening of the public space in Mozambique for both the indigenous population and foreigners, and their companies. Thus, the height of state intervention and increased numbers of *assimilados* (a Portuguese term referring to 'people who had social and economic intelligence and good manners') under Salazar resulted in the introduction of a broadened compulsory national insurance and the shrinkage of the associations and their racial cross-membership, limited in terms of race and geography.

Unlike the adversarial social protection relationships that the colonial state bolstered, separating whites from the black majority, and private charity which the Catholic Church and emerging protestant churches mainly provided, associations based on reciprocity and solidarity faced many obstacles. By 1901, the colonial government passed the Overseas Regulations for the Exchequer, and it signed the First Labour Agreement (renewed in

---

1    Serra & Cossa, 2007:433-456., Serra, 2000; Covane, 2001; Neves, 1998; Newitt, 1995.

1928 and 1963) with the Transvaal Witwatersrand Native Labour Association (WNLA) to recruit 80 000 workers from southern Mozambique for the mines in South Africa. The rest of central Mozambique was awarded to the British South Africa (BSA) Company in the former Southern Rhodesia and the Mozambique Chartered Company in the current provinces of Manica and Sofala. The *Companhia da Zambézia* ('Zambezia Company') and the Sena Sugar Estates got leasing contracts for parts of the Tete and Zambézia Provinces, and the northern region was awarded to the Nyassa Company, corresponding to almost 75 per cent of the country, in terms of generated revenues in foreign currency, from hut taxes and African labour.

The Overseas Regulations for the Exchequer was directed at the Portuguese public servants who worked in Mozambique and who could afford to contribute to the social pension fund and be integrated into Portugal upon their return home for their old age retirement and medical care. The agreement with WNLA transferred the costs of social protection to the miners and the South African Chamber of Mines. The rest of the country's social protection system was vested in the chartered companies and fraternal associations and religious charities, and by 1910 the first trade unions were set up in the ports and railways of Mozambique, widely known as *Caminhos de Ferro de Moçambique* ('Mozambique Railways') in Portuguese.

Following the development of self-help societies and mutual aid associations inside and outside Mozambique, the Salazar regime set up fake associations and societies such as the Sena Portuguese Native Association (*Associação dos Indigenas Portugueses de Sena*) in Harare and the Portuguese Imperial Native Club (*Clube dos Indigenas do Império Português*) in Bulawayo. They did this to undertake surveillance and attract Mozambicans from the more progressive associations such as the Tete Society and the Mozambique Native Association. The Salazar regime used *curadores* ('trustees'), and agents from the *Polícia Internacional e de Defesa do Estado* ('International and State Defence Police') who established intelligence networks and communities which were supposed to oversee the migrants and convert their social organizations into political organisations.

Nevertheless, during this period, international pressure increased, especially from the United Nations (UN):

➢ UN Resolution 1514 XV: the Declaration on the Granting of Independence to the Colonial Countries and Peoples in 1960.

▷ UN Resolution 1542 on 'Transmission of Information under Article 73C of the Charter' related to Portuguese 'overseas provinces' and stated that 'overseas territories' were colonies rather than metropolitan Portugal.

▷ UN Resolution 1669 XVI: the Special Committee.[2]

The Salazar regime thus made cosmetic changes by creating 'overseas provinces' in 1953 and then making all natives, *assimilados* and *mestiços* (people of European and African descent) Portuguese citizens. However, as far as social development was concerned, the country lagged behind as 346 505 African students were in rudimentary primary schools, and 17 642 in the common primary schools, in contrast to 400 000 white pupils in primary schools in 1957/58 and 430 000 pupils in 1960/61. The numbers in church schools of white students were 385 304 and 401 581 in 1957/8 and 1960/61, respectively.

By the 1960s, Portugal passed a new Colonial Development Policy focused on education and health and the budget for these two sectors increased to 'conquer the hearts and minds' of Africans. Forced labour was banned through the new Rural Labour Code and the Social Action Fund for Rural Workers (*Fundo de Acção Social para o Trabalhador Rural*) was created in 1963 through the Legislative Diploma 2368 of May 25. This legislation extended the social security and protection coverage to most *mestiços* and *assimilados* while the trade unions, set up in 1966, wanted the expansion to cover indigenous Africans. The trade unions from the ports and railways and other companies, however, managed to get a Family Allowance for the indigenous population, which was supposed to be claimed at the Department of the Exchequer as a non-contributory social-security programme.

Social development in Mozambique was important for raising residents' political awareness but also for economic development and military counterinsurgency since it resulted in the reversal of the policy of economic nationalism. It was important to open foreign direct investment to Western countries culminating in the setting up of the *Banco Nacional de Investimento* ('National Investment Bank') in 1959. For counter-insurgency the Decree-Law 43896 was issued, envisaging the subdivision of colonial administration at the lowest levels and the restructuring of the *regulado* ('regulated' natives) and traditional chiefs, but under the colonial government's strict control.

---

2    Afonso & Gomes, 2000:55.

Furthermore, as part of social development and counterinsurgency against the Front for the Liberation of Mozambique (*Frente de Libertação de Moçambique* - Frelimo) movement, the Villagenisation Strategy (*Estrategia de Aldeiamentos*) was introduced in 1966. It was called strategic hamlets or protected villages and aimed to gain the loyalty of the rural populations, especially the war-prone zones. Since *Aldeiamentos* ('villages') became part of the then social policy, the colonial authorities tended to exaggerate their numbers and residents confined in there. For instance, it is reported that by 1969 160 000 people lived in 114 *Aldeiamentos* in the region of Nyassa and that 55 primary schools, 68 primary health centres, 64 wells, six houses for the traditional chiefs and six militia bases were constructed.[3] Besides, much money was invested in providing food, clothes and educational materials for areas recaptured from Frelimo.

The colonial state strived to build a health centre for each district to provide services, but they could not cope with the demand from the residents at large and the wounded or injured from landmines. War efforts led the local authorities to resort to military provided medical services – which were of better quality due to top priority allocated equipment, medicines and medical staff – as well as Portuguese armed forces' support in social development, incurring a huge public debt by the end of the war.

The above-mentioned show that social development in northern Mozambique and elsewhere in the country resulted from international pressure and the war. However, the information and the figures provided of the *Aldeiamentos* and Frelimo Liberated Zones and the number of people, and social conditions should be used with caution since both sides tended to exaggerate for public relations. War ended in 1974 and, according to Middlemas (1975), the basis for negotiations for the Lusaka (Zambia) Accord for Frelimo was:

- a guarantee of Independence
- recognition of Frelimo as the sole representative of the people of Mozambique
- transfer of power, and
- all other outstanding issues.

---

3    Henriksen, 1983:16-17.

The Caetano regime wanted a ceasefire and a referendum before the constitutional change and the handing over of power and granting Independence.

## Post-Independence Era

Although the general perception is that Frelimo won the War for Independence, in many circles it is said that it only took over the political and economic system that the Portuguese colonial administration left, since Frelimo only controlled less than 30 per cent of the territory and the least populated provinces. Frelimo managed to impose a single-party system in the Lusaka Agreement and inherited the centralised economic system. Frelimo subordinated the social sector to the party-state coming to power after Independence and nationalised social services.

In winning the struggle against settler colonialism and racial discrimination in Mozambique, Frelimo served as a role model to other Southern African states, not yet independent of white settlers' colonialisation. Rather than achieving a military victory in the field, the political and economic change was obtained first, by a coup in Portugal, and at the negotiation table in Lusaka, with the support from the broader anti-colonialist forces such as the Portuguese Communist Party; the Southern Africa liberation movements; part of the rural population; the *mestiços*; white intellectuals from the left; and other socialist countries with a vested interest in the peaceful transfer of power to Frelimo.

Between the coup of April 1974 in Portugal and the Independence of Mozambique on 25 June 1975, about 100 000 Portuguese settlers and part of the Indian, Pakistani and Chinese community, responsible for running almost the entire economy, left the country for Portugal and the neighbouring countries especially South Africa, Malawi and Zimbabwe. The country was left in disarray and crisis, not only due to decolonisation and Independence but also due to Frelimo's policies towards state domination and socialism. Frelimo nationalised the private health network, schools, housing; prohibited private operation of doctors, teachers; allowed property rental without specific criteria; and collectivisation through communal villages. As far as social security and protection were concerned, the early policy measures aimed at reversing the economic downfall and keeping the abandoned companies and farms economically viable through bank funding and money printing. Policies followed that deepened the crisis, such as the prohibition of dismissals and massive recruitment of workers without the necessary skills, given that 90 per cent of the indigenous population was illiterate. Later, these policy measures became part of the central planning established in 1977, that did not include econometric models of inputs and outputs and indicators such as exchange and interest rates, credit and economic performance.

It can be argued that the hopes and expectations of an egalitarian society vanished in the first decade of Independence, due to the lack of know-how and experience, despite some success in ensuring preventive health through massive vaccination campaigns and the reduction of illiteracy rates. Authoritarianism and populism became the order of the day, and the challenge of bringing together disparate peoples and ethnic groups in socialism and a planned economy was much more complex and difficult than uniting against colonialism and winning Independence through war, economic destabilisation and destruction. The 1975 Constitution of Mozambique stated that there were main political and economic principles that were relevant for social welfare and social protection. First, in Article 31, it was stipulated that, "... employment and education constitute rights and duties of every citizen" and second, in Article 32 that, " ... each citizen has the right to social assistance in case of disability and old age." The constitutional provisions above show that policy measures taken had a double-edged impact in the sense that they tried to contain the decolonisation crisis. The government wanted to avoid the collapse of production, restoration of transport and communication, and trading and marketing networks (through People's Shops). The government, however, closed companies and increased employment, with funding from banks for 'nationalised companies' without adherence to economic criteria.

There was the appointment of administrative commissions made up of persons without managerial skills and business experience; the prohibition of layoffs aimed at containing social welfare problems for households and continued payment of wages and salaries and other current expenditures. Without significant production and productivity, it resulted in a worsening crisis. These policy measures coupled with other new policies for the reorganisation of public administration, such as the amendment to the 1901 Overseas Exchequer Regulation through the *Decree-Law 52 of 1975*, which set the retirement age at 35 years of work (rather than 40 years), included the compensation for work accidents, disability and sickness, death and funeral subsidies and retirement. The new socio-economic system was based on excessive state intervention and collective ownership at large; a central planning system for the public sector (state-owned companies and parastatals); production and consumption cooperatives; the residual private sector; and the family and small farming sector.

Furthermore, central planning was based on the assumption that the State or public sector will become the dominant economic force by transforming the nationalised enterprises into engines of growth and development, supporting individual peasants, households and farmers by making them cooperative members and agro-industrial workers (worker-peasant alliance) living in communal villages. The private sector would be part of joint-ventures with State-Owned Enterprises (SOEs) whose ultimate goals and objectives were full employment and social protection for all Mozambicans. However, the realisation of those assumptions, in turn, would require a peaceful domestic and Southern African environment; the fast-tracking of skills development; good neighbourhood relations; and trade and cooperation with former South Rhodesia and apartheid South Africa. They would depend on support and aid from socialist countries in the short- and medium-term:

> It is noted that the benefits from the welfare state and social protection did not focus on the indigenous population. Since the colonial era and after Independence they focused on the formal economy and the employed, a legacy that continues in present-day Mozambique.[4]

Thus, the following changes characterised the first decade of Independence (1975-85):

▷ The 1966 colonial legislation related to the public sector and servants' social protection was amended through the *Decree-Law 8 of 1982*, including the indigenous workers and focusing on medical care and retirement.[5]

▷ The new State Owned Enterprises (SOEs) and parastatals increased their labour force based on the departure of the Portuguese and massive recruitments. As such, they had to provide social protection through training and skills development, medical care, and affordable housing.

▷ A new regulatory framework for the private insurance firms was passed – the

---

4    Francisco, 2002:27.

5    Quive, 2007:15.

*Decree-Law 3 of 1977*, a merger of three formerly nationalised firms: Nauticus (established in 1943); Lusitania & Tranquilidade; and Mundial & Confiança (who ran out of business). The merger resulted in the Empresa Moçambicana, a monopoly and regulator in the insurance and reinsurance business.[6]

▷ The cooperatives and communal villages had to run their social protection schemes but also benefitted from free public education, health and welfare programmes and special literacy projects, based on voluntary work. The collapse of the State's political and economic model by 1985 led to a rethinking of the then socialist-oriented model in a context of a protracted civil war and nationwide food shortage.

Thus, the main characteristics of the second decade of Independence (1986-1996) were:

▷ A significant withdraw or rollback of the State from the economy, especially firm state intervention in the local economy and markets, while using the price mechanism, market institutions and the decentralisation of economic policy and decision-making.

▷ The reallocation of economic resources, from the public sector and SOEs to private cooperatives and family sectors, based on the redirecting of the State budget and banking credit but also using the newly allocated foreign aid at large and food aid, in particular, following the opening of the country to Western countries and joining the Bretton Woods institutions and the Lomé Convention in 1984.

▷ The public sector was restructured by deconcentrating and decentralising political power to provincial and strategic district levels. Non-strategic SOEs were gradually reorganised and liberalised or privatised based on economic and financial autonomy; parastatals were separated from productive and trading SOEs.

▷ Private sector development and the opening up to Foreign Direct Investment, were due to pressure from international donors and creditors, especially in the production of cash crops; export-import trade; the tourism and hospitality industry; transport; communications; banking and finance.

Furthermore, as far as social protection is concerned, a new Labour Act was introduced in 1985, providing for the public and private sector with, for example, the disability

---

6    Muchena & Jauch, 2011:54.

and old age grant and medical care. However, the family allowance was phased out with the introduction of harmonised systems of wages and salaries, previously by the *Decree-Law 4 of 1980*.

Later, the government amended the *Decree-Law 8 of 1982* and the *Decree-Law 3 of 1983* relating to public servants, through passing and consolidating them into *Estatuto Geral dos Funcionários do Estado* ('the General Statute for State Officials') with the *Decree-Law 14 of 1987* that streamlined former administrative procedures and strict compliance to legislation into force. The general statue was updated in 1996.

Following the introduction of the Economic Recovery Programme in 1987 or the Mozambique Structural Adjustment Programme, the National Institute for Social Security (*Instituto Nacional de Segurança Social*, INSS) was established through the *Decree-Law 17 of 1988*. The INSS would manage the pension scheme, maternity leave and other workers' constraints from SOEs, parastatals and private sector, based on a compulsory contributory system, ensuring workers' generational solidarity. The INSS contributed towards the production of the *Social Security Act 5 of 1989*, which enabled the compulsory contribution from public and private employers, and workers to a new pension scheme alongside international labour conventions.

## Neoliberal Social Protection Reforms in the 1990s

Mozambique had been embroiled in a civil war from 1977-1992. Before the 1992 General Peace Agreement between the ruling Frelimo party and the rebel *Resistência Nacional Moçambicana*, ('Mozambican National Resistance', Renamo) group, a further process of political, economic and social reforms ensued. Politically it included the drafting of a new Constitution; the creation of multi-party electoral democracy provisions; economic liberalisation and privatisation; and social policy and insurance business. For social protection, the food ratio system and price decontrols were abolished, and social measures were added to the Economic Recovery Programme as part of the social dimensions of the Structural Adjustment Programme.[7] As such, the Office for Support of Vulnerable Population (GAPVU) was set up in the then Ministry of Finance. It was later

---

7    Correia et al., 1993.

upgraded and transferred to the Ministry for the Coordination of Social Action in 1995, responsible for policy and oversight of social programmes.

GAPVU was the main urban safety net programme whose goal was to provide food support and later cash transfers to reduce urban poverty among destitute households. It was funded through a government budget and other bilateral arrangements as well as UN agencies such as the UN Children's Fund and the World Food Programme. It benefitted over 100 000 people in 1997 when it became the National Institute for Social Action (*Instituto Nacional de Acção Social*, INAS), part of the Ministry for Social Action with funding directly from the Ministry of Finance. Furthermore, the private Insurance Law 24 of 1991 was passed and paved the way for the end of state monopoly and allowed new entrants into the insurance sector from 1991, such as the *IMPAR-Companhia de Seguros de Moçambique* ('IMPAR-Insurance Company of Mozambique'), the *Companhia Geral de Seguros de Moçambique* ('General Insurance Company of Mozambique') and later Hollard from South Africa in 2001.

The first National Social Policy was adopted in 1998, and the first Social Protection Law was passed almost a decade later in 2007 with the *Social Protection Law 4 of 2007*, comprising three sub-systems:

- The Compulsory Social Protection (CSP) – a contributory system for public and private enterprises and their employees and informal sector workers;

- The Basic Social Protection (BSP) – a non-contributory system for the destitute and poor elderly; people with disabilities unable to work and meet basic needs; the chronically ill due to hypertension, diabetes, epilepsy, bronchial asthma, chronic renal insufficiency; and later tuberculosis except HIV/Aids; and orphans and vulnerable children (OVC); and

- Complementary Social Protection – for workers or people who can afford to pay for life and non-life insurance themselves, provided by public and private business.

There is no cross-fertilisation, communication, and linkages among the three social protection sub-systems and the government are working towards the setting up of a coordinating board. The CSP and the BSP are, therefore, the main social protection mechanisms alongside households, community, and church-based mutual aid schemes.

However, both systems are marred by problems such as occasional mismanagement and corruption. CSP is affected by a range of intertwined problems such as low-intensity citizenship; poor employment levels; weak state institutions; and different modes of economic rationality. For instance, low-intensity citizenship is reflected in a wide range of economic sectors and levels through citizens' limited knowledge:

▻ political (weak participation in public policymaking and a demand for transparency and accountability);

▻ economic (making choices, business start-ups and taxation)

▻ social rights (workers' rights and association and social protection); and

▻ duties (payment of taxes and compliance with legislation).

Low-intensity citizenship is expressed in the culture of non-payment of taxes and not paying for basic services such as education and health since the socialist era, and now water and electricity, coupled with illiteracy rates of nearly 50 per cent of the population. According to Rosário Fernandes, the former Chairman of the Mozambican Tax Authorities, in 2014, only 3.25 million people were registered for tax purposes, corresponding to 13 per cent of the entire Mozambican population estimated at 25 million.

Despite forecasts of high economic growth and macroeconomic success, Mozambique is still one of the poorest countries in the world. It has not so far delivered huge socio-economic benefits in terms of job creation, especially in the rural areas and outside southern Mozambique, resulting in high social tensions and a rise in the living costs. The jobs created are not quality jobs that can lift most people out of poverty and bring gains in social welfare. Furthermore, the INSS is responsible for the CSP system that includes the old-age pension scheme, maternity and paternity leave and work accidents. Neopatrimonialism and corruption have marred the CSP system since its establishment, and the last case reported in the media was the bankruptcy of Nosso Banco ('Our Bank'). This financial institution, the main shareholder in the pension scheme with a 76 per cent stake, was involved in speculative housing deals and bad investment decisions.

According to António Francisco, in 2010, the CSP only made up 38 per cent of the formal social protection budget, and it covered only 10 per cent of the working-age population estimated at 11.5 million people.[8] Also, it is marred by a low contribution to the compulsory system due to poverty and tax exemption schemes and because of political reasons, for example, those involved with the Frelimo party-state elites. Frelimo runs a parallel taxation system that feeds the party coffers.[9] Besides, there are cases of tax evasion along the porous Mozambican borders with neighbouring countries, especially South Africa, Zimbabwe, Malawi and illicit financial flows involving multinational corporations and local cross-border traders. Their revenues are not taxed and thus do not go to state coffers.

The INAS is responsible for the non-contributory basic social protection system, that the State budget and foreign donors and creditors, and some international non-governmental organisations fund. The BSP is a social assistance programme based on social principles such as universality, progress, equity, social inclusion, solidarity, transparency, accountability, and efficiency. In practice, the BSP is based on discriminatory, selective and social assistance criteria to meet the needs of some vulnerable and poor groups such as elderly women aged 55 and men aged 60 or above, who live in urban and peri-urban areas.[10]

INSS manages four different social protection programmes:

- ▻ the Food Subsidy Programme (*Programa Subsídios de Alimentos*, PSA),

- ▻ the Direct Social Action Programme (*Programa Apoio Social Directo*),

- ▻ the Social Benefit through Work Programme (*Programa Benefício Social Pelo Trabalho*), and

- ▻ the Income Generation Programme (*Programa de Geração de Rendimentos*).

We will focus only on the PSA because it is the most important social assistance programme, and it dates back to the GAPVU days. PSA is an unconditional government-funded cash transfer programme rather than a food provision subsidy that, despite a call for its expansion in scale and scope nationwide, is fragmented with limited coverage and provides low benefits at household levels. By 2009, 166 824 PSA beneficiaries

---

8    Francisco, 2013.
9    Nhachote, 2010.
10   Francisco, 2013; Francisco & Sugahara, 2014.

included 93.8 per cent of the elderly, 5.3 per cent disabled persons and 0.9 chronically ill; expanded to provinces but only 30 of the 153 districts nationwide.[11] PSB is criticised on several grounds:

- The amount provided is not enough (300 Meticiais per beneficiary, corresponding to less than 60 South African Rand and 4 US dollars in 2016).

- PSB has a limited impact on their lives.

- The monthly cash transfers to beneficiaries are irregular.

- Patronage from INAS delegations is without a commensurate increase in human and financial resources to staff to operate them fully, according to the Department for International Development.[12]

The government approved the National Basic Social Security Strategy (*Estratégia Nacional de Segurança Social Básica*) in 2010, based on the 1998 National Policy for Social Action. The goals and objectives of the Social Security Strategy (2010-2014) were to:

- increase social coverage and impact;

- improve efficiency;

- ensure the harmonisation and coordination of programmes; and

- cover OVC and child-headed households.

The strategy's cost was estimated at 2.2 per cent of total government expenditure in 2014, but it sought to be a more inclusive and better-targeted programme.

As the title of this chapter suggests, Mozambique does not have a welfare state, and the government is still considering having a social protection system for all. Thus, the ruling party says that since June 1975 it is struggling to ensure social protection benefits for the orphaned, aged, sick, vulnerable and destitute members of society, illustrated, it is argued, by enshrining of the right in the Constitution and other social protection policy documents:

---

11   INAS, 2010.

12   DFID, 2014.

➤ the Economic and Social Rehabilitation Programme;

➤ the Social Action Policy;

➤ the Poverty Reduction Strategic Papers;

➤ the Food Subsidies Programme (PSA); and

➤ the Social Benefit through Work Programme.

However, local scholars and actors from civil society organisations (CSOs) are pushing for discussions and debates about universal access to social protection based on democratic values, and economic and social inclusion. These groups have provided alternatives from the current discriminatory, fragmented, and care-based system to a progressive one that looks at social protection as part of social and sustainable human development. Furthermore, scholars and CSOs argue that the debates in this arena should go beyond the shortage of economic and human resources and that social protection should not be seen as a marginal public policy issue but something that needs to be brought into the centre; both for poverty and vulnerability reduction, and sustainable human development. They envisage a cross-regional social protection learning based on the experiences of Lesotho, South Africa and Swaziland as far as children and the elderly are concerned, and better domestic coordination and governance within and among state institutions such as INAS, the National Aids Council, the Food Security and Nutrition Secretariat, the National Disaster Management Institute and other contributory social protection systems for the graduation of beneficiaries.

Furthermore, there is no linkage between non-contributory social protection and contributory systems to avoid duplication and multiplication of economic efforts in a context of growing informality, unemployment and under-employment; and even within the public assistance and income-generating programmes of INAS. Besides the principles of universal pension and progress, there are issues related to equity, inclusion, efficiency, solidarity, transparency, and sustainability. Mozambique's system of enlisting beneficiaries from among the most vulnerable is selective, and there seem to be no set fairness criteria. Inclusion seems to be based on closeness to INAS offices' catchment areas, patronage and *clientelism*, while efficiency and effectiveness are unattainable due to red tape and corruption. As far as solidarity and transparency are concerned, the elderly usually rely on their children and the extended family. However, since most of them did not join any pension scheme, they risk their children confiscating their assets or accusing them of witchcraft, while politicking and red tape mar the entire system in the context of limited and ineffective coverage and targeting.

According to Francisco and Sugahara (2015), the overhead costs for INAS programmes were 31 per cent (Food Subsidy), 27 per cent (Social Work Benefit) and 24 per cent (Income-generation), in most cases including per diem, safety, jobs and bonus for its administrative staff. The last issue is sustainability, since most of the international donors fund the social protection system (6.5 per cent) and few taxpayers, but there are discussions and debates about other options. The options available are to increase the tax base especially by collecting taxes from households; the informal sector; the mining houses; new foreign investors; and the political elite, exempted from some duties, and because of a decline in foreign aid and aid fatigue as well as mismanagement and corruption in both INAS and INSS. Despite the growing interest and studies about social protection, there are several barriers to tackling the issues mentioned above. These include the political establishment's and vested interests' resistance to change; the lack of political will; the belief that the destitute are responsible for their fate and that their extended families should care for them rather than the State agencies; lack of thorough and comprehensive approaches; weak public policy analysis on poverty and vulnerability and deprivation; and social protection in Mozambique. The former is due to a shortage of social workers, public policy analysts, economists and lawyers interested in those issues outside of public assistance and philanthropy in a context of the fiscal crisis of the State, budgetary constraints, aid fatigue, complex institutional settings made up of different state agencies and under different state ministries and the overlapping mandates and competition for the same sources of funding and shortage of social workers.

One proposed solution to the above-mentioned is the political decentralisation of state function to the provincial and district levels and the strengthening and development of private sector providers along with limited government interference; the scaling up of social work degree programmes and the use of a fiscal policy that can partly contribute to overcoming the obstacles to a universal system.

## Social Work Education and Training in Mozambique

Social protection and social work resulted from late developments in Portugal and the intensification of colonisation in Mozambique, with the enactment of the 1933 Colonial Act. However, the consolidation of social protection as an area of state intervention was subordinate to the mission that colonial Mozambique was supposed to raise public monies to pay for its native population's social protection. Furthermore, social work became an academic course and part of a pool of professions that supported the ideology of the New State, envisaging the Portuguese civilising mission based on a stronger role for the Catholic Church in education, social protection and health for the indigenous populations and *assimilados*; reinforced by the extension of women's domestic chores and work in private and religious education.[13]

The academic training models of social work, from the beginning of the last century, were based on the view of social work as an art based in science.[14] The first school of social work was an outreach course of the Lisbon Catholic University in 1962, after the introduction of tertiary education in 1961, influenced by scientific positivism and American functionalism in Sociology and Anthropology within the broader context of Christian humanism and remedial curative group; and community health and social problems such as diseases, disasters and deprivation.[15] Thus, the institutionalisation of social protection and social work, as well as the development of social workers as professionals, became part of the colonial administration's mission in general and the social doctrine of the Church, in particular. It served mainly urban and suburban areas, and was fragmented along race and class lines.[16]

At Independence, the new Frelimo party-state continued with most of the colonial social protection programmes and 'nationalised' the other private assistance and church-based ones while expanding to all other races. Thus, the Department of Social Welfare became mainly part of the Ministry of Health, and as such it lost visibility, and public assistance was granted only after checking if the applicant could not obtain assistance from their families and neighbourhoods or even community. This process did not make the training

---

13    Correia & Mathabatha, 2001; Meneses, 2010.

14    Rwomire & Radthokw, 1996; Strier, 2007.

15    Moreira, 2009; Kaseke, 1991.

16    Santana, 2013.

of social workers a top priority until 1993 when it was discontinued since it was assumed the extended family would take care of the destitute. Despite the enactment of the Social Action Policy (Resolution 2 of 1998), envisaging the need and inclusion of social workers and other private, religious and non-profit social protection providers in basic service delivery, healthcare, and social support, there was no reference to the establishment of an institution for the training of social workers and the further recruitment and selection of future graduates.[17]

## Conclusion

In 2002, the *Instituto Superior Maria Mãe Africa* ('Higher Institute of Mary Mother Africa'), a Catholic Church institute of higher education, was established to train social workers based on the Church's high ethical and moral standards and standing for professionals to solve communities' social, ethical and moral problems; train educators and social welfare agents and religious and pastoral health staff. Churches and CSOs employ most graduates, despite the staff shortage in the Ministry of Social Welfare; the main excuse not to recruit these professionals being lack of funds. Thus, staff recruitment into the ministry is from the ruling party's social organisations, especially the Women's League. Eduardo Mondlane's University Department of Sociology only introduced a Social Work degree in 2013 to train social workers to bring social change at the household, community, national and regional level and solve a wide range of social problems based on human behaviour theories and social systems.

Furthermore, social work graduates are supposed to promote social change and solve problems by performing a wide range of roles such as counsellors, advisers, educators, trainers, human rights advocates, public managers, and consultants. However, there is little known about the future role of graduates in the discussions and debates about social action policy and basic social action strategy; and having visibility at the household, neighbourhood, corporation, community, NGOs and state institutions levels, despite the inclusion of an internship programme in schools, hospitals and other service providers from its beginning. Therefore, it looks like future graduates should not rely too much on state institutions and agencies for employment but they also need to find jobs in other markets and institutions such as pension funds, private insurance agencies, and

---

17    Pfeiffer, 2003; Serra & Cossa, 2007:62-68.

in areas of corporate social responsibility in a context of a neo-liberal Mozambique. The CSOs and NGOs could provide an opportunity to raise the challenges of the social question in Mozambique and bring about active citizenship since the destitute and others are currently seen only as rights holders and not duty bearers as voters and social change agents.[18]

18    Ulriksen & Plagerson, 2014.

# References

Afonso, A. & Gomes, C.d.M. 2000. *Guerra Colonial*. Lisbon: Notícias.

Carvalho, M.I. & Pinto, C. 2014. *Serviço Social Teorias e Praticas*. Lisbon: Practor.

Correia, J.I. 1993. The Social Dimensions of Structural Economic Programmes in Southern Africa with special Reference to Mozambique, Harare. University of Zimbabwe, POLAD Winter School June 4-23.

Correia, J.I. & Mathabatha, S. 2001. The Roman Catholic Church and Education under Colonialism and Apartheid: The Mozambican and South African Experiences. Paper presented at the International Burden of Race Conference, University of the Witwatersrand, Johannesburg, 5-8 July.

Covane, L.A. 2001. Southern Mozambique: Migrant labour and Post-Independence Challenges. In: De Wet, C.J. & Fox, R.C. (eds), Transforming Settlement in Southern Africa. Edinburg: Edinburgh University Press. pp.48-64.

DFID (Department for International Development) 2010. *Annual Review 2009-2010: DFID Social Protection Project*. Mozambique. London: Department for International Development (UK).

Francisco, A. 2002. A Evolução da Economia de Moçambique da Colónia â Transição para a Economia de Mercado. In: Rolim, Cássio, S. António Franco, Bolnick, Bruce and Anderson, Per-Ake (eds), *A Economia Moçambicana Contemporânea-Ensaios*. Maputo: Ministério do Plano e Finanças.

Francisco, A. 2013. *Acção Social Produtiva em Moçambique: Uma falsa solução para um problema real*. Maputo: IESE

Francisco, A. & Sugahara, G. 2014. *Why Mozambique still does not have a universal pension for the elderly?* [https://bit.ly/3jfcG3p] (Accessed 21 May 2015).

Francisco, A. & Sugahara, G. 2015. *Porque Moçambique Ainda Não Possui Uma Pensão Universal para Idosos*. Maputo: IESE

Henriksen, Thomas 1983:16-17. See his Revolution and Counterrevolution: Mozambique's War of Independence, 1964-1974. Westport: Greenwood Press.

INAS (2010). *Relatório de Actividade de Apoio ao Programa Subsídio de Alimentos (PSA) do Exercício Económico de 2009*. Maputo: Instituto Nacional de Acção Social

INE (National Institute of Statistics). 2009. *Mozambique Household Budget Survey 2008-2009*. Global Health Data Exchange. [https://bit.ly/2SbBIEW]. (Accessed 12 August, 2011).

Kaseke, E. 1991. Social Work Practice in Zimbabwe. *Journal of Social Development in Africa*, 6(1):33-45.

Meneses, I.J. 2010. *Exclusão social e políticas sociais: os casos dos municípios de Maputo e Beira.* PhD thesis. Lisboa, Portugal: New University of Lisbon. [http://run.unl.pt/handle/10362/6104]. (12 August, 2011).

Middlemas, K. 1975. *Cahora Bassa: Engineering and Politics in Southern Africa.* London: Wiedenfeld and Nicolson.

Moreira, D.A. 2009. A espuma do tempo: memórias do tempo de vésperas. *Cadernos CERU,* 2(1):307-310.

Muchena, I. 2011. *Development of Insurance in Mozambique.* Oklahoma: Tate Publishing.

Nhachote, L. 2010. Industria de Mineração atrai várias figuras da Nomenclatura dominante. *CIP Newsletter.* Maputo: Centro de Integridade Pública.

Neves, J.M.d. 1998. Economy, Society and Labour Migration in Central Mozambique, 1930-c1965: A case study of Manica Province. PHD dissertation, School of Oriental and African Studies, University of London.

Newitt, M. 1995. *A History of Mozambique.* Bloomington, IN: Indiana University Press.

Pfeiffer, J. 2003. International NGOs and primary health care in Mozambique: The need for a new model of collaboration. *Social Science and Medicine,* 56(4):725-738.

Quive, S. 2007. *Protecção Social em Moçambique: Uma Rede Furada de Protecção Social.* Maputo: CIEDIMA.

Rocha, A.R. 2006. *Associativismo e Nativismo em Moçambique.* Maputo: Texto Editora.

Rwomire, A. & Raditlhokw, L. 1996. Available through a partnership with Social Work in Africa: Issues and Challenges Introduction: Conceptual and Contextual Background. *Journal of Social Development in Africa,* 2:5-19.

Santana, J.S. 2013. 'O branco não tem panela para nos cozer': eco popular dos movimentos panfricano e nacionalista no sul de Moçambique. *Sankofa. Revista de História da África e de Estudos da Diáspora Africana,* 6(11):96-114.

Serra, C. (ed). 2000. *Racismo, Etnicidade e Poder.* Maputo: Promédia.

Serra, C. & Cossa, D. 2007. *Colectânea de Legislação de Saúde.* Maputo: Ministry of Justice, Ministry of Health & Legal and Judicial Training Centre. pp.62-68.

Strier, R. 2007. Anti-Oppressive research in social work: A preliminary definition. *British Journal of Social Work,* 37(5):857-871.

Ulriksen, M. & Pagerson, S. 2014. Social Protection: Rethinking Rights and Duties. *World Development,* 64:755-765.

# 08

# SOCIAL WELFARE AND SOCIAL WORK IN NAMIBIA: SYSTEMS IN PROGRESSION

*Ndumba Jonnah Kamwanyah, Rachel Johanna Freeman*
*and Hetty Rose-Junius*

## Introduction

Namibia was Africa's second last colony, liberated on 21 March 1990. In 2017 it celebrated 27 years of Independence. After 1990, the country became an independent, democratic, and unitary state, whose governance is based on democracy, the rule of law, solidarity, and justice. Its history has passed through several distinct stages such as the pre-colonial era (1400-1800); the Christian Missionary Era (1805-1840); German rule (1884-1915); South African rule (1915-1990) and the post-colonial period (1990-present). Formerly known as German South-West Africa before Independence, the country was proudly named after the Namibian Desert that covers about one-fifth of the country. The name Namibia derives from a Nama/Damara word meaning 'shield' or 'protector' that long protected the Namib Desert's interior - from access by sea. This thinly populated, vast and largely arid country shares borders with Angola and Zambia (north), Botswana (east), South Africa (south), and the Atlantic Ocean (west).[1] The size of Namibia's territory is 824 268 km². Namibia is a land of diversity with 11 different ethnic groups, namely: Ovaherero; Aawambo; vaKavango; Namas; Damaras; Caprivians; Basters, Coloureds,

---

1    Van Rooyen & SWA/Namibia Information Service, 1980:4.

Germans, Afrikaners, and San people. Every ethnic group has its distinct traditions and cultures. The country's official language is English, but less than 7 per cent of Namibians speak it as a first language.

The end of colonial rule in 1990 left Namibia with fragmented social welfare and social work systems and the country's traditional and indigenous systems and institutions of social welfare service provision disrupted and destroyed. The colonial social welfare and social work systems, with a strong Christian influence, were deeply rooted in the legacy of apartheid. Consequently, the social welfare system and social work inherited from the apartheid South African colonial administration lacked inclusiveness and the promotion of the wellbeing of all Namibians. Although, like in South Africa, many welfare policies during South African rule did not specifically exclude black people, however, the government's allocation of welfare resources was based on racial differentiation, with the 'white' administration on top of all others. Under the South African rule, Namibia was divided into 11 ethnic administration where whites had their administration, followed by the coloured administration, and various black ethnic group administrations. For example, just like in South Africa, public assistance was not provided to Africans even if they qualified for such assistance as Bernstein and Gray (1997) state. The same is true for Africans in Namibia; only limited state help was available for them. In reversing the legacy of apartheid, Namibia, at Independence, opted to align social welfare provision with the country's new Constitution based on liberal democracy. In line with that, the country signed and ratified several African and international conventions to advance human rights and human dignity; emphasising democratic participation, social justice and a human rights approach in the promotion of people's social wellbeing; and the protection of vulnerable and marginalised groups.

Emerging out of the need to record the history and produce scholarly work, which contextualises the development and evolution of social welfare and social work in Namibia, this chapter describes the development of social welfare and social work practice in the Namibian context. It identifies three periods in Namibian history as far as the development of social welfare and social work over the centuries are concerned. The three periods that can be demarcated are the time of the indigenous human services, the period under colonial rule, and the current period after Independence. The chapter further provides an overview of the challenges and opportunities for social welfare and social work in Namibia today. Hopefully, this contribution will fill the existing gap of written work about social welfare and social work in Namibia. The authors are academics with practical and theoretical experiences in public policy, social work, casework, group work, community work, research and teaching and learning. They have more than 50 years of experience altogether with exposure to different fields of practice, knowledge and teaching in academia.

## Socio-Economic Opportunities and Challenges

Namibia has made great strides since Independence, and it is often heralded as one of Africa's greatest success stories for its stable democracy, peace and stability, and progressive social welfare policies and institutions. The country is ranked as an upper-middle-income country and has recorded steady economic growth over the last two decades. According to the International Labour Organisation, poverty declined in official estimates from 69.3 per cent in 1993-1994 to 28.7 per cent in 2009-2010.[2]

This enormous socio-economic progress has been accompanied by equally vital changes in the social welfare field in terms of:

- systems and organisational structure
- the size of social work professional membership
- the educational systems of all professions in the human services
- the sophistication of their practice methodologies
- social work as a profession within this wide ambit of socio-economic development.

It needs to be noted, while recognising the intrinsic connectedness of the total social welfare institution and social work profession, that social work developed out of the need for agents to carry out the welfare programmes developed to address people's living conditions throughout the country. However, like other countries in Africa, the country faces certain socio-economic problems requiring some adjustment in social welfare and social work provision. Globally, Namibia is considered as suffering one of the highest income inequalities, despite its upper-middle-income country status. Key social

---

2    ILO, 2014.

problems facing Namibia include poverty, HIV/Aids, vulnerable children, gender-based violence, unemployment and substance abuse.

In addition, Namibia faces a human resource crisis in the public health sector, characterised by:

▷ a shortage of health professionals

▷ high vacancy rates for all categories of staff

▷ high attrition rates (mostly due to resignations)

▷ lack of human resources retention strategy

▷ staff burn-out (and incomplete implementation of the Employee
  Assistance Programme)

▷ inadequate capacity at local health academic institutions to produce the required
  number of needed health workers, according to the Ministry of Health and
  Social Services.[3]

There are three health workers for every 1 000 people in Namibia, above the World Health Organisation (WHO) recommendation of 2.5 health workers per 1 000 population. Some specific health worker-population ratios include 1:13 519 for social workers; 1:2 952 for doctors; 1:704 for registered nurses; 1:10 039 for pharmacists; and 1:28 562 for health inspectors. These figures, however, ignore a shortage in the public sector – barely two health workers per population of 1 000. Moreover, within the public sector, there are chronic shortages of frontline workers, including social workers, doctors, and nurses. The country depends on the recruitment of expatriate doctors. There is a direct relationship between the ratio of health workers to the population and survival of women during childbirth and children in early infancy. In Namibia, the health worker shortage has been a major impediment to attaining the former health Millennium Development Goal.

Based on this background, the development of social work education at the University of Namibia (UNAM) is an important part of social work professionalisation. The first professional training of social workers, called welfare workers then, started in 1983 at

---

3    Namibia Statistics Agency, 2014

a learning institution called Academy for Tertiary Education.[4] Collectively, therefore, it can be argued that since gaining Independence, many opportunities and avenues shaped and changed the landscape of social welfare and social work in Namibia to respond effectively and efficiently to the citizens' welfare needs. As Compton & Galaway (1989) observe: "... today the profession of social work is much more than the agent of the welfare system. It is charged both with the delivery of services to individuals, families and groups and with attending to the institutional structure within which such services are offered."[5] Therefore, we believe that for Namibia to address the myriad of socioeconomic challenges, its welfare system must be robust and holistic and be geared towards addressing structural and institutional inequality as well.

## Definitions of Social Welfare and Social Work

Literature defines social work in many ways, but in this chapter, we operationalise it to mean a helping profession that utilises professional approaches to help the vulnerable groups in society – such as women, persons with disabilities, children and the elderly as well as people living with HIV/Aids; and to empower people to solve their social problems.[6] However, we argue that social work's virtues of helping and empowering people cannot be narrowly defined to include professional approaches only. The ability to help and ameliorate social problems is inherently present in informal helping systems, referred to as an indigenous human service system. Since time immemorial, societies throughout every civilisation had some types of indigenous helping methods and social assistance to take care of each other. An example of indigenous helping systems is the extended African family continuing to address the social welfare needs of a sizeable number of Africans throughout the continent, who lack any form of social protection.[7]

By broadening the concept of social work to extend or apply to indigenous helping systems, therefore, we see social welfare as a formal and informal system of arrangements, programmes and mechanisms by governmental/non-governmental/community – that try to meet the needs of individuals and families who cannot fulfil such needs with

---

4    UNAM, 2008.

5    Compton & Galaway, 1989:16.

6    Chitereka, 2009; Mupedziswa, 2005.

7    Apte & Grieco, 1994; Chitereka, 2009.

their resources.[8] In this respect, human needs must be met through some form of system (whether formal or informal) that guarantees protection when people become vulnerable. Citizens are part of many systems, and those systems combine to form the larger society. For example, a person is part of his or her family, neighbourhood, school or workplace and social class, and different identities define each person. In this respect, 'welfare' speaks to the wellbeing – the state of having a healthy balance. For the sake of this chapter, social welfare will mean the wellbeing of society.[9]

Another definition of social work to note is that of Hormer (2012), who regards social work:

> ... as a profession that promotes social change, problem-solving in human relationships and the empowerment and liberation of people to enhance wellbeing. Social work intervenes at the point where people interact with their environment, utilising theories of human behaviour and social systems. Principles of human rights and social justice are fundamental to social work.[10]

The International Association of the Schools of Social Work (IASSW) and International Federation of Social Workers (IFSW) in 2014 agreed on the following definition of social work:

> Social work is a practice-based profession and an academic discipline that promotes social change and development, social cohesion and the empowerment and liberation of people. Principles of social justice, human rights, collective responsibility and respect for diversities are central to social work. Underpinned by theories of social work, social sciences, humanities and indigenous knowledge, social work engages people and structures to address life challenges and enhance well-being.[11]

## Three Periods of Social Welfare and Social Work Development in Namibia

Social welfare and social work in Namibia have undergone various changes influenced by the country's socio-political landscape, ranging from the pre-colonial period, Christian

---

8    Johnson, Schwartz & Tate, 1997.
9    Segal, 2010.
10   Hormer, 2012:3.
11   IFSW/IASSW, 2014.

missionary era, the colonial and post-colonial eras, altogether playing an important role in the development of the Namibian social welfare system and social work. In the following section, the authors will be addressing the various stages in social welfare development in Namibia.

## Indigenous Human Service Systems in Pre-Colonial Era

Contact with Christian missionaries (1805-1840), and subsequent German colonial rule (1804-1915) and then South African rule (1915-1990), not only introduced the indigenous people of Namibia, previously known as South-West Africa, to foreign rule and domination but also disrupted and undermined Namibia's traditional and indigenous systems and institutions of social welfare and human service provision. That is to say that the Christian Church heavily influences Namibia, as we know this country today, with over 90 per cent of Namibians subscribing to the Christian faith as Anglicans; Lutherans; Roman Catholics; African Methodist Episcopalians Orora; Seventh Day Adventists; Jehovah's Witnesses; Dutch Reformed Church; and Pentecostal.[12] The early missionary churches evangelised and converted the indigenous people of Namibia to Christianity through the Gospel of God; through the efforts of the first missionary societies such as the London Missionary Society; the Wesleyan Methodist Missionary Society; the Rhenish Missionary Society; and the Finnish Missionary Society, arriving in Namibia in 1805. This process heavily influenced the social identity of the indigenous people.[13] As a religious duty, the missionaries provided evangelisation, education, and religious, medical and some sort of social work services, to the indigenous people to help the poor and the 'unrepentant'. Therefore, the missionaries used evangelisation, education, medical and social services, to win the hearts and minds of the indigenous people and sway them away from their traditional practices and value systems, including their traditional social welfare services.

At the same time the arrival, respectively, of both German settlers and later, South African rule in the country, would further undermine the indigenous human services systems. Apartheid and stereotypical views informed the German and South African colonial system of social welfare provision, attributing social issues and challenges affecting the indigenous majority in Namibia to personal and moral failing of their

---

12    Diescho, 2014.

13    Buys & Nambala, 2003.

own, instead of looking at broader structural and institutional contributory factors. The provision of social services and programmes were mainly clinical, individualistic and symptom-driven, instead of addressing the underlying causes of social welfare problems. Therefore, professional social work education and practice in Namibia might be closely tied to the country's missionary and colonial history, but it did not necessarily start with colonialism.

What colonialism did was to undermine, disrupt and destroy Namibia's traditional and indigenous systems and institutions of social welfare service provision. Consequently, the missionaries' churches and subsequent colonial rules of German and South African social welfare systems and social workers failed in recognising, incorporating and utilising the available wealthy indigenous human service help systems that characterised pre-colonial Namibia. Like the rest of the African continent, before the contact with colonial rule, pre-colonial Namibia had rich political and social welfare systems such as the extended family; and other mechanisms to assist the needy and vulnerable. For example, the *vaKavango* people used the concept of *ndjambiNzambi* to collectively cultivate each other's field to ensure that every community member's needs were met, especially those who lacked means or resources to cultivate for themselves. This concept puts them on an equal basis with everybody in the community as far as cultivation is concerned. Namibia is a vast country and has 11 ethnic groups, with varying social, economic, and political situations. Therefore, a generalisation of the indigenous human service system is thus difficult and might not give the true picture of each indigenous system of social welfare. However, one cannot shy away from the reality of certain conditions and situations, common to the pre-colonial Namibian indigenous human services systems. A significant portion of this pre-colonial Namibian existence was people living in small-scale, clan-based, and egalitarian societies in which members of the community depended on each other for their wellbeing. Discourses about pre-colonial Namibian human services may be linked to three broader historical events discussed below.

## Indigenous Human Services in Pre-Historical Period: BC to 1485

In the pre-historical period (BC to 1485), for example, the San people (!Kung, /Xam, ≠Khomani, Nusan, Khwe (Khoi, Kxoe), Naro, Hai//om, Tsoa, Auen, Ju/'hoan, Kua and G/u and G/ana), the first inhabitants of Namibia, hunted and gathered food from the grasslands; painted rocks; and collectively took care of each other by moving from place to place in search of food, water and protective shelter for every member. Their existence was serene, simple and in harmony with nature in the sense that they consumed according to what 'one needs, not what one wants'.[14] The concept here is that each member's wellbeing depended on being non-materialistic and leading a simple life that did not destroy nature but conserved it for the wellbeing of everybody, including the future generation. In this type of society, greed was not common as each member consumed no more than what he or she needed.

## Indigenous Human Services in Period of Bantu Expansion: 1400-1800

The San people's simple way of taking care of each other was followed by the period of Khoisan and Bantu – Namas, Damaras, Ovaherero, Aawambo, vaKavango, Mafwe/Subia/Lozi expansion. The Bantu and the Khoisan worked the soil, cultivated the fields, and herded cattle. Theirs was a stateless society in which the elders were respected, revered and enjoyed hierarchical advantages over the young ones; the elders played the important roles of counselling, coaching and mentoring the rest of the community.[15] They primarily communicated with God – Kalunga, Nyambi, Mukuru, Nyambe – through ancestors, instead of prayer. They believed the dead did not completely disappear from the earth but continued to take an interest in the wellbeing of the living.[16] Therefore, an ancestor as a medium to reach God had the power and ability to influence life-changing events such as birth, sickness, death, seasonal change and everything human reason could not explain. Communal ethos characterised their existence in the sense that one's wellbeing was nothing without the existence of the other; the ability to imagine life from the perspective of others, collectively responsible to take care of each other in action – the notion of *ubuntu* ('I am because we are') common throughout Africa. A society cannot function fully if one of their own is struggling, hence the taking care of each mechanism built in their political and social system such as the extended family arrangement and the collective cultivation arrangement of the Ndjambi/Nzambi.

---

14    Kamwanyah, 2016.

15    Ibid.

16    Ibid.

## Role of Indigenous Human Service Systems in Independent Namibia

Today, the indigenous human service systems in independent Namibia through the extended family and social network continue to work parallel to governmental public assistance programmes in providing social protection to many Namibians, especially in rural areas where resources and facilities are scarce, and poverty is rampant. Namibia's poor, especially the previously disadvantaged blacks, largely depend on their employed relatives for social security in terms of food, shelter, healthcare and education because they lack governmental social protection. In conclusion to this section, the pre-colonial system of helping was not curative or medically oriented but more socially rooted in the African *ubuntu* sense of taking care of each other.

## Social Welfare and Social Work during the South African Colonial Era

During this colonial period, social workers, medical doctors, and nurses in the then South-West Africa shared their concerns for people's quality of life in the remote areas of the country. One of the authors, who was heavily involved in the setting up of social welfare systems, and working with other health professionals and training social workers, recalls how the medical staff went out in the districts, staying and setting up the most basic medical services in tents so that they could attend to health problems brought to their attention. The government addressed medical services in this period through the building of state hospitals in various towns in the country. In Windhoek, the capital city, two separate state hospitals served white patients and other (ethnic groups) respectively. Large state hospitals were built in the northern part of Namibia (Oshakati and Eenhana); in the southern part of the country (Keetmanshoop); central north (Rundu) and far north-eastern (Katima Mulilo). Although these hospitals served all the patients in those respective areas, they were cared for in separate wards. State and private clinics were erected in towns and rural areas caring for the poor who could not afford hospital fees.

## Legal Social Welfare System during Colonial Rule

While South Africa colonised Namibia, at the time known as South-West Africa, the South African legal system, based on Roman-Dutch Law, was applied in the country. The main statutes governing the work of social welfare services in Namibia were:

▻ The *National Social Welfare Act 25 of 1956*, as amended in South Africa before Namibia's Independence, regulated friendly societies, associations of persons established to provide relief to children, the aged, and sick widows.

▻ The *National Welfare Act 79 of 1965*, as amended in South Africa, established a National Welfare Board of Namibia providing for the registration and control of certain welfare organisations.

▻ The *Aged Persons Act 81 of 1967* before Namibia's Independence provided for the protection and welfare of certain aged and debilitated persons.

▻ The *Blind Persons Act 26 of 1968* concerned the promotion of blind people's welfare.

▻ The *Criminal Procedures Act 51 of 1977* and the *Children's Act 33 of 1960*, were some of the legal statutes governing the court system and the total social welfare scene during colonial rule.

According to Aisindi (2013), the social work profession has developed as a scientific discipline since the early 1950s. At this time, churches mainly facilitated and carried out social work. During the 1950s non-governmental organisations (NGOs) that specialised in specific services were established.[17]

## Education and Training of Social Workers

According to the Ministry of Education (2013), unequal access to education and training at all levels of education characterised the educational situation before Independence. There was a fragmentation of education along racial and ethnic lines and lack of democratic participation within the education and training system. One of the authors, Rose-Junius, narrates that Namibian social workers were originally trained in South

---

17    Maree, 2012.

Africa since there were no tertiary institutions in Namibia.[18] They were trained at the Universities of Cape Town, Stellenbosch, Witwatersrand and South Africa (Unisa, a distance training institution). The University of the Western Cape (UWC) opened in Belville South, Cape Town, in 1960, and catered for the so-called non-white students (or the mixed-raced population group) from South Africa and the countries in Southern Africa, including Namibia. The UWC was a university college of Unisa, with students receiving degrees. Psychologist, teachers, and dentists were trained at these institutions.

The Academy for Tertiary Education was established in the early 1970s in Windhoek, Namibia, as a university college of Unisa. While its curriculum started as a three-year Bachelor of Arts degree in Social Work (BSW), it advanced to a four-year training degree around 1991. The then Department for Education and Training initiated the training of welfare workers, already commencing in 1975 at the Augustinium Training College. The minimum requirement was a standard 8 (grade 10) certificate, although a matriculation certificate was preferred. It is estimated that 37 welfare workers completed the welfare training course by 1979, and were mainly employed in the southern rural areas. The training mainly prepared them for court work and home visits leading to the assessment of the needs of the poorest people in the country. They functioned like friendly visitors in early American social work. In later years, immediately after Independence through the newly proclaimed UNAM, the Ministry of Health and Social Services appointed them as social workers.

The various church denominations played an important role in the development of the social welfare programmes in the country such as the Dutch Reformed Church Welfare Organisation, appointing the first social worker, Mrs C.M. Truter, in 1954 in Grootfontein, Namibia. At that time, this welfare agency only served white communities.

The Roman Catholic, Lutheran, Anglican, and various other denominations were more involved in all Namibian cultures in need of some form of assistance. This system only changed after Independence. The Catholic Aids Action became the leader in the field of addressing HIV/Aids in the country. It, over time, built hospitals and brought doctors and nurses, mostly nuns from Germany to serve in towns and the most remote areas of the country. The Catholic and Lutheran denominations, having the financial support

---

18    Rose-Junius, 2016.

of Germany, played leading roles in building schools and hostels to secure education, specifically for the families who could not afford school fees and accommodation away from their places of residence. During the colonial era, the Ministry of Health and Social Services registered private welfare agencies in various towns of the country, functioned under the supervision of this Ministry. These welfare agencies worked very well because they knew the local social needs and cultural practices.

## Social Welfare and Social Work Systems in Independent Namibia (1990 – to the present)

Since Independence, Namibia's social welfare and social work landscapes have changed dramatically, shifting from a clinical approach to broader issues of nation-building and socio-economic development. The Namibian government, after Independence in 1990, committed to a constitutional responsibility to address the inequalities and discrimination in access to services and to meet the basic needs of people through a social development approach. The Constitution provides a strong backdrop for equal access to social welfare and social work services in Namibia. The Namibian Government developed the National Development Plan, placing social welfare provision at the centre of service delivery. Post-Independence Namibia's social welfare approach differs from the social welfare model during the colonial and apartheid eras that focussed on institutionalising policies for whites and a residual system for blacks. At the moment, the Namibian Government has charged various governmental ministries and departments such as the Ministry of Poverty Reduction and Social Welfare, Gender Equality and Child Welfare, and the Ministry of War Veterans to address vital social welfare needs in the country. Social workers currently work in several government ministries, such as the Ministry of Poverty Reduction, the Ministry of War Veterans, the Ministry of Safety and Security, the Ministry of Youth, the Ministry of Gender Equality and Child Welfare, the Ministry of Prisons and Correctional Services, and the Ministry of Health and Social Services. They also work in NGOs such as Regain Trust, Catholic Aids Action, ChildLine/LifeLine; Red Cross and international organisations such as the United Nations Children's Fund, United Nations Development Programme; United Nations Fund for Population Activities; United States Agency for International Development and private practices. There have been several legal reforms to address gender inequalities, gender-based violence; poverty; strengthening social protection; improving care coordination; confronting underdevelopment and economic inequality; therefore, changing the landscape of social welfare and social work in the country. Examples include the *Local Authorities Act 23 of 1992* which institutes affirmative action for women to participate in local government elections, including several statutory bodies such as the Social Security Commission, the Namibia Sports Commission and the National Council for Higher Education. The *Labour Act 6 of 1992* prohibits discrimination in any respect of employment based on sex, marital status, family responsibilities and sexual orientation.

The *Married Persons Equality Act 1 of 1996* eliminates the discriminatory Roman-Dutch law concept of marital power previously applicable to civil marriages in Namibia. With the shocking levels of gender-based violence in Namibia, the Parliament passed the *Combating of Rape Act 8 of 2000*, a very progressive law. Law reform on rape was followed by the *Combating of Domestic Violence Act 4 of 2003*, which covers a range of forms of domestic violence, including sexual violence, harassment, intimidation, economic violence, and psychological violence. It covers violence between husbands and wives, parents and children, boyfriends and girlfriends and close family members. Another major family law reform was the *Maintenance Act 9 of 2003* that made significant changes to the child maintenance system. The *Children's Status Act 6 of 2006* deals with the position of children born outside of marriage and provides simple procedures for appointing a guardian for any child whose legal custodian or guardian has died. All these law reforms show that Namibia is seriously committed to improving the quality of life and wellbeing of its citizens.

Internationally speaking, in 1997, Namibia adopted a social development focus in line with the UN Copenhagen Declaration of 1995. The Namibian government, after Independence, set its agenda and objectives out in its developmental objectives of the Millennium Development Goals.[19] Namibia is a no-reservations signatory to the UN Convention on the Elimination of All Forms of Discrimination against Women, and the UN Convention on the Rights of the Child. Regionally, Namibia has adopted the Protocol to the African Charter on Human and People's Rights, and on the Rights of Women in Africa. In combatting the social challenges facing Namibia, the government introduced free primary healthcare, no-fee paying schooling and social grants.

---

19    UN, 2013:13.

In 2004, the Namibian Government passed the *Social Work and Psychology Act 6 of 2004*, to regulate the field of Social Work in Namibia. This also recognises the role that social work plays in achieving the Sustainable Development Goals (DSGs).[20] However, to date, the country has yet to develop a unique social welfare system and social work profession authentic to the Namibian situation. Instead, the country's social welfare and social work systems in terms of principles, philosophy, and practice, predominantly mirror colonial-apartheid practice and to some extent reproduce similar patterns of clinical, casework and symptom-driven response interventions.

## Social Work Education and Training in Independent Namibia

Freeman (2017) narrates that the training of social workers is currently done at UNAM. On 31 August 1992, an Act of Parliament established UNAM, as a Commission on Higher Education recommended. The Faculty of Humanities and Social Sciences has been represented at the university from the start, offering the Bachelor of Social Work (BSW) degree.[21] Thirty years after Independence a lot has changed, with the establishment of the Social Work, Psychology and Sociology Departments at UNAM, providing social work training. UNAM upgraded a group of welfare workers to social workers. In this regard, the authors argue that Namibia's post-independent social welfare system and social work are still work in progress. UNAM and the Social Work and Psychology Council have played major roles in the professionalisation of social work in Namibia. The *Social Work and Psychology Act 6 of 2004* constituted the Council for the Registration of Social Workers and Psychologists to ensure professionalism among practitioners in the given fields. Registration is needed to practice social work in Namibia legally. Social workers are required to keep abreast with their professional development through the earning of continuous professional development units, offered by registered CPD providers under the Health Professions Council, to ensure that professionals in Namibia are up to date with the latest developments in the profession.

---

20    Republic of Namibia, 2004.
21    UNAM, 2013a&b.

UNAM's social work curriculum complies with the university's quality assurance requirements and the Namibian Qualifications Authority's standards. Schenck, Mbedzi, Qalinge, Schultz, Sekudu and Sesoko (2015) state that to perform as a social worker:

> ... one needs education and training in a wide range of areas and disciplines, such as values, ethics, diversity, human behaviour, health, social pathologies, Sociology, Psychology, Anthropology, Economics, and Development Studies to effectively deal with the developmental challenges faced by individuals, groups, families and the larger community.[22]

In response to this, the Department Social Work at UNAM reviewed its social work curriculum, in the recent past, to move away from the colonial-apartheid curriculum, towards a robust, and more uniquely Namibian model of social work practice. It offers a BA Honours, a Master of Arts and doctoral degrees. The newly revised 2016 Social Work curriculum and internship programme offers work-integrated learning components that transform students to become practitioners who can render social services to the diverse Namibian society. Professional exposure and experimental learning are offered through a Field Education Programme where students can work directly with community partners, getting valuable experience on the ground, while offering countless hours of capacity to those organisations.

In a short time, social work in Namibia has and continues to develop into a well-established field. The social work programme in the Department of Social Work in the Faculty of Humanities and Social Sciences at UNAM, became popular over the years and attracted students from all over Namibia, Southern Africa, and internationally (USA, Sweden, Finland and Germany). In most cases, after graduation, these international students choose to remain in Namibia. In past years, the UNAM social work student population increased from an average of 18 first-year students in the early 1990s to 60 first-years in 2009.[23] UNAM roughly educates approximately 205 social work students per year.

The post-Independence social work programme aims to provide students with the necessary knowledge, skills and understanding to deal positively with problems that arise in the interaction between people and their environment, and to empower those

---

22    Schenck, Mbedzi, Qalinge, Schultz, Sekudu and Sesoko, 2015:12.
23    Ananias & Lightfoot, 2009.

involved to deal with their problems in a self-reliant way. The students should acquire theoretical knowledge, professional skills and adhere to the ethical code of the profession. After training, students should perform in social work methods, including working with individuals, groups and communities, as well as researching and management. These methods should be applied according to the integrated social work model and are tailored to the specific needs of a client, group, or a community system. Social workers in Namibia serve as:

▻ counsellors (e.g., in adoption, bereavement, domestic violence, vocational and rehabilitation, hospice, mental health, substance abuse, and youth services)

▻ service coordinators and case managers (e.g., in healthcare, child welfare, housing, human resources, public affairs, student life, employee assistance programmes)

▻ therapists (e.g., child, adolescent, marriage, and family)

▻ administrators (public and private human service agencies)

▻ community development workers

▻ public policy analysts, to name a few.

They work in juvenile and adult justice systems, governmental agencies, private institutions, as well as in voluntary welfare organisations and non-governmental organisations.

## Conclusion

According to Schenck et al. (2015): "... social welfare and social work originated many years back, but yet face adversative conditions that require transformation even in the present times."[24] The colonial period under German rule, proceeding to the colonial incursion under the South African rule to professional social work in the post-colonial era, altogether played an important role in the transformation and development of a Namibian social welfare system. Schenck et al. (2015) state that the "formalisation of social work as a profession evolved social services in the sense that services were rendered by qualified professionals".[25] As the authors demonstrated in this chapter, there is yet no unique and authentic Namibian social welfare system and social work.

24    Schenck et al., 2015:59.
25    Ibid.

Any such provisions still rely on colonial and Western theories, practices, books, and teaching in social work pedagogy. The Namibian social welfare system and its social work profession still face many challenges in addressing the past inequalities caused by unstable economic factors, such as poverty, unemployment, and corruption. All these challenges in the development of effective social welfare and a social work system in Namibia need to be addressed to improve people's quality of life, promote wellbeing, and enhance social functioning and social justice for all human beings.

# References

Aisindi, J. 2013. *The Marginal Social Worker. Exploring how Namibian social work students perceived and implement knowledge from a study exchange in Sweden.* MA thesis. Växjö, Sweden: Linnaeus University. Department of Social Work.

Ananias, J.A. & Lightfoot, L. 2009. Promoting Social Development: Building a Professional Social Work Association in Namibia. *Journal of Community Practice*, 20(1-2):196-210. [https://bit.ly/2GKR0OU]. (Accessed 15 November 2016).

Bernstein, A. & Gray, M. 1997. Social Work, a beginner's text. Kenwyn, South Africa: M. Juta and Company.

Buys, G.L. & Nambala, S.W. 2003. *History of Christianity.* Windhoek: Gamsberg Macmillan.

Compton, B.R. & Galaway, B. 1989. *Social Process.* Belmont, CA: Wadsworth.

Diescho, J. 2014. Diescho's Dictum – The role of the church in Namibia. *New Era*, 29 July. [https://bit.ly/371DWPy]. (Accessed 15 November 2016).

Freeman, R.J. 2017. *Social workers' perspectives of their role in providing palliative care to patients with life-limiting illnesses: A Qualitative Study among Social Workers in Primary Care Settings in Namibia.* PHD thesis. Pretoria, South Africa: University of South Africa (UNISA). Department of Social Work.

Hormer, N. 2012. *What is social work?* London: SAGE.

IFSW (International Federation of Social Workers). 2014. *Global definition of social work.* [https://bit.ly/30ZTRds]. (Accessed 19 March 2015).

ILO (International Labour Organisation). 2014. *World Social Protection Report 2014-15: Building economic recovery, inclusive development and social justice.* [https://bit.ly/3iOOHak]. Accessed 19 March 2015).

Johnson, L.C., Schwartz, C.L. & Tate, D.S. 1997. *Social Welfare: A Response to Human Need.* 4th Edition. Boston, MA: Allyn and Bacon.

Kamwanyah, N. 2016. Indepth with Ndumba – The rock on which Namibia is built. *The Namibian*, 30 September. [https://bit.ly/34WHGQ1]. (Accessed 20 August 2017).

Malan, J.S. 2004. *Peoples of Namibia.* 4th Edition. Pretoria: Rhino Publishers.

Maree, M. 2011. *1st Year Student Social Work Class Powerpoint Presentation on: History of Social Work in Namibia.* 25 March. University of Namibia.

Mupedziswa, R. 2005. Challenges and prospects of social work services in Africa. In: J.C. Okeibunor, & E.E. Anugwom (eds). *The social sciences and socio-economic transformation in Africa.* Nsukka: Great AP Express Publishing. pp.271-317.

Namibia Statistics Agency. 2014. *Namibian Demographic and Health Survey*. Windhoek: Namibia Statistics Agency.

Patel, L. 2015. *Social Welfare and Social Development*. 2nd Edition. Oxford: Oxford University Press.

Peterson, R. 2009. *Families First: Keys to successful family functioning: Communication*. Virginia Cooperative Extension: Publications and Educational Resources. [https://bit.ly/3iY4q6W]. (Accessed 3 September 2012).

Republic of Namibia. 1960. *Children's Act 33 of 1960*. [https://bit.ly/3dnrg6N]. (Accessed 15 November 2016).

Republic of Namibia. 1965a. *Friendly Societies Act 25 of 1956*. [https://bit.ly/2Iu0BtX]. (Accessed 15 November 2016).

Republic of Namibia. 1965b. *National Welfare Act 79 of 1965*. [https://bit.ly/3nKC2cb]. (Accessed 15 November 2016).

Republic of Namibia. 1967. *Aged Persons Act 81 of 1967 (RSA)*. [https://bit.ly/3jVXc4H]. (Accessed 15 November 2016).

Republic of Namibia. 1968. *Blind Persons Act 26 of 1968 (RSA)*. [https://bit.ly/3lGQQGP]. (Accessed 15 November 2016).

Republic of Namibia. 1977. *Criminal Procedures Act 51 of 1977*. [https://bit.ly/34RYeZp]. (Accessed 15 November 2016).

Republic of Namibia. 1990. *Namibian Constitution*. [https://bit.ly/310060S]. (Accessed 15 November 2016).

Republic of Namibia. 1992. *Labour Act 6 of 1992*. [https://bit.ly/3nPmR1A]. (Accessed 15 November 2016).

Republic of Namibia. 1996. *Married Persons Equality Act 1 of 1996*. [https://bit.ly/3iUS7sb]. (Accessed 15 November 2016).

Republic of Namibia. 2000. *Combating of Rape Act 8 of 2000*. [https://bit.ly/3jUXicJ]. (Accessed 15 November 2016).

Republic of Namibia. 2003a. *Combating of Domestic Violence Act 4 of 2003*. [https://bit.ly/3jTFnTS]. (Accessed 15 November 2016).

Republic of Namibia. 2003b. *Maintenance Act 9 of 2003*. [https://bit.ly/33SPcvD]. (Accessed 15 November 2016).

Republic of Namibia. 2004. *Social work and Psychology Act of 2004*. [https://bit.ly/310Q3J3]. (Accessed 18 November 2013).

Republic of Namibia. 2006. *Children's Status Act 6 of 2006*. [https://bit.ly/3iWNOMZ]. (Accessed 15 November 2016).

Republic of Namibia. Ministry of Education, Arts & Culture. 2013. *About the Ministry of Education, Arts and Culture*. [http://www.moe.gov.na/m_ab_aboutus.php]. (Accessed 17 December 2013).

Schenck, R., Mbedzi, P., Qalinge, L., Schultz, P., Sekudu, J. & Sesoko, M. 2015. *Introduction to Social Work in the South African context*. Cape Town: Oxford University Press Southern Africa.

Segal, E.A. 2010. *Social welfare policy and social programmes: A values perspective*. Belmont, CA: Brooks/Cole.

UN (United Nations). 2013. *The Millennium Development Goals: Report: We can end poverty 2015*. New York: United Nations.

UNAM (University of Namibia). 2008. *Human Sciences: Social Work*. [https://bit.ly/33U7EEv]. (Accessed 11 October 2013).

UNAM (University of Namibia). 2013a. *About UNAM: History*. [https://bit.ly/315kM7U]. (Accessed 23 November 2013).

UNAM (University of Namibia). 2013b. *About UNAM. Vision and mission*. [https://bit.ly/3nLGkQB]. (Accessed 23 November 2013).

Van Rooyen, I. & SWA /Namibia Information Service. 1980. *SWA/Namibia Today*. Windhoek: The Service.

# 09

# EVOLUTION OF SOCIAL WELFARE AND SOCIAL WORK IN SOUTH AFRICA

*Ndangwa Noyoo, Boitumelo Seepamore,*
*Mpumelelo Ncube, and Mzwandile Sobantu*

## Introduction

This chapter examines South Africa's social welfare system and the profession of social work since their inception. It traces the beginnings of social welfare initiatives and social work in the country and then illuminates how the former responded to human needs in previous epochs. After that, the chapter attempts to ascertain the current standing of social welfare and social work in South Africa. In its discussions, the chapter covers three historical eras, namely: the pre-colonial, colonial-apartheid and post-apartheid periods. At the outset, it is important to state that social welfare and social work in South Africa are inextricably bound up with South Africa's history of colonial conquest and occupation on the one hand, and apartheid on the other. It is also important to assert that social welfare and social work cannot be divorced from the indigenous social fabrics of the various African populations of South Africa. However, Africans were forcibly incorporated into the colonial system of exploitation and subjugation for close to 350 years. In this regard, the genesis of social welfare and social work is linked to the initial occupation of the Cape peninsula by a European settler population that eventually dispossessed most of the land of various African indigenous polities. Colonial conquest, industrial development, and the institutionalisation of racism, after the apartheid state was created in 1948, are all important antecedents that shaped social welfare and social work in South Africa. Before colonial rule, different indigenous societies had various ways of meeting the needs of their members. It is a universal fact that almost all societies had created mechanisms, over the centuries, to safeguard the wellbeing of people. Thus, in the pre-industrial age where communal existence defined social interaction, indigenous systems that responded to human needs predominated. All societies at the time had indigenous modalities to look after the disadvantaged who could not fend for themselves. In pre-colonial Africa, individuals' needs were met through the extended family system.

The caring of the old, infirm, and at times people with disabilities (because some cultures were extremely hostile towards these individuals) was a core function of the family, the pillar of pre-colonial Africa. In this context, family ties were based on the kinship system, where each member had a specific role to play. Families were organised as clans and were held together by the mutual-aid system, underpinned by solidarity and reciprocity. However, it must be noted that African pre-colonial polities were not homogenous and had exhibited different levels of social and political organisation. Unfortunately, when the pre-colonial period is mentioned in academic discourse, there is sometimes a misconception by those who seem to suggest that it was Utopia and, in line with this account, this state of 'bliss' was only disrupted by colonial conquest. This description of pre-colonial Africa is erroneous and misleading.[1] Wars of conquest between different indigenous polities defined pre-colonial Africa, like in other parts of the world at that time.

Colonial penetration in South Africa began with the establishment of a Dutch settlement, pioneered by Jan van Riebeeck in 1652 at the Cape of Good Hope. When the Dutch landed on the African shores, they first introduced two new and unambiguous forms of inequality: slavery and the reduction of the Khoisan people to landless labourers. Cape slavery lasted about 175 years, and at abolition in 1834, there were over 36 000 slaves, and some 59 000 colonists and 42 000 Khoisan and 'bastaards'.[2] Later and more significantly, the Anglo-Boer war (1899-1902) – now called the South African War, because there were

---

1     Noyoo, 2015.
2     Bundy, 1992.

many Africans who fought and died on both sides – had profoundly led to the dislocation of the Afrikaner community and therefore served as the initial impetus to the creation of a phenomenon known as the 'poor white problem'. According to Fourie (2006), the poor white problem's cause, first noted at a Dutch Reformed Church (NGK) Synod in 1886, was unclear; later many blamed the inadequate education system, urbanisation, cheap wages or cultural factors, while others argued that external events such as the rinderpest disease and the South African war had increased the numbers of poor whites. Religious organisations such as the Dutch Reformed Church and organs of civil society, for example, the Afrikaans women's group, the Afrikaans Christian Women's Association (*Afrikaanse Christelike Vroue Vereniging*, ACVV), were primarily actively involved in the amelioration of the harsh living conditions of poor whites. The colonial state only became involved in earnest in meeting the needs of poor whites in 1910 after the Union of South Africa came into being. For the Africans, their indigenous social security systems still catered to their needs:

> Before the 19th Century, social welfare services were no[t] organised as such. For blacks, the extended family system provided for the needs of all people under tribal custom. During the first two centuries of colonial rule, white pioneer families also provided for their needs. In the 19th Century the Dutch Reformed Church, to which most Afrikaners belonged, was active in early efforts to establish a variety of social welfare services, and other religious denominations, Protestants, Catholics, and Jews, followed suit. Gradually, voluntary welfare organisations, some with international affiliations, such as the Red Cross and the Salvation Army, appeared in the Cape Colony.[3]

It is safe to say that the discovery of vast mineral deposits of diamonds and gold in South Africa unleashed forces of social change which transformed the South African society in significant ways and continue to shape the country to this day. The harnessing of mineral deposits for commercial use resulted in the industrialisation of South Africa. Regarding the Afrikaners, who were the descendants of the early Dutch settlers from the Netherlands, the former twin forces led to the erosion of their livelihoods. As industrialisation unfolded, there was an influx of foreign, mainly British capital that put the mining industry on the world map and spearheaded the highly centralised character of the industry. Secondly, there was a rush of European immigrant labour, supplying the

---

3    Hare & McKendrick, 1976:76.

semi-skilled and skilled labour the mines needed. Thirdly, there was the dismantling of the African peasantry, becoming the chief source of cheap unskilled labour.[4]

Nevertheless, it must be stated that even though most Afrikaners lost out in the country's industrialisation, Africans suffered the most from this process. Lester (1996) observes that with the industrialisation of the Rand, commercial farmers across the country began to utilise the land they owned fully to supply the expanding urban markets.[5] Therefore, landless Afrikaners found their rural options narrowed as landowners began to evict unprofitable tenants, and their drift to the cities began, as individual families felt the broad shifting structures of economic development impinging upon their lives. Equally, the global Great Depression of the late 1920s and 1930s negatively impacted South Africa and further compounded the poverty of the white population, especially that of the Afrikaners. What can be said of the Africans and other races such as the so-called 'coloureds' and Indians, was that if white people were impoverished in this way, the worst circumstances could be assumed for the other race groups, especially Africans, who ranked the lowest on the colonial socio-economic and political ladder.

Thus in 1928, at the instigation of the Dutch Reformed Church, the Carnegie Corporation of New York was persuaded to fund a new approach to white indigence, referred to as "a scientific investigation into the causes of white poverty, its extent, and the means by which it could be reduced".[6]

## Social Work Education Development and Welfare System Establishment in South Africa

The reason for establishing social work practice was crystallised after the National Conference on the Poor White Problem at Kimberley in 1934, resulting in the creation of a State Department of Social Welfare (DSW) in 1937. The new DSW employed social workers as well as subsidised similar posts in the voluntary sector.[7] The DSW's functions were as follows:

---

4       Marais, 2001.
5       Lester, 1996:68.
6       McKendrick, 1987.
7       Hare & McKendrick, 1976.

▷ To assist towards proper adjustment, people and families who are socially maladjusted (the rehabilitation aim).

▷ To study and take appropriate steps to deal with the conditions that may cause or contribute towards maladjustment (the preventative approach).

▷ To coordinate the activities of government bodies, carrying out, among other things, services of a social welfare nature with those of the DSW (the coordination of government services).

▷ To coordinate the activities of voluntary welfare organisations (the coordination of voluntary welfare work).[8]

However, before South Africa could have social workers, infrastructure and expertise for their training had to be put in place. Hence in 1929, the Pretoria branch of the voluntary association, the South African Women's Federation (*Suid-Afrikaanse Vrouefederasie*) decided to finance a Child Guidance Clinic at the Transvaal University College. In 1930, its name was changed to the School for Child Study and Social Welfare Training, the forerunner of the Department of Sociology and Applied Sociology at the University of Pretoria. Elsewhere, departments of social work were already established at the University of Cape Town in 1924 and the University of Witwatersrand in 1931.

However, the first direct formal request for trained workers on a national scale came from the Carnegie Commission of Enquiry in 1932. The Commission observed that:

> ... the scientific study of individual cases of destitution and proper differentiation between various types are essential. For this purpose, thoroughly trained social workers that are capable of making sound diagnoses will be required. There is a grave shortage of such social workers.[9]

Racist values of white supremacy informed residual social welfare in apartheid-South Africa. Mainly, social welfare services were remedial in focus and were not attuned to the development of human capacities of all South Africans, but rather only came into play, for the European populations, when the normal structures of supply, such as the family and the economic system broke down. The colonial-apartheid social welfare system was founded on four principles:

---

8    RSA, 1968:33.
9    Muller, 1968.

▷ racial division in the provision of welfare services

▷ a rejection of socialism

▷ a partnership between state and community

▷ movement from residential and therapeutic services towards community-based and preventative facilities.[10]

## Rise of the Apartheid State: Social Welfare and Social Work

When the National Party came to power in 1948, it institutionalised its policy of apartheid or racial segregation. However, this does not mean that racial injustice did not exist in South Africa. Apartheid, which the National Party introduced, was only codified through policies and legislated through various laws after 1948. Despite this, by 1947, moves had already been underway to formalise the welfare sector. Thus, the *Welfare Organisations Act 9 of 1947* and amended, Act 3 of 1949, provided a foundation for the apartheid state's future interventions into the welfare sector. The Act of 1947 required all welfare and other fund-raising organisations to register with a National Welfare Board, to prevent the duplication of services – albeit in the European sector only. An amendment was then passed in 1949 that made provision for the appointment of regional welfare boards to oversee the coordination of welfare services.

Social welfare mirrored the wider ideology of apartheid through its responses to human needs:

> In line with the Republic's policy of separate development for the different national groups, separate departments of State provide social amenities and services for each group. Thus, there are the Departments of Social Welfare and Pensions, for the White Nation, Bantu Administration, and Development, for the various Bantu nations, Indian Affairs for the Indian population groups and Coloured Affairs for the Coloured nation. Not only is this a logical development of the policy; it is the most practical way of ensuring efficiency and success, as it allows for welfare measures to be designed to take into account the diverse circumstances and needs of South Africa's diverse peoples.[11]

---

10     McKendrick & Dudas 1987 in McKendrick, 1987.

11     RSA, 1968:4.

Apartheid policies and legislation heavily impacted the social welfare system of the country, in turn, influencing social work education and social work practice. For instance, the *Republic of South Africa Constitution Act of 1983*, enabled social welfare to be based on race and meant that social workers could only operate in areas where the clients were from their racial or ethnic groups. State social welfare services were not only residual but fragmented:

> As the senior partner in a joint enterprise, the state assumes responsibility on a national basis for the country-wide planning and coordination of social welfare programmes and the formulation and administration of social legislation. Although organised at the national level, state-sponsored social welfare services are delivered regionally and locally. State welfare provision is not centred in any single government department, and major welfare functions are shared by four different departments, each serving the needs of different groups in the population. Thus, in the case of most statutory social services, white persons would receive service from the DSW and Pensions, 'coloured' (i.e., mixed-race) persons from the Department of Coloured Affairs, and black persons from the Department of Bantu Administration and Development. The nature of services offered by these four departments is generally similar and falls into the two categories of social welfare: security provision and the delivery of service programmes.[12]

## Formalisation of Social Security in South Africa

Before the formalisation of apartheid in 1948, four main population groups comprising Africans, Indians, whites, and people of mixed-race, often referred to as 'coloured' were already living apart. Through the promulgation of legislation such as the Native Urban Areas Act (1923), people were grouped according to population group, and Africans lived in the reserves.[13] Rapid urbanisation and industrialisation led to the disruption of socio-economic mechanisms for some population groups with no measures put in place to help the needy. The Dutch Reformed Church (NGK), state, and community sought solutions to the poor white problem as earlier mentioned. The church and state's interventions were aimed at supporting only poor whites and some support to coloureds, but not Indians and Africans. Africans were driven from their lands to work in white-owned farms and the mines. The election campaign by the Pact Government formed between the Labour Party (LP), and the National Party (NP) peddled the idea of a 'civilised' life

---

12    Hare & McKendrick, 1976:78.

13    Sagner, 2000.

for coloured and white people, meaning that whites and coloureds needed to live above the standard of Africans and Indians.[14] This idea appealed to most party supporters as it justified their superior economic, political and social status against the *Swartgevaar* or "menace of black physical, occupational and social mobility".[15] Therefore, whites and coloureds had to be paid higher wages for the same job as Africans and Indians, and lived a higher standard of life.[16] There was pressure on the government to protect the jobs of white and coloured workers, and the Minimum Wages Act was passed in 1925 immediately after the new Pact Government came to power in 1924.[17] The Minimum Wages Act (1925) effectively removed competition from black labourers and prevented them from joining or forming unions. This Act appealed to most coloureds, who helped the Pact Government to win the elections.

The Pact Government, led by General J.B.M. Hertzog, presented the James Collie's report on social security options to Parliament. This report outlined possible options, including universal access to social security to the exclusion of Africans; however, the government sought further options for addressing the poor white problem.[18] In 1926 the Pienaar Commission, tasked with investigating the feasibility of developing a comprehensive system to address the social support needs of citizens, recommended an old-age pension. This pension would benefit the aged and those who were permanently incapacitated or had no other means of providing for themselves.[19] The Pienaar Commission was further tasked with exploring the feasibility of a national social insurance pension to mitigate against the risk of old age, ill-health, disability, invalidity, and unemployment.[20] The NGK heavily influenced the Committee that prioritised the needs of poor whites. Other racial groups, such as Africans, and those of Indian descent were excluded from pensions. Following a presentation of the first Pienaar Commission report in 1927, recommending non-contributory, means-tested old age and invalidity pensions for 'civilised' persons, the Old Age Pension Act was passed in 1928, introduced in January 1929 and amended

---

14    Seekings, 2007; Van der Berg, 1997.

15    Seekings, 2007:375.

16    Bhorat, 2002.

17    Seekings, 2007.

18    Ibid.

19    Van der Berg, 1997.

20    Seekings, 2007.

in 1931, giving the State increased discretionary powers.[21] The aim was to rehabilitate the destitute and poor, and to eliminate the scourge of laziness, idleness and the poor's feeling of entitlement to state support. The role of the NGK was central not only in the provision of material benefits but also moral and religious instruction.[22]

The intention was to have minimal state involvement in the provision of social security, with an emphasis on the family to take primary responsibility for their destitute or needy. In 1929 the Carnegie Commission was tasked with investigating the causes of the poor white problem as articulated earlier. Some of its recommendations in 1932 shaped the provision of social welfare services in South Africa. Although this Commission recommended that professionally trained and salaried social workers establish social work services, it was the ACVV that shaped the profession of social work in South Africa.[23] Dr Hendrik Verwoerd, later the Minister of Native Affairs, working with his student and ACVV leader Erica Theron, established the Department of Sociology and Social Work (DSSW) at the University of Stellenbosch in 1932. It was anticipated that this DSSW would 'diagnose' social problems and respond appropriately using scientifically proven methods.[24] Because the focus of social security was to rehabilitate the needy into being productive members of society, the training and education of social workers mirrored this approach. Social work has historically emphasised individual, therapeutic methods to deal with social problems.[25]

Following a national congress in 1933, it was recommended that the ACVV work with the State and the church to address the poor white problem. The NGK held a national congress on the poor white question in 1934. Although all these stakeholders had different views, all had a vested interest in the provision of welfare services to poor whites. The church advocated a moral regeneration stance to welfare with the State and the ACVV working under its directives. While the ACVV based interventions on the needs of poor rural women, the State relied on the findings of investigations by bodies such as the Pienaar and Carnegie Commissions. The Department of Labour, established in 1924, managed social security; however, a separate section for social welfare was established

---

21    Sagner, 2000; Seekings, 2008.

22    Seekings, 2007.

23    Seekings, 2008.

24    Seekings, 2008; Sagner, 2000.

25    Mamphiswana & Noyoo, 2000.

in 1935. Its role was to provide welfare services in all local councils, and professionally trained social workers staffed it. A separate DSW was subsequently established in 1937, and by 1938 there were 30 trained social workers with this number doubling the following year.[26] Although private agencies employed social workers, the State heavily subsidised their salaries. The Department of Labour continued to pay social grants until 1958 when this function moved to the DSW and Pensions.[27] From the beginning, social grants were targeted at the needy and were not universal; a means test was carried out to ascertain the level of need.[28]

Further, to qualify for the old-age pension, the applicants had to demonstrate indigence and be 'deserving' of the grant. The applicant's income, assets and those of children were considered in the decision to award the pension.[29] The residual nature of pensions emphasised the obligation of family and kin in caring for their elderly parents, and the age of eligibility was 65 years for men and 60 years for women.[30] An invalidity pension scheme was introduced in 1937 to cater for the needs of employed people who suffered ill-health or had a disability; however, it was only available to whites.[31] If the person was not able to manage their pension, then another more responsible adult could be appointed to manage this money as they saw fit. The State had no means of monitoring use of the old-age pensions; however, the NGK had welfare committees with the power to make decisions on the provision of pensions and monitoring thereof. Initially, the NGK staffed and controlled these committees; however, state employees gradually gained more power and control. The old-age pension was directed at white and coloured persons, and only extended to Indians and Africans in 1944. Whites and coloureds were paid higher pensions than Indians who, in turn, were paid slightly higher than Africans. It was such that the benefit levels of Africans were less than one-tenth of those of whites, and the means test was far more stringent.[32]

---

26    Seekings, 2008.
27    Lund, 2009.
28    Seekings, 2007; Mckendrick, 1987.
29    Sagner, 2000.
30    McKendrick, 1987.
31    Seekings, 2007.
32    Van der Berg, 1997.

Pensions were introduced to assist the poor and vulnerable with the establishment of a DSW in 1937. Previously, the Blind Pensions Act was promulgated in 1936; in 1944, Africans and Indians were included. The invalidity pension scheme for white people who could not work as a result of disability was introduced in 1937, together with the Children's Act (1937).[33] This Act enabled the provision of material aid to families with many children to ensure an adjusted home life and to prevent social challenges as a result of poverty. This pension was meant to help rehabilitate children in conflict with the law, help those in need of care and supervise referred cases. Military pensions, dating from 1919, and war veterans' grants were instituted in 1941 to make provision for the elderly.[34]

Furthermore, family allowances were introduced in 1947 for the poor who had large families. It is significant to note that the pensions laws were amended in 1944 to include Africans and Indians. Nevertheless, they were not eligible for a non-contributory pension for disability and old age, albeit the maximum payment was less than one-third of the amount payable to whites.[35] Single mothers, widows and divorcees, those who were never married or women who had been abandoned by partners could claim child maintenance grants from the State (until 1997) if together with their children, did not have any means of support.[36] The Lund Commission reviewed the provision of this grant in 1995. It was phased out over three years until 1998 when the child support grant was introduced.

Following apartheid's institutionalisation under the NP in 1948, the Departments of Coloured and Indian Affairs were formally established in 1951 and 1961, respectively.[37] It should be mentioned that progressive forces, at the time, were determined to turn the tide of racial and economic oppression around for the advancement of all, especially the oppressed majority. More and more formations emerged with a diverging vision from that of the apartheid state, and that alone became a unifying force, seen with the anti-apartheid movement consisting of, among others: the African National Congress (ANC); the South African Indian Congress; and the South African Coloured People's Organisation. The fact that a fragmented social security system had predominantly favoured one racial group agitated the anti-apartheid movement. They envisioned a

---

33    Pauw, Mncube & UCT, 2007; Lund, 2009.

34    Van der Berg, 1997; Seekings, 2007.

35    Seekings, 2007.

36    Van der Berg, 1997; Khosa, 2013; Khosa & Kaseke, 2017.

37    Lund, 2009.

social security system that would equally cater for all racial groups. In 1955, the alliance gathered in Kliptown, a township, south-west of Johannesburg, where the Freedom Charter was agreed to and drafted. The Freedom Charter of 1955 articulated a vision of a non-racial and democratic society with much emphasis on issues of social security that, among others, included: health insurance, old-age pensions, unemployment benefits, disability grants and child grants. Despite the segregated nature of the social security system at that juncture, it was still residual, leaving families largely responsible for the wellbeing of their members.

Later, in the 1970s, specifically 1971, the Homelands or Bantustans were created as self-governing areas − each according to an ethnic group.[38] The *Bantu Homelands Citizens Act of 1970* allocated Homelands for different ethnic groups, each with its welfare department. The emphasis that no black person could apply for permanent residence in South Africa meant that they could only access pensions and grants in their Homelands. These departments were often chaotic, with no systems in place and generally inefficient.[39] Although there were amendments in legislation regarding the provision of welfare services, the beneficiaries were almost exclusively white. Later, the Republic of South Africa Constitution Act (1983) included coloureds and Indians, albeit all population groups were represented separately in Parliament with the House of Assembly (whites), the House of Representatives (coloured people) and the House of Delegates (Indians). Africans were not represented, and therefore, the Department of Education and Development Aid handled their affairs.[40]

The political upheavals of the 1960s and 1970s brought legislative change affecting social services, although welfare provision was still segregated with all race groups, except Africans, having political representation. Africans were represented in self-governing states with departments to provide social assistance. In 1978, important legislation was passed governing social work services. The Social and Associated Workers Act controlled social work and allied workers, the National Welfare Act monitored the registration of welfare organisations, and the Fund-Raising Act controlled the collection and receipt of donations from the public.[41] Other laws regulating the provision of services in the

---

38    McKendrick, 1987.

39    Lund, 2009; McKendrick, 1987.

40    McKendrick, 1987.

41    Ibid.

relevant sectors were the Aged Persons Act (1967), the Blind Persons Act (1968), the Child Care Act (1983), the Mental Health Act (1973), the Social Pensions Act (1973), and the Abuse of Dependent Producing Substances and Rehabilitation Centres Act (1971). McKendrick (1987) explains that the funding of non-contributory social welfare services came from personal tax.

In the 1980s, all race groups received social grants for old-age; war veterans; disability; the blind; those in special care; those receiving parent allowances; child maintenance; single parent; and foster care grants.[42] However, in unequal proportions, for instance, in 1986, Africans who formed 65 per cent of the population received only 20.9 per cent of welfare services, expenditure on coloureds who constituted 12 per cent of the population received 26.3 per cent, Indians 7.1 per cent and the expenditure on whites, who made up 19.5 per cent of the population, was 45.8 per cent. This allocation of the budget went towards the administrative costs, salaries, and capital expenditure on new facilities.[43] Workers with formal employment could claim social insurance based on a contributory system, for instance, the Unemployment Insurance Fund, civil servants' pensions, private retirement insurance, workmen's compensation aimed at employers making risk-related contributions to the accident fund.[44]

## Democratic South Africa and the Welfare Sector

In the late 1980s and early 1990s, the apartheid forces eventually succumbed to a host of pressures including political activities unfolding within and outside the country as well as international economic and political sanctions. In 1985, the Congress of South African Trade Unions (Cosatu) was formed, and in 1987 it endorsed the Freedom Charter for its labour friendly posture. After the unbanning of political organisations in 1990, Cosatu entered into negotiations with the African National Congress (ANC) and the South African Communist Party. Stemming from the ideological underpinnings of the Freedom Charter, the ANC and Cosatu developed a Reconstruction and Development Programme (RDP) that the ANC adopted as the basis for its manifesto leading to the first democratic elections in 1994. Mamabolo and Moyo (2014) reflect that the RDP

---

42    Van der Berg, 1997; McKendrick, 1987.
43    McKendrick, 1987.
44    Van der Berg, 1997.

was among the first comprehensive development programmes introduced in 1994. Through the RDP, the ANC-led government purported to create sustainable growth and development and thereby addressing unemployment, poverty, and inequality. One of its key strategies entailed the provision of basic social services including housing, education, healthcare and various forms of social grants.[45] In essence, the RDP was not only a broader policy framework but also an ideological reference that confirmed the political-historical continuity between the Freedom Charter and the prevailing circumstances of the new political dispensation.

In 1996, the country adopted a new Constitution thereby transitioning to an era of constitutional democracy. The new Constitution had a whole chapter dedicated to human rights encompassing socio-economic rights. Of importance, in the Bill of Rights, Section 27(1C) provides for the right to access appropriate social assistance according to the Republic of South Africa (1996).[46] The section provided the shift in social welfare policy, that was, up to that point, completely residual. Henceforth, South Africa would join the few countries worldwide, whose Constitution made it the government's duty to cater to the socio-economic needs of citizens.[47] The institutionalisation of welfare services in this manner, through the adoption of the RDP and promulgation of the Constitution, was at this point, viewed a resounding success, especially by the labour movement. The new government published a draft White Paper for Social Welfare in 1995, underpinned by principles of developmental social welfare, to consolidate a turn-around strategy in social welfare. The draft was subsequently formalised in 1997 as a guiding policy for social services in South Africa - a product of extensive consultations in the welfare sector.

The White Paper was significant because it broke with the apartheid era's inequitable, inappropriate, and undemocratic welfare policies. The approach adopted by the White Paper for Social Welfare (1997) was developmental social welfare or social development. It is important to note that various scholars have defined social development varyingly. Nevertheless, its under-girding principles remain relatively the same. Social development seeks the integration of social and economic dimensions of development as articulated by Midgely (1995). While the White Paper complemented the RDP, as a national policy framework, both policy documents were arguably compatible with the

---

45    Mamabolo & Moyo, 2014.

46    RSA, 1997.

47    RSA, 2003.

social development approach. Indeed, it can be noted that the former were informed by participatory approaches to development and saw citizens as playing active roles in their development. Equally important in the post-1994 era, were the efforts made to reform social security in order to establish a comprehensive social security system in 2000. This work is reflected in the Taylor Commission Report, named after the Chair of the aforementioned Commission.

Furthermore, after South Africa became a democratic country, social work education became crucial in propagating the new welfare system, believing it would impact positively on practice. Bourdieu and Wacquant (1992), emphasise the importance of professional guiding rules and value systems, referred to as Doxa. It was expected that these social work value systems, when put into practice, would promote human wellbeing "towards ever new possibilities of fuller and richer life individually and collectively".[48] Social work education institutions endeavoured to transform social work curricula. The government came on board, raising concerns about:

- the low recruitment of social work students

- low marks of social work students at universities

- the mismatch between education and practice

- the lack of international social work exchange programmes, and

- the high turnover of social workers.[49]

During this period, the Department of Public Service and Administration declared the social work profession a critical skill after the Department of Social Development's instigation, paving the way for the development of the Recruitment and Retention Strategy (RRS) for social workers in 2003.[50] The policy was aimed at curbing the shortage of social workers as a result of poor working conditions and the challenges in social work education.[51] The high turn-over of social workers had negative repercussions on the implementation of the government's Comprehensive HIV/Aids strategy.[52]

---

48   Freire, 1972:12.
49   RSA, 2003.
50   Ibid.
51   Ibid.
52   Ibid.

Through the RRS strategy, the government committed itself to provide scholarships for students enrolled in social work.[53] In an endeavour to increase the intake of social work students, the government encouraged social work education institutions to look closely at their selection criteria to ensure that it was "balanced with the need and demand for social workers in the country".[54] To this end, the admission of students into the social work degree dramatically improved over time. To further keep the profession relevant to global trends and those on the African continent, as well as the new dispensation, social work education institutions began improving their curricula, underlined in the RRS.[55] However, the curricula reformations progressed slow, as reflected in Noyoo's (2003) study, where most students testified to the largely rehabilitative and remedial theories, despite the students' interest in empowerment and people-centred initiatives.[56] Noyoo (2003) and Chikadzi and Pretorius (2011) argue that there is little that social work practice in the new dispensation would achieve without a major shift from the normative to reflect largely African epistemologies, cultures and traditions. It is interesting to note that Noyoo's (2003) proposition of Africanising both social work practice and education is regaining momentum, not only in the profession but across all disciplines.

The government has made strides in responding to the plight of the poor in the new dispensation. The introduction of the different types of grants is helping to cushion the beneficiaries from abject poverty, and an empowerment exit strategy will be more important to wean the beneficiaries off the system. The country's post-1994 legislative framework advances the government's commitment to democracy, an inclusive welfare system that is underpinned by a matching social work curriculum and responsive practice. The continued struggle for Africanising and indigenising social welfare, social work education and practice should be understood as a process that seeks to instil pride into the profession and foster hope and dignity in the black majority and poor South Africans.

The new dispensation has reiterated the need for coordinated planning and partnerships as this is essential for uplifting people's wellbeing, given the protracted entrenchment of apartheid that gave birth to deep poverty and marginalisation. The collaboration of

53    Ibid.
54    Ibid:27.
55    Patel, 2005; RSA, 2003.
56    Noyoo, 2003.

different professionals within the welfare sector and beyond has great benefits for fiscal planning, sharing of expertise and coordinated delivery of welfare services and broad service delivery. This network includes professionals from both the public and private sector and civil society, and this is a boost for nation-building and driving the country's social and economic agenda. Social work as a profession cannot survive without this collaboration.

## Transformation of the Social Welfare Sector and Social Work in South Africa since 1994

Social welfare policies and programmes that provide for cash transfers, social relief and empowerment, and developmental services ensure that people have adequate economic and social protection during times of unemployment, ill-health, maternity, childrearing, widowhood, disability, old age and so on. Social welfare programmes of this nature contribute to human resource development by enabling impoverished households to provide adequate care for their members, especially children and those who are vulnerable. When such programmes are combined with capacity building, people can be released from the poverty trap.[57]

The White Paper for Social Welfare (1997) was largely viewed as a turn-around strategy in redressing injustices of the past. While the government made significant strides in the implementation of the White Paper, especially in the light of social protection, the implementation has seemingly remained at a social treatment level and struggling to transform to a social development approach. This struggle has, at times, been attributed to lack of capacity and social workers' inability to comprehend the approach and how it could translate into viable programmes for which it was designed. Thus, this policy framework has not realised the objectives, envisioned from the onset.[58] On the other hand, barely two years after its adoption as a government policy framework, the RDP was abandoned owing to numerous challenges. Chiefly, due to many office-bearers' inexperience regarding their implementation skills, poor governance as well as overall fiscal constraints. As a result, the government's commitment to the RDP diminished as it had to focus on fiscal discipline. The government replaced the RDP with a less

---

57    RSA, 1997:5.
58    Midgley, 2014; Patel, 2014.

credible but conservative macroeconomic policy framework, the Growth Employment and Redistribution (GEAR) strategy. Many critics argued that GEAR was not inclusive and developed by a technical team.

Thus, the ideological underpinnings of GEAR were tilted towards achieving social development through economic growth. As such, the priorities of the government were skewed towards fiscal prudence and economic growth. GEAR limited the State's involvement in economic development and opened a way for privatisation of state-owned entities. Heintz (2003) argues: "A central tenet of the GEAR policy was to keep inflation low while liberalising financial markets."[59] The strategy implied that the State had to reduce spending on welfare services and social commitments, thereby derailing the agenda of social development. At this time, social workers, whose main task is to implement social welfare policy, were relegated to statutory service administrators while still working from a curative perspective. While economic growth was registered in subsequent years, the envisaged jobs were not created. Also, the levels of inequality and poverty were not reduced. GEAR did not meaningfully raise social development in the country. Some even dubbed it as an era of 'jobless growth'. The GEAR policy had to be complemented by new policies introduced from 2006-2011 such as: the Accelerated and Shared Growth Initiative for South Africa (ASGISA) and the New Growth Path (NGP). The two policy initiatives were, to some degree, aligned to the redistribution thrust of the RDP, albeit with an equal emphasis on economic growth.[60] Although there was regular maintenance of social security services, the developmental aspects remained significantly below par. Heintz (2003) indicates:

> ... to realise the real potential for growth, employment, and redistribution, economic policies should move away from market-friendly, inflation-targeting strategies but move towards a developmental, employment-targeting approach.[61]

In 1998, the Social Work Act of 1978 was amended to the *Social Service Professions Act 110 of 1978*, which signified an amalgamation of various pieces of social services legislation. Its promulgation gave provision for the establishment of the South African Council for Social Service Professions (SACSSP). In sharp contrast to the apartheid epoch, the Council was established chiefly to coordinate interests of social service professions

---

59    Heintz, 2003:3.

60    Mamabolo & Moyo, 2014; Heintz, 2003.

61    Heintz, 2003:6.

in the country. In other words, it meant that fragmentation of services in the sector would be halted in favour of a unified approach. The Council is charged with promoting a developmental approach to social welfare as opposed to the curative approach that characterised the previous epoch. While progressive policy instruments appear to be in place, the realisation of the ideals of developmental social welfare still seems far-fetched.

## Conclusion

The transition from residual social welfare to developmental social welfare is still unfolding. In 2011, the country adopted the National Development Plan (NDP) Vision 2030. Broadly, the plan seeks to enhance and widen political freedoms and human rights, unleash social opportunities arising from education and healthcare, develop a sound social security system as well as widen economic activities.[62] The implications of the plan, among others, are the mobilisation of people's efforts from all sectors, including the civil society towards the identified objectives. Notwithstanding the need for remedial services, the platform for developmental social work practice is more conducive than before.

---

62    NPC, 2011.

# References

Bhorat, H. 2002. A Universal Income Grant Scheme for South Africa:
An Empirical Assessment. In: G. Standing & M. Samson (eds.) *A Basic Income Grant for South Africa*. Cape Town: University of Cape Town Press.

Bourdieu, P. & Wacquant, L.J.D. 1992. *An invitation of reflexive sociology*. London: University of Chicago Press.

Bundy, C. 1992. Development and Inequality in Historical Perspective. In:
R. Scherie (ed). *Wealth or Poverty? Critical Choices for South Africa*. Oxford: Oxford University Press. pp.1-14.

Chikadzi, V. & Pretorius, E. 2011. Unhelpful help: Social work profession's response to mass poverty in South Africa. *Social Work/Maatskaplike Werk*, 47(3):39-56.

Freire, P. 1972. *Pedagogy of the Oppressed*. London: Penguin.

Fourie, J. 2006. *The South African poor white problem in the early 20th century: Lessons for poverty today*. Stellenbosch: University of Stellenbosch.

Hare, I. & McKendrick, B. 1976. South Africa: Racial divisions in social services. In:
D. Thursz & J.L. Vigilante (eds). *Meeting Human Needs, 2: Additional Perspectives from Thirteen Countries*. Beverly Hills, CA: SAGE Publications. pp.71-96.

Heintz, J. 2003. *Out of Gear? Economic Policy and Performance in Post-Apartheid South Africa*. Political Economy Research Institute (PERI) Research Brief, 1. [https://bit.ly/2H8hlWA]. (Accessed 2 September 2011).

Khosa, P. 2013. The Utilisation of Child Support Grant by Caregivers:
The Case of Ba-Phalaborwa Sub-District in the Limpopo Province of South Africa. Doctoral dissertation. Johannesburg, South Africa: University of the Witwatersrand.

Khosa, P. & Kaseke, E. 2017. The Utilisation of Child Support Grant by Caregivers:
The Case of Ba-Phalaborwa Sub-District in the Limpopo Province of South Africa. *Social Work/Maatskaplike Werk*, 53(3):356-367.

Lester, A. 1996. *From Colonisation to Democracy: A New Historical Geography of South Africa*. London: Tauris Academic Studies.

Mamabolo, M. & Moyo, T. 2014. The National Development Plan (NDP): A Comparative Analysis with the Reconstruction and Development Programme (RDP), the Growth, Employment and Redistribution (GEAR) programme and the Accelerated and Shared Growth Initiative (ASGISA). *Journal of Public Administration*, 49(3):946-959.

Mamphiswana, D. & Noyoo, N. 2000. Social Work Education in a Changing Socio-Political and Economic Dispensation: Perspectives from South Africa. *International Social Work*, 43(1):21-32.

Marais, H. 2001. *South Africa: Limits to change: The political economy of transformation.* Cape Town: University of Cape Town Press.

McKendrick, B.W. 1987. The development of social welfare and social work in South Africa. In: B.W. McKendrick (ed). *Introduction to Social Work and Social Welfare in South Africa.* Pretoria: HAUM. pp.5-19.

McKendrick, B.W. & Dudas, E. 1987. South Africa. In: J. Dixon (ed). *Social Welfare in Africa.* London: Croom Helm. pp.184-217.

Midgley, J. 1995. *Social Development: The developmental perspective in social welfare.* London: Sage Publications.

Midgley, J. 2014. *Social Development: Theory & Practice.* London: Sage Publications.

Muller, A. 1968. A historical review of university education for social work in South Africa. *Social Work/Maatskaplike Werk,* 4(1):3-10.

Noyoo, N. 2003. Social welfare policy, social work practice and professional education in a transforming society: South Africa. Doctoral dissertation. Johannesburg, South Africa: University of the Witwatersrand.

Noyoo, N. 2015. Social Development in Southern Africa. In: L. Calvelo, R. Lutz & F. Ross (eds). *Development and Social Work: Social Work of the South,* 6. Oldenburg: Paulo Freire Verlag. pp.167-185.

NPC (National Planning Commission). 2011. *The National Development Plan: Vision 2030 – Our future – make it work.* Pretoria: NPC.

Patel, L. 2005. *Social Welfare & Social Development in South Africa.* Cape Town: Oxford University Press.

Patel, L. 2014. Social workers shaping welfare policy in South Africa: The White Paper for Social Welfare and Lessons for Policy Practice. In: CSD Perspective. St. Louis, MO: Washington. pp.14-23.

Pauw, K., Mncube, L. & UCT (University of Cape Town). 2007. *Expanding the Social Security Net in South Africa: Opportunities, Challenges and Constraints.* Cape Town: Development Policy Research Unit, UCT. [https://bit.ly/315ZwPh]. (Accessed 2 May 2011).

RSA (Republic of South Africa). 2003. *Recruitment and Retention Strategy for Social Workers in South Africa.* Pretoria: Government Printing Works.

RSA. Department of Information. 1968. *CARE: Welfare Services for South Africans.* Pretoria: Government Printing Works.

RSA. Department of Social Development. 2013. *Framework for social welfare services.* Pretoria: Government Printing Works.

RSA. DSW&P (Department of Social Welfare and Pensions). 1962. *Report of the Interdepartmental Committee of Inquiry into the Treatment of the Alcoholic.* Pretoria: Government Printing Works.

RSA. Department of Welfare and Population Development. 1997. *The White Paper for Social Welfare.* Pretoria: Government Printing Works.

Sagner, A. 2000. Ageing and Social Policy in South Africa: Historical Perspectives with Particular Reference to the Eastern Cape. *Journal of Southern African Studies*, 26(3):523-552.

Seekings, J. 2007. *The Carnegie Commission and the backlash against welfare state-building in South Africa, 1931-1937.* Cape Town: Centre for Social Science Research, University of Cape Town.

Seekings J. 2008. The Carnegie Commission and the Backlash against Welfare State-Building in South Africa, 1931-1937. *Journal of Southern African Studies*, 34(3):515-537.

Van der Berg S. 1997. South African Social Security under Apartheid and Beyond. *Development Southern Africa*, 14(4):481-503.

# 10

## TRACING THE ORIGINS OF SOCIAL WELFARE AND SOCIAL WORK IN SWAZILAND (ESWATINI)

*Lungile Mabundza*

## Introduction

The Kingdom of Swaziland (now known as Eswatini) is a landlocked country in Southern Africa, with the Republic of South Africa and Mozambique forming its borders. Swaziland has a land area of just 17 364 km$^2$, making it the second smallest country in Africa (after the Republic of the Gambia).[1] According to the 2017 census results, Swaziland has a population of 1 093 238.[2] In the first part of the nineteenth-century parts of Africa south of the Limpopo River experienced a lot of turmoil and nation-building wars, known as *Mfecane* in SiSwati/Zulu languages. Among the powerful names of this period were Shaka, king of the Zulus; Sobhuza, king of the Swazis; and Moshoeshoe, king of the Basotho.[3] During this period, the power of the monarchy was ensured by his prerogative to appoint representatives in all regions, and also, by establishing a system of regiments which periodically assembled at the king's royal residences and directly paid homage and allegiance to him [king] not the local chiefs, although they were followers of their respective chiefs in the different regions (Magagula, 1988; Kuper, 1976).

---

1    Davies, O'Meara & Dlamini, 1985.
2    UNFPA, 2017.
3    Magagula, 1988.

Before colonialism, Swaziland had a rich history of a micro-nation, and the Swazi people created informal networks that sustained and cared for them.[4] The kinship institution was significant to the survival of the people of Swaziland. As a nation, Swazis had their cultural stories, practices, and story-telling traditions; meaningful and rich in transmitting culture from one generation to the next. Swazi people lived in harmony, and deviation from the norm was sanctioned.[5] The infrastructure, in use at the time, met the economic, social and political needs of the nation.[6] From time immemorial, Swaziland was under the leadership of a king. Life in rural Swaziland and "hereditary succession, age as a basis of status and rigid adherence to custom were the characteristics of this kingdom".[7]

The extended family was significant in maintaining the acceptable welfare standards of its members. As the main institution tasked with providing psychological, emotional, physical, economic, and social support and moral upliftment to all members, the extended family was a revered institution in Swaziland.[8] Through the extended family, all members considered weak or vulnerable were protected from social exclusion and discrimination.[9] The preoccupation of the extended family was ensuring food security to avoid any form of deprivation; traditionally no child was an orphan because of the belief that 'it takes a village to raise a child' and so familial adoptions were common as members fulfilled their duties to ensure that all children grew well. In many ways, children were a surety and social security in old age, and therefore the welfare of children was the kinship network's concern. In a similar vein, everyone highly esteemed and honoured older persons.

When Swaziland was colonised, the indigenous forms of social welfare and security were significantly compromised. One of the significant deeds of the colonialists was to tamper with the original boundaries of the kingdom; an intrusion that weakened the kingship's strong base.[10] With a shrinking territory and colonial masters imposing ridiculous rules, the standard of social welfare was significantly compromised. The British managed to

---

4   Maathai, 2009.
5   Ibid.
6   Apt & Blavo, 1997.
7   Nukunya, 1992:7-8.
8   Kreitzer, 2004.
9   Kumado & Gockel, 2003.
10   Ray, 1986.

impose taxes on the indigenous people, compelling men to work for colonial masters to pay 'hut taxes'. These taxes imposed on the indigenous people were so harsh that men were forced to migrate to cities or work for the colonial masters.[11] These and other developments severely impacted the ability of the extended family to provide adequate welfare for its members. The monarchy was not spared as colonialists' manipulation continued. The British were not interested in the welfare of locals; there were no family-oriented policies and programmes.

## Formal Social welfare/Security

Even though social welfare or security is not a new phenomenon in the Swazi society, yet "social security schemes can never hope to carry the full burden of achieving social equality or raising the general standard of living. At present, the system favours urban moderate- and high-income earners".[12] With the significant breakdown of the family structure and an increase of people migrating to urban areas, the British began to use social welfare programmes to attract more labourers, especially men.[13] As more men migrated to the cities, women were pressured to maintain and provide social protection to the rest of the kinship. It can be argued that these factors (urbanisation, migration, and education) contributed to the weakening of the indigenous social welfare /social safety net and these cracks are still visible decades post-Independence. Institutions such as social insurance are examples of formal social security.

Missionaries introduced Christianity in Swaziland in the latter part of the nineteenth century, and there were clashes between Christianity and ancestry worship. Christianity further sowed the first seeds of a new social and economic order through education. "The indigenous missionary workers, catechists, lay preachers, deacons and priests were the backbone of the missionary enterprise. With them, the white missionaries would have achieved nothing".[14] Reverend James Allison came to Swaziland in 1884, leading the Methodist Church after king Sobhuza I had sent a delegation to Thaba Nchu to ask for missionaries to come to Swaziland to offer education and the gospel. The king acted on

---

11    Nukunya, 1992.

12    Asamoah & Nortey, 1987.

13    Kuper, 1947.

14    Jones, 1957:181.

his grandfather Somhlolo's earlier dream; a vision of white people coming out of the sea. In one hand, they had a book (*umculu*), and in the other, they had money (*indilinga*).[15] Then his aunt advised him not to accept the money but the book. The king allocated the reverend land at Mahamba, in southern Swaziland, where the community under the command of their chief built the first Methodist church.[16]

King Sobhuza II later confirmed that these fears (towards the white settlers) were not just limited to the commons when he warned the Swazis to take the good from the whites and discard what was perceived as bad.[17] The king went on to establish government schools with the sole purpose to accommodate Swazi culture and traditions in their curriculum, for instance, the Swazi National High School. In 1948 the king organized a Zion group, an indigenous church that accommodates worshippers who maintained their traditional beliefs. The king's actions indicated that the total disregard of the Swazi way of life, as Western Christianity advocated, was frowned upon and these actions counteracted the missionaries' preaching to the Swazis to discarding their beliefs. Maimela (1985) asserts:

> Africans reluctantly broke ties with the African transitional religious practices. The religion wedded in their worldview, in which salvation was traditionally understood within the religious practices and cultural norms. Therefore, traditional leaders tried to exert force to accommodate traditional rituals.[18]

Landau (1995) observed that the missionaries did not have a solid understanding of Swazi worldview and values, and, did not realise that their preaching was tainted with Norwegian values that did not have any meaning in the Swazi context.[19] Those few Swazis who embraced religion, as the missionaries portrayed, became strangers in their own country; they were isolated, and the community viewed them as deviants because they broke Swazi values, norms and religious heritage.[20] The influx of the white settlers resulted in a new form of dispensation; the few people to be recruited into formal employment were either sent abroad to further their education or to work in South African mines while the missionaries were working hard in ushering development into

---

15    Matsebula, 1987:41.

16    Ibid.

17    Kuper, 1972.

18    Maimela, 1985:72.

19    Landau, 1995:231.

20    Kasanene, 1983:16.

the Swazi society. The few people in formal employment were also eligible for formal social security or social welfare. Most importantly, even the civil service jobs targeted men while women were left to take over their roles (minding the homes, cattle, ploughing and upkeep of children while the husbands were away).[21]

Consequently, education was ushered in through the religious apparatus. The value systems the Judea-Christians introduced were a direct assault on the familial value system. Religious values were against the indigenous modes of worship and beliefs, and this triggered clashes between the settlers and the indigenous people.[22] In the end, some of the Swazi people embraced the values of the white settlers creating a further rift between the different generations. Furthermore, those individuals who embraced the education and religious values of the settlers were ostracised because they had accepted something different from the indigenous beliefs.[23]

The Judeo-Christianity value system, caused more damage to the already destabilised institution of the family, resulting in a significant shift from the indigenous way of life to an ambiguous one that challenged the status quo. European religion supplanted indigenous African religion, not by any means a smooth transition – there was resistance as the two different cultures and religious values clashed and collided, confusing the populace. These changes altered life in many ways; in particular, the family was undermined. Furthermore, the Swazi nation's sovereignty was greatly compromised and resulted in the king being demoted to the rank of a paramount chief.[24] These trends led to structural changes in African economies, including increases in commodification, wage labour, industrialisation, urbanisation, male migrant labour, and female involvement in subsistence agriculture.[25] These features of late colonial 'development' were associated with changes in patterns of poverty, with lack of access to land emerging in many areas as a second significant driver of poverty, alongside lack of (access to) labour.

What is noteworthy during this period is that the British policies were built on the foundation of the British Poor Laws [1901] – where the poor were classified as either

---

21    Mkhonza & Kanduza, 2003.
22    Vilane, 1986.
23    Ibid.
24    Magagula, 1988.
25    Bevan, 2004.

deserving or undeserving poor. In the end, the people perceived as abled-bodied were encouraged to seek formal employment rather than expect to receive handouts from the State. In contrast, those seen as deservingly poor were supported, such as the aged, disabled, and young children. This approach was extended to Swaziland. For example, old age institutions were never introduced in most British colonies because of the strong belief that the family was capable of providing care to its people (Illife, 1987). For a long time in Swaziland, the missionaries were the conduit for formal welfare for the needy in communities and provided food, medicine and education.

Even though the history of social welfare in Swaziland coincides with the development of formal welfare systems through colonial regimes, it is noteworthy that social welfare existed before the colonial era. It was after the indigenous structures of governance and welfare were tampered with that more formalised structures of social welfare provision emerged. According to Kaseke, the origins of formal social welfare services in Swaziland can be traced back to 1952, with efforts to formalise social welfare services beginning during the colonial era but expanding after Independence.[26] At that time, Local Administration was responsible for providing social welfare, and care services, and later this function moved to the Ministry of Home Affairs. The Social Welfare Department was transferred to the Ministry of Health in 1996, having been gazetted under the Legal Gazette 147 and renamed the Ministry of Health and Social Welfare.[27] In 2008, the Department of Social Welfare (DSW) was moved from the Ministry of Health and Social Welfare to the Deputy Prime Minister's Office where it is currently located. Some of the vulnerable groups the DSW focuses on are orphaned and vulnerable children, the elderly, and persons with disabilities. The services provided include public assistance to the destitute; maintenance payments; foster care; adoption; military pension; family counselling; and disaster relief.[28]

## Contemporary Trends

At Independence in 1968, Swaziland maintained both the traditional and Westminster systems of governance, resulting in a dual system of government. "The 'Westminster'

---

26    Mkhonza & Kanduza, 2003.

27    Kaseke, 1997.

28    Ibid.

system comprises of a bicameral Parliament, a judiciary, and an executive". Members of Parliament are elected through the voting process at the different constituencies, and the monarchy appoints some. "The traditional system of governance consists of traditional institutions of local government called *Tinkhundla* (in singular form *inkhundla*) in the rural areas". The monarchy is at the apex of both political governance structures. Swaziland is divided into four administrative regions – Hhohho, Manzini, Lubombo and Shiselweni, administered by four regional administrators.

This form of governance relies on, among others, a Queen Mother. The significance of the Queen Mother is that she can assume the role of leading the country in case the king dies.[29] She is the biological mother of the king and thereby advises and counsels him.

> Traditionally, the role of the king at the divisional level was to administer the division, look after the spiritual, physical and emotional welfare of the people; maintain law and order, consult with elders, lead the army into battle and act as a mediator between ancestors and the clans.[30]

On the other hand, the role of the Queen Mother is that of mothering the nation; she is the she-elephant (*indlovukati*); she was [and still is] responsible for the social welfare and upkeep of the Swazi nation. The Queen Mother always plays the role of the social welfare officer (SWO) and social worker. In the Queen Mother's courts, lots of social issues are reported because she is seen as the problem solver and solution giver. She is seen as the liaison between the people and social welfare and care services and ensures that there is fairness in the distribution of resources. Everybody pays attention whenever she gives directives, and her authority in society is quite significant. The Queen Mother also acts as a role model for women and girls. She has spearheaded several initiatives, allied to social work and intended to empower women. For instance, the Old Age Grant can be attributed to her efforts in trying to influence policies on behalf of the aged. There are social gatherings where women are involved, enabling them to socialise, rejuvenate and strengthen bonds. Most of these initiatives are meant to benefit women economically and socially. Even though the Queen Mother is not a formally trained social worker, her activities lean to what professional social workers do. In this regard, if Swaziland wants the social work profession to take root, perhaps there is a need to create some synergies

---

29    Blavo, 2003.

30    Busia, 1951.

between the Queen Mother and social workers. As Kreitzer (2004) puts it: "... queen mothers need social workers and social workers need queen mothers."

All the historical forces mentioned earlier affected the social work profession in Swaziland, and the country has struggled to professionalise the social work profession. Social workers constantly struggle to be a voice for the voiceless and vulnerable populations. The challenge began at the inception of social work in Africa, taking place during the colonial era, where the church focused mainly on the deserving poor. "Social workers are struggling to empower clients and are fighting against the negative efforts to neo-liberal economic policies including cutbacks in health, education and welfare".[31] Social work education in most of the African context continues to borrow heavily from the West.

Nonetheless, African social work should have its roots in the continent; indigenous and not imported.[32] Instead, most social welfare policies influencing the social work profession:

➤ fail to take a holistic view of human conditions;

➤ neglect that politics matters in the formulation of policies; and

➤ ignore the good practices in indigenous structures and approaches.[33]

In this chapter, social work is defined as:

> ... a practice-based profession and an academic discipline that promotes social change and development, social cohesion, and the empowerment and liberation of people. Principles of social justice, human rights, collective responsibility and respect for diversities are central to social work. Underpinned by theories of social work, social sciences, humanities and indigenous knowledge, social work engages people and structures to address life challenges and enhance well-being.[34]

For several years Swaziland did not have a Bachelor of Social Work (BSW) degree, and that meant anyone interested in social work had to receive training from countries such as South Africa, Botswana, Lesotho and Zimbabwe. Social work faces challenges in Swaziland because mobilising relevant people to go through the process of examining

---

31    Sewpaul, 2006.
32    Asamoah, 1995:223.
33    Ibid.
34    IFSW, 2014:2.

assumptions, critiquing, and building a culturally relevant social work curriculum is difficult. Therefore, taking the best of Western theory and practice and balancing it with African indigenous knowledge and traditions is an important step in this process.[35] Similarly, this approach is needed in the formulation of social welfare legislation and policies and programmes in Swaziland. Despite these challenges, Swaziland has come a long way in professionalising and training social work professionals. In 2014-2015, the University of Eswatini (or UNESWA; formerly known as the University of Swaziland), as well as other tertiary institutions, introduced the BSW degree. The importation of Western social work theories and knowledge has helped in the introduction of social work programmes. According to Kreitzer (2004), the rationale behind this was that theory and practice are universal and transferable and that a Western social work curriculum is the best in the world. Three years into the programme, there are warning signs that theories and methods transplanted directly from the West might present some implementation issues for the future. A direct transplant of the Eurocentric social work programme disregards the cultural, political, and social differences that exist between the developed world and a developing country such as Swaziland. The inability of the education system to cultivate logical reasoning and critical thinking reflects some of the Western concepts' challenges to translate into the local context.

Therefore, Swaziland needs a culturally relevant social work training and practice for social workers to be relevant, effective and fill the gap the social work cadre's lack of proper training created. Furthermore, social workers in touch with the issues vulnerable populations face, are more desirable and more likely to respond efficiently to the needs on the ground. It can be proposed that Western education was neither offered to Africans to encourage critical thinking, nor was it meant to influence critical consciousness and awareness, but instead, it was presented as a tool for further enslavement.[36]

Indeed, colonial tertiary education was crafted to let African children memorise and regurgitate what they learnt – nothing more and nothing less. This 'enslavement of the mind' was a tool used [and still] used to control how Africans perceive themselves as people. This situation succeeded in producing students, to be 'black from the outside but white on the inside [so-called coconuts]'.[37] In this mind-set, anything from the West

---

35    Kreitzer, 2004.

36    Kreitzer, 2004.

37    Van Hook, 2004.

is ideal and indigenous knowledge is not cultivated. This mind enslavement and other reasons are signposts for Swazi scholars and educators to come up with learning material, relevant to the context of a developing country. There should be a desire to develop case studies using local examples for students to begin to assimilate the issues that they will face once they complete their education.

## Prospects and Way Forward

The social work profession places emphasis on the commitment to fight all social injustices, especially in Swaziland, where the gap between the haves and have-nots continues to widen. The lack of a comprehensive social security system has resulted in discrimination and marginalisation of poor, vulnerable populations. Swaziland needs a universal and comprehensive programme, informed by the needs of older persons and other vulnerable members of society. Providing services that uphold the dignity and worth of individuals can enhance the poor's overall outlook of life. Swaziland needs to appreciate the fact that addressing some of the social problems will demand a multitier approach and coordination between different stakeholders. There is an urgent need for government to support the new BSW degree through sponsorship of all social work students as one way to increase enrolment for the programme. Instead of falling into the same trap as other social work programmes in Africa, Swaziland as a latecomer has an opportunity to come up with a programme that celebrates Africanism, and an evidence-based programme, relevant to the Swazi society. This opportunity is a huge challenge, but a decision must be made.

As the social work and social welfare fields take root in Swaziland, there is a crucial need to use African material and, where possible, instructors must take steps towards publishing papers that present social work in the context of Swaziland. The issue of lack of African focused textbooks is another issue that makes it difficult to teach African-based social work. Teaching materials (from the African and Swazi perspectives) are not easily available; technologically equipped classrooms to make it easy to do demonstrations, watch videos and do role plays are few and compromise the quality of the teaching and learning experiences in this newly established programme. There is an even greater need for connecting the indigenous approach to social work and welfare practised by the Queen Mother and Eurocentric inspired social welfare and social work practice. Swaziland, with its vibrant culture, stands at the polar opposite to the Eurocentric welfare approach and therefore finding synergies for the two approaches is the key to a smooth infusion of the old and new way of teaching and practising social work. Swaziland does not have to reinvent the wheel; she can use evidence generated in other African countries where Queen Mothers have been partners in the formalisation of the social work profession.

Currently, social work is seen as an activity that just anyone can do. Thus, the need to establish professionalism is paramount, and there is still a lot to be done. Swaziland needs to ask itself if it will adopt the Western approach to social work, welfare and social development or a hybrid that will be a foundation for the formal social welfare system in Swaziland. There is a need to make this profession relevant to the development objectives of Swaziland since social workers:

▷ enhance the social functioning of individuals, groups, families, organisations and communities

▷ link clients to resources

▷ improve the operations of social service delivery networks, and

▷ promote social justice throughout the development of social policy.[38]

These roles seem quite similar to those of the community Social Welfare Officer (SWO) which the Queen Mother traditionally performed. Both the social workers and the Queen Mother are involved in social welfare, healthcare, housing, schools, workplaces, corrections, and community development. Thus, the question of how the profession can liaise with the Queen Mother to gain access to the community, remains. As it is, there is a gap in terms of how social workers in the communities should handle domestic abuse cases. If the police are called to a domestic abuse case in communities, they normally ask that the family tries to reconcile the two parties and then if all fails, arrests are made. In other words, the indigenous social security structures are still viewed as vibrant and in existence. Therefore, if social workers are not conversant with all these cultural issues, they might feel ineffective and incompetent, especially when their interventions clash with cultural expectations.

---

38    Dubois & Miley, 2005:11.

A question that is beyond this chapter is whether or not Swaziland should embrace an integrated social welfare approach where it borrows the good from the West and incorporates traditional approaches to have well-balanced curricula and relevant and vibrant social workers within the context of Swaziland.

## Conclusion

In this chapter, it was argued that colonialism undermined the indigenous social security and welfare mechanisms that had been there from time immemorial in Swaziland. Restoration of these systems has proven to be an uphill battle for Swaziland because of lack of formal social security coverage to protect people from day-to-day hardships. It is worth mentioning that the British system of governance compromised a sovereign self-governing state in the pre-colonial era, resulting in a significant shift in the roles of the State with the advent of the coming of the white settlers in the nineteenth century. The hut tax incapacitated the Swaziland state and rendered it vulnerable to the dictates of its colonial masters. The focus shifted from conquering territories to a position where the kingdom was worried about its survival. Even though the British's indirect rule over Swaziland did not completely destroy the indigenous institutions, it resulted in an underdeveloped social welfare system, favouring those in paid employment. Such a system exposed women and children to poverty because men had to migrate in search of formal employment. This situation indirectly relegated women to a lesser status compared to men who now had formal employment and had some form of formal protection.

Furthermore, Swaziland needs to consider strengthening family policies, which will ensure that all family members are protected throughout the lifecycle. Decades post-Independence, many Swazis are living in poverty, and most are elderly, orphans and vulnerable children and people living with disabilities. One of the notable weaknesses in the implementation of the DSW programmes is the limited number of legislative frameworks backing the social welfare programmes being implemented. With the introduction of the BSW degree, the issues of shortage of qualified technical and support staff may be responded to in a few years. Between now and then, it will be key for the DSW to create social work posts which qualified social workers can fill. Also, the on-the-job training for the SWOs who do not qualify to study social work is needed. They can be viewed as para social workers and can be the face of social work in Swaziland because of their years of experience. Swaziland needs to strengthen the social welfare workforce strategically for efficiency and effectiveness.

Coordination of sector players is equally weak as a robust mechanism for this is absent, both at the national and regional level. Coupled with this is the absence of a clear referral system to appropriate service provision, leading to a duplication of effort and wastage of resources. Therefore, Swaziland needs to design welfare and care programmes to address needs for all and move towards a comprehensively integrated system for social welfare provision in the country. All services and service providers need to coordinate their activities for effectiveness, efficiency, and timeliness of services.

Tertiary institutions need to come up with curricula that addresses the developmental needs and challenges the country faces. For instance, the impact of cultural issues on practice need to be clear for students to address them in the field. The goals of tertiary institutions should be enhancing research to assist policymakers in coming up with evidence-based policies and programmes. On the other hand, curricula must benefit from field experiences to address real issues on the ground adequately. The country needs to educate people to uphold and respect the traditional systems that currently exist in the communities, families, and society at large. If such indigenous practices are neglected, social work professionals will continue to be inefficient and irrelevant in whatever they do. There is an opportunity to present themselves as an extension of the Queen Mother's traditional SWO's role, making her the channel to introduce social work to the chiefs and communities, to avoid resistance whenever social workers undertake their different roles in the communities and countrywide. Momentarily the country is in the process of finalising a new White Paper on Social Development.

# References

African Development Bank. 2013. Kingdom of Swaziland. Country Strategy Paper 2014-2018. *Southern African Regional Resource Centre* (SARC).

Apt, N.A. & Blavo, E.Q. 1997. Ghana. In: N.S. Mayadas, T.D. Watts & D. Elliot (eds). *International handbook on social work theory*. Westport: Greenwood Press.

Asamoah, Y.W. 1995. Africa. In: T.D. Watts, D. Elliott & N.S. Mayadas (eds). *International handbook on social work theory*. Westport: Greenwood Press.

Asamoah, Y.W. & Nortey, D.N.A. 1987. Ghana. In: J. Dixon (ed). *Social welfare in Africa*. Beckenham: Croom Helm. pp.22-68.

Bailey, C. & Turner, J. 2002. Social Security in Africa. A brief review. *Journal of Aging Social Policy*, 14(1):105-14.

Bevan, P. 2004. The Dynamics of Africa's In/Security Regimes. In: Gough, I., Wood, G., Barrientos, A., Bevan, P., Davis, P. & Room, G. *Insecurity and Welfare Regimes in Asia, Africa and Latin America*. Cambridge: Cambridge University Press.

Blavo, E.Q. 2003. Personal Interview, 23 May, Accra, Ghana.

Busia, K.A. 1951. *The position of the chief in the modern political system of Ashanti*. London: Oxford University Press.

Davies, R.H., Omeasa, D. & Dlamini, D. 1985. *Kingdom of Swaziland: A Profile*. London: Zed Book.

Dror, Y. 1974. *Public Policy Making Re-Examined*. Bedfordshire: Leonard Hill.

DuBois, B. & Miley, K.K. 2005. *Social Work: An empowering profession*. 5th Edition. New York: Pearson Education.

Dzobo, N.K. 1981. The indigenous African theory of knowledge and truth: Example of the Ewe and Akan of Ghana. *Phenomenology in Modern African Studies*, 13(1&2):85-102.

Hickey, S. 2005. T*hinking about the Politics of Social Protection in Africa: Towards a Conceptual and Theoretical Approach*. Manchester: Institute for Development Policy and Management.

IFSW (International Federation of Social Workers). 2004. *Proposals for a new ethical document*. Presented at the IFSW General Meeting, Adelaide, Australia, 29 September-1 October.

Iliffe, J. 1987. *The African Poor: A history*. Cambridge: Cambridge University Press.

Jones, S.E. 1957. *Christian Maturity*. Nashville: Abingdon.

Kasanene, P. 1983. *Ecumenical Progress in Swaziland: 1880-1982*. PhD Dissertation. University of Cape Town.

Kasanene, P. 1993. *Religion in Swaziland*. Braamfontein: Starkville Publishers.

Kaseke, E. 1991. Social work practice in Zimbabwe. *Journal of Social Development in Africa*, 6(1):33-45.

Kaseke, E. 1997. A Situation Analysis of Social Welfare Services in Swaziland. A paper presented at the Social Welfare Stakeholder's Meeting, Nhlangano, February.

Kaseke, E. 2001. Social work education in Zimbabwe: Strengths and weaknesses, issues and challenges, *Social Work Education*, 20(1):101-9.

Kreitzer, L.M. 2004a. Indigenization of social work education and practice: A participatory action research project in Ghana. Doctoral dissertation. Calgary, Alberta, Canada: University of Calgary.

Kreitzer, L.M. 2004b. Queen Mother and social workers: A potential collaboration between traditional authority and social work in Ghana. *Chieftain, 1*.

Kreitzer, L.M. 2012. Social Work in Africa: Exploring Culturally Relevant Education and Practice in Ghana. Calgary: University of Calgary Press.

Kumado, K. & Gockel, A.F. 2003. *A study on social security in Ghana*. Accra: Friedrich Ebert Stiftung.

Kuper, H. 1947. *An African Aristocracy: Rank among the Swazis*. London: Oxford University Press.

Kuper, H. 1972. A royal ritual in a changing political context. *Cahiers d'Etudes Africaines*, 12(48):593-615.

Kuper, H. 1978. *Sobhuza II: Ngwenyama and King of Swaziland*. Duckworth: London.

Kuper, H. 1986. *The Swazi: A South African Kingdom*. New York: CBS College Publishing.

Landau, P. 1995. *The Realm of the Word: Language, Gender and Christianity in a Southern African Kingdom*. Portsmouth: Heinemann.

Maathai, W. 2009. *The challenge for Africa: A new vision*. United Kingdom. Heinemann.

Magagula, P.Q. 1988. *Swaziland's relations with Britain and South Africa since 1968*. Doctoral thesis. Durhan, England: Durham University. [http://etheses.dur.ac.uk/6640/].

Maimela, S.S. 1985. Faith and ideologies. *Missionalia*, 13(2):88-89.

Marzui, A. 1983. Francophone Nations and English-Speaking States: Imperial Ethnicity and African Political Formation. In: D. Rothchild & V. Olorunsola (eds). *State versus Ethnic Claims: African Policy Dilemmas*. Boulder, Co: Westview Press.

Matsebula, J.S.M. 1987. *A history of Swaziland*. Cape Town: Longman.

Mkhonza, S.T. & Kanduza, A.M. 2003. Issues in the economy and politics of Swaziland since 1968. Kwaluseni, Eswatini: Organization for Social Science Research in Eastern and Southern Africa Swaziland Chapter, University of Swaziland.

Midgley, J. 1981. *Professional imperialism: Social work in the Third World*. London: Heinemann.

Midgley, J. 1999. Social development in social work: Learning from global dialogue. In: C. Ramanathan & R. Links (eds.), *All our futures: Principles & resources for social work practice in a global era*. Belmont, CA: Brooks/Cole. pp.193-205.

Mouton, P. 1975. *Social security in Africa: Trends, problems and prospects*. Geneva: International Labour Organisation.

Mupedziswa, R. 2005. Challenges and prospects of social work services in Africa. In: J.C. Okeibunor & E.E. Anugwom (eds). *The social sciences and socioeconomic transformation in Africa*. Nsukka, Nigeria: Great AP Express Publications. pp.271-317.

Mzizi, J. 2004. *Religion and Politics in Swaziland: The contributions of Dr J.B. Mzizi*. Cape Town: African Sun Media.

Mzizi, J. 2005. *Strengthening parliamentary democracy in SADC countries. Swaziland country report: The South African Institute of International Affairs*. Pretoria. South Africa.

Northrup, D. 1988. *Beyond the bend in the river: African labour in eastern Zaire, 1865-1940*. Athens, Ohio: Ohio University Press.

Nukunya, G.K. 1992. *Traditional and change in Ghana: An introduction*. Accra: Ghana Universities Press.

Nyawo, S. 2004. *The early encounter between the missionaries: the establishment of the Evangelical Church in Swaziland, 1894-1950*. Masters thesis. University of KwaZulu Natal: Pietrmaritzbug.

Obeng, E.E. 1988. *Ancient Ashanti chieftaincy*. Tema: Ghana Publishing Company.

Philip, A. 1989. *The enigma of colonialism: British policy in West Africa*. London: James Currey.

Rattrap, R.S. 1929. *Ashanti law and constitution*. Oxford: Clarendon Press.

Ray, D.J. 1986. *Ghana: Politics, economics and society*. Boulder: Lynne Rienner.

Sewpaul, V. 2006. The Global-Local Dialectic: Challenges for African Scholarship and Social Work in a Post-Colonial World. *British Journal of Social Work*, 36(3):419-34.

Smith, L. 2008. South African social work education: Critical imperatives for social change in the post-apartheid and post-colonial context. *International Social Work*, 51(3):371-83.

United Nations. 1958. *Training for social work: Third international survey*. New York: United Nations Department of Economic and Social Affairs.

UNFPA (United Nations Population Fund). 2017. *African Union Roadmap on harnessing Swaziland's demographic trends*. Mbabane: UNFPA.

Vanbalkam, W.D. & Goddard, T. 2007. Sustainable and dynamic development. In: G. Anderson & A. Wenderoth (eds.), *Facilitating change: Reflections on six years of education development programming in challenging environments*. Montreal: Universalia Management Group. pp.253-267.

Van Hook, J. 2004. A decomposition of trends in poverty among children of immigrants. *Demography*, 41(4):649-670.

Vilane, J. 1986. Ideology and Ideological Struggles in Swaziland. In: J. Daniel and M.F. Stephen (eds). *Historical Perspectives on the Political Economy of Swaziland*. Selected Articles. Kwaluseni: University of Swaziland.

# 11

# EVOLUTION OF SOCIAL WELFARE AND SOCIAL WORK IN TANZANIA

*Leah Natujwa Omari*

## Introduction

This chapter discusses the development of social welfare and social work in Tanzania, from the pre-colonial, colonial to the present time. First, the chapter explains more about the social work professional development in pre-colonial times where services provided to people in need were mostly at individual, family, group and community levels. Second, it highlights how the profession changed into more basic social functioning by focussing on persons as social human beings. Nevertheless, the profession has been confused with sociology and community development, where the traditional social work approach in Tanzania has waned. Hence, the development of the profession needs more people's commitment to initiating change in order to enable people to identify their needs and social problems in their day-to-day lives. Social work in Tanzania focusses on creating positive changes in people's lives; at the same time, however, it is not fully utilised in preventing visible challenges and providing accessible services to people who need it.[1]

---

1    Mabeyo, 2014.

## Historical Background

Social work in Tanzania began in 1947 following the British Colonialists' introduction of probation services.[2] The profession emerged as a means of social control that helped to transform the so-called 'law abiders' into 'ordinary people' who could work and produce what was needed at a particular time.[3] Initial services focused on the protection of the colonialists' interests and not the colonised people. Therefore, the social work profession in Tanzania was established to respond to Europeans' direct pressing needs. Later the needs of indigenous Africans; and the country's social problems such as vulnerable children and their families, and children who needed foster care or adoption, necessitated the extension of social work services to Africans. On the other hand, social work was developed to ensure that the law was enforced and violators followed behaviour modification, so that every member of the society looked after their families, for instance, children.[4]

After Tanzania (it was known as Tanganyika during colonial rule) became independent in 1961, the scope of social work expanded and started to offer services to children and children out of wedlock, facilitated by an amendment to the Affiliation Ordinance of 1949. The National Council for Social Services was established after Independence; however, it could not last long due to lack of civil society support and members' commitment. In 1969 a *Resettlement for Habitual Criminal Offenders Act 8* was enacted and used against people not following society's established regulations; they were resettled at Kitengule in Bukoba, Songwe in Mbeya, and Wami in Morogoro for rehabilitation and behavioural changes.[5] The trend shows how social work grew and continued to offer services to all people including the development of Elderly Houses at Nunge, Dar es Salaam, as well as Remand Homes and other services, necessary at that time. Currently, the Department of Social Work (DSW) oversees social work with social welfare officers (SWOs) providing all social work services.

---

2    Njimba, 2011.
3    Ibid.
4    Mabeyo, 2014.
5    Njimba, 2011.

## Communal Ways of Life: Social Welfare Delivery during Pre- and Post-Colonial Rule

The history of social welfare in Tanzania can be traced back to pre-colonial times, where people lived in communities and assisted each other in times of need. Children, regarded as belonging to the society, obliged the community to raise children as its own; the same for the elderly and the disabled. In early ages, there were indigenous social welfare systems that responded to the needs of the people, for instance, the *Boma* that the head of the kin or family leads. Everything was reported to him, and all the requirements for the communities were derived from him. He called all the families in the community together to listen to and come up together with solutions. If a child needed to go to school, the Boma head had to come up with a solution, agreed to by all. The family worked according to the concept of common interest in the family property. Under normal circumstances, property ownership was decentralised among family members, and decisions became communal. All the needy and the ageing members of the family were able to receive adequate support from the family when they retired from active farming. On the other hand, family members perpetuated themselves through maintaining links with the old parental family and new family offshoots, expressed through parental support to sons in establishing themselves occupationally and setting up their family households.

In Tanzania, indigenous social welfare forms were there to protect family members from harm or any other forms of abuse possible within a community. Not only the family but family members carried out most recreational, educational, political, protective, and social activities in socially organised groups. Kinship systems that traditional rural Tanzanians operated, sometimes offered financial and moral assistance, primarily from parents to children in the early years of marriage. For other members of the community, it played the role of providing mutual aid that included the exchange of services and gifts and giving and receiving advice from various community members.[6] The kinship system acted as an indigenous social welfare system that maintained ties among the people and even in regulating the behaviour of family members. For instance, it was well known that older women's roles were to look after the younger children, by feeding, washing, and caring for them in all aspects. Younger women had the task of fetching water, collecting firewood, cleaning the house, feeding, and caring for their babies. Therefore, domestic

---

6    Odetola, Oloruntimehin & Aweda, 1983.

roles and responsibilities within a family were based on gender and age.[7] Each member of the community respected each one's roles; when there were quarrels, families were able to give guidance and resolve the problem peacefully. When tracing the history of social work in Tanzania, we include the traditional and indigenous forms of social welfare as a way of maintaining social conditions and providing services to all Tanzania's community members.[8]

The indigenous social welfare system was exposed to colonial rule after colonialists came to the country to exploit raw materials, labour, and open markets. Colonialists invested in schools, hospitals, and basic infrastructural rail-lines to enable them to ease work on plantations and in the mines. The social welfare system changed with the introduction of new developments during and after the Second World War, when the German colonies, including Tanganyika, were redistributed among Europeans powers. Tanganyika became a mandated territory under British rule that used the traditional intermediate chiefs who ruled ethnic groups. The British administration system had several chiefs or headmen, who were just colonial paid servants, to lead small units. The African unit leaders (chiefs) had no power; they were subjected to removal from their positions if they could not fulfil the colonial duties they had to perform on behalf of the colonial administration. Among other things, they mobilised their fellow Africans on behalf of the colonialists to produce cash crops, and participate in the construction of roads, railways, and bridges.

To take advantage of more African labour and natural resources in the colonial time, the British opted to use local ruling chiefs (where they existed) due to the following reasons:

- They could easily mobilise their people to participate in colonial economic activities.

- In the case of grievances, the Africans could directly face their chiefs and not the British administrators, because they were the immediate people implementing the colonial policies.

- The British were instilling tribalism to divide Africans and finally rule them, fulfilled by creating local tribal chiefs at grassroots level.

---

7    Ibid.

8    Ibid.

The colonisation of the African labour force led to the German and British rule overpowering the indigenous administration. The colonial administration was pyramidal; at the top was the governor, the highest-ranking official in charge of the political and administrative matters in the colony. The governor saw to it that the colonial policies were implemented, and he had to account to his government in Britain. Below the governor were provincial commissioners; then district commissioners who administered districts and were helped by the traditional local chiefs assisted by the councils of elders. British colonial administrators were mostly middle-class citizens who had a moderate educational background. Some of them were geographers, political scientist, historians, sociologists, and anthropologists. The indirect rule applied various administrative instruments, including the social welfare system, to function efficiently. Some of the instruments were the native courts, treasuries, and local authorities. The colonial administrators created the native courts for Africans, and then classified and supervised the African chiefs. The courts were conducted through traditional African laws, though the Europeans considered them to be barbaric. For example, the Hehe ethnic group had a sub-chief known as Vanzagila; under his control were the Jumbes; then the Lunanzi, traditional village court processors who solved cases for the Hehe at the grassroots level.

It is on the same basis that laws such as the *Children and the Young Persons Ordinance of 1937*, the *Affiliation Ordinance of 1949*, the *Probation of Offenders Ordinance of 1947*, and the *Foster Care and Adoption Ordinance of 1955* were developed. These had laid a foundation for social welfare and social work in the pre-Independence era. As a result of the Second World War, these systems developed and expanded into the government which decentralised them, thus creating a movement that searched for the right social welfare system to accommodate Tanzanians' needs. Social work started to develop primarily as an instrument of social control, and never seriously addressed the root causes of social problems. The social work profession expanded and grew during the same period simultaneously with the expansion of social welfare services. Social work methods expanded to encompass group work, community work, and administration in addition to casework with individuals and families.

## Social Welfare during Mwalimu Julius Nyerere's Rule

Tanzania became independent on 9 December 1961. At Independence, social provision was private, and the social services were limited in scope and content as they were for those who could afford to pay for them. Social and economic policies were thus interlaced to serve the purse of the inherited capitalist economy, although this was fundamentally contrary to the thinking and philosophy of the founding president Julius Kamabarage Nyerere.[9] *Mwalimu* ('Teacher') Nyerere saw the widening gap in social provisioning and became eager to establish an equal society and guarantee the equality of the people. He had the idea of vesting the critical means of production in the hands of the majority and nationals, hence ensuring collective ownership of wealth and equal social provisioning to all.[10] In efforts to maintain equality in Tanzanian society, Nyerere established his policy of *Ujamaa* ('familyhood') during the Arusha Declaration of 5 February 1967. Nyerere translated the *Ujamaa* concept into a political-economic management model through several means, including the institutionalisation of social, economic, and political equality. He created a central democracy, abolished discrimination, and nationalised the economy's key sectors, namely production, service provision, and distribution.[11] His main goals were collective agriculture, generated under a process called villagisation; the nationalisation of banks and industries; and an increased level of self-reliance for individuals and nationally. His philosophy was to develop a country where everyone could own and enjoy the 'fruits' of Independence.

Villagisation was a key issue in this policy, emphasising the overcoming of the problem of 'tribalism', emerging in some communities of independent Tanzania. However, his philosophy was unsuccessful because of the large population. The country could not increase its productivity, which was supposed to emanate from collectivisation. Thus, productivity fell to less than 50 per cent to that achieved at Independence, meaning the social welfare system was negatively impacted as accessibility to the educational, medical facilities and other services was difficult. *Ujamaa* was brought to an end in 1985 when Nyerere stepped down from the presidency and his vice-president, Ali Hassan Mwinyi, was selected as the new president of Tanzania for five years. Under the *Chama cha Mapinduzi* ('Party of the Revolution'), the ruling party for Tanzania, small-scale private

---

9    Boddy-Evans, A. 2019a.

10   Aikaeli & Moshi, 2016.

11   Ibid.

enterprise and local economic investment were allowed. From 1981-1984, the economy collapsed, and the emphasis changed to social welfare at the expense of production reform. At this time rural dwellers abandoned communal villages. The government encouraged the privatisation of various companies, including those that offered social services to people in need. The DSW remained the sole government entity, offering social services at no cost to the community.

Between 1987-1991 the new president, Mwinyi, allowed the international donor community to support his reform programme with significant financial aid. However, rural communities and the urban poor were under strain due to the devaluation of the country's currency; the shilling lost 80 per cent of its value. This devaluation constrained the social welfare system and even more social services the government delivered under the economic austerity package of the International Monetary Fund (IMF). The period, 1996-1998, saw the third elected president, Benjamin William Mkapa, continually committing himself to follow IMF policies based on market reforms and securing more aid from internal financial agencies. This commitment allowed the establishment of more non-governmental organisations offering social welfare services. More service delivery agencies were developed, and new ones provided services such as children's homes and counselling centres, with consultation from professional social workers who studied at the Institute of Social Work.

By design, this paradigm change sounds good regarding social development and equity. Nevertheless, the policies pursued in the 1980s and the late 1990s led to poor economic performance, in turn, undermining or weakening the government's capacity to provide adequate social services, not only in terms of quantity but also in quality. All these indicators showed signs of deterioration. Although reforms triggered some efficiency improvements and growth started to regain momentum, ordinary people in rural areas remained poor, and the provision of social services was inadequate. While there was a consideration of social aspects in the reform process, the bifurcation, between economic and social policies as separate sectors, was still apparent.[12] There was no coherent integration of social goals into economic policy formulation as part and parcel of the transformation process. A lot of emphasis and effort were devoted to structural changes and economic stabilisation as if social provisioning would automatically emanate from an efficient market system. However, this was not the case.

---

12    Aikaeli & Moshi, 2016.

Over time, the State gradually assumed a greater role as the principal source of social provision. Although the family and the church are still important actors in the welfare field, they are no longer considered adequate to meet social problems, emerging as a result of rapid social and technological change. Modern society has become so complex that state intervention in social welfare has become a universal phenomenon. Numerous social welfare services and institutions have sprung up to replace earlier sources of social provision. At the government level, there has been a proliferation of policies, plans and programmes aimed at improving and expanding social welfare. However, due to limited resources, government has continued to support voluntary social welfare organisations. Despite increased government responsibility for social welfare, there has not been much development of partnership and cooperation with voluntary and private organisations, at local, national, and international levels. In fact, from the 1980s, social workers engaged in new fields of practice and began to conceptualise a generic or generalist professional practice. Even the DSW was developed, although curatively. The formal response to meeting human need influenced the basic institutions and legislation that facilitated social services provision.[13] Therefore, it is clear that even after attaining Independence, Tanzania continued to use the remedial or curative approach in dealing with its social problems. Most social workers are employed in DSW while others are employed in correctional services, hospitals, police and defence force where the remedial approach is usually used. Non-governmental organisations employ a few. Social workers in the employ of NGOs normally use the community work method and are recognised by the government since the DSW falls under the Ministry of Health, Community Work, Gender, Children and Elderly.

## A Paradigm Shift in Social Welfare Provision in Tanzania

The paradigm shift has brought socio-economic development, especially in the delivery of social welfare services to people in need. The different approaches the country adopts, depend on the political system the country embraces. For example, the coherence of the *Ujamaa* policy and strategies was crucial for social welfare service provision and the growth of the social work profession in Tanzania. The experiences of the past show that the kind of policy the country developed and implemented, determined the changes in social welfare provision. Nevertheless, what the government needed to understand is that

---

13    Asamoah, 1995 in Chitereka, 2009.

the *Ujamaa* policy could not create opportunities to increase social welfare provision in the country. However, as the country entered the 1990s and 2000s, Tanzania had no clear development vision to guide social development through forging people's minds and diverting efforts and resources towards the attainment of specific development goals. One main reason behind this was that the liberalisation process made policy frameworks incoherent which further blunted policy implementation.[14] Notwithstanding its weaknesses, the *Ujamaa* policy, had an ideological perspective which was aligned with the country's development goals. This was not the case during the liberalisation era. Thus, this is an important missing link in the contemporary development process in Tanzania.

Furthermore, Tanzania was involved in various policy regimes not focused on the strengthening of social welfare. Several policies and strategies, implemented in an attempt to reform the economy through International Monetary Fund (IMF) packages, were either incoherent or resulted in duplication and the dilution of economic and social policy stances. This implementation hindered the development of the social welfare system which needed at that particular time to help individuals, groups and communities suffering from social ills. This deficiency was noticed when measures were made to abolish the *Ujamaa* policy aimed at providing social services such as education, health, water, and sanitation to enhance human development. Social provision for Tanzanians is not destined to remain unchanged since it has varied through different political regimes. Therefore, an efficient social welfare system can only be achieved in a country where there are sound public policies and specific social service provision systems, based on economic, social, and political factors. Thus, political will is needed from the government to see the importance of having a useful social welfare system, accessible to all citizens. Economic and social policies should be tied together in the sense that whatever is economically achieved has a cause and effect on the adopted approach to social service provision. This argument means that poverty is critical in determining the social provisioning approach. Therefore, to bring about changes in poverty entail changes in the social provisioning approach.[15]

Tanzania needs to build a stable economy and mobilise resources to be able to provide basic social services to all people. The government needs to take a role in the provision

---

14    Aikaeli & Moshi, 2016.

15    Aikaeli & Moshi, 2016.

of resources in case people have limited access. The problem with social welfare services is that they do not reach everyone due to limited resources, implying that as resource mobilisation efficiency increases, there may be leverage for more public provision of basic social services, coupled with enhanced fiscal discipline for all Tanzanians.

## Recent Trends in Social Welfare and Social Work Practice in Tanzania

The DSW in the Ministry of Health and Social Welfare is tasked with protecting orphans and vulnerable children (OVC) and ensuring that they access basic services. The DSW is responsible for policy guidance about social welfare with a focus on ensuring adequate and quality care, and timely provision of social welfare services to vulnerable groups. Its key targets are the elderly, people with disabilities and OVC. The DSW, however, faces several challenges and inadequacies in fulfilling these functions: technical, managerial, organisational, financial, and human capacity. The Act that established the DSW does not provide enough details about its roles, and improvements are needed in:

- data collection, management, and utilisation
- training and staff development
- documentation, research, and analysis
- resource mobilisation
- advocacy strategy.[16]

There is an over-dependence on external funding from international organisations or foreign countries to deliver on its mandate. Understaffing seriously impinges on service delivery at national and local levels. Many districts do not even have one SWO. The DSW has a low profile within the Ministry and an inadequate understanding of its functions and roles; with low visibility impacting on resource allocation from the government.

Many social welfare resources and functions were recently decentralised from the national to district levels to address OVC's and other vulnerable groups' needs more effectively. Currently, there is no formal strategy for strengthening the social welfare

---

16    Njimba, 2011

workforce in Tanzania. However, the DSW led the development of the first phase of a National Costed Plan of Action (NCPA), a guide to:

▷ outline the identification of most vulnerable children

▷ coordinate the efforts of NGOs

▷ mobilise resources

▷ create a national data management system.

The second phase of the NCPA is underway, and it includes plans for developing a Social Welfare Workforce Strategy for Tanzania, a response to strengthen the social welfare workforce since only half of Tanzania's districts have district SWOs. To fill this gap, the government has been largely relying on paraprofessional or auxiliary social workers, including community volunteers, and community justice facilitators. Other developments are the Tanzanian Social Work-HIV/Aids Partnership Project for OVC, piloted in 2006. This model used to train community-based caregivers in key social work and child development skills and is currently replicated in Ethiopia and Nigeria. The programme was established as a result of the DSW's assessment that para social work training, as a strategy, decentralises social welfare services to ensure quality OVC services to communities and families.

However, the HIV/Aids epidemic severely overstretched Tanzania's welfare system, and it lacks sufficient social workers to respond to needs. There was a notable shortage of trained human resources in the health and social service sectors. On account of this, para-social workers were trained at the village and ward level to help SWOs working at the district level. The para-social workers assess the needs, provide care and support, undertake referrals to clients to various services and provide on-going follow-up care in the delivery of foundational social welfare services in the community.

## Creation of the First School of Social Work and Professional Association in Tanzania

The *Miscellaneous Act 3 of 2002* established the Institute of Social Work (ISW), formerly known as the 'National Social Welfare Training Institute'. This Act amended the *National Social Welfare Training Institute Act 26 of 1973*. The ISW provides training, consultancy services and conducts research and is the National Council for Technical Education accredited to provide National Technical Awards: certificates, ordinary diplomas and a degree programme in Social Work, as well as a post-graduate Diploma in Social Work.[17] The Institute opened in 1974 under the DSW's auspices as the DSW's founding and the oldest academic unit, entrusted with the task of training social workers, most of whom the DSW then employed.

In that regard, the Institute was charged with the responsibility of training qualified human resources who could strengthen the existing workforce in Tanzanian society after colonial rule.[18] The Institute started to offer an Ordinary Diploma in Social Work in 1975; an Advanced Diploma in Social Work in 1977; and a Social Work Certificate in 1979. In 1999, the ISW started a post-graduate Diploma in Social Work, as provided for in the Miscellaneous Act; the Act that also gives the ISW the mandate to administer Board of Governors-approved examinations and award certificates.[19] The ISW is producing between 205-506 students per year in the social work field. Enrolment has been increasing since 2010 due to more awareness about the social work profession throughout the country with the ISW advertising its programmes through para-social work training and the revitalising of the Tanzania Social Work Association in 2010. Changing its name in 2012 to the Tanzania Social Workers Organization (TASWO), the association aims to stimulate, foster and promote the growth of the social work profession in Tanzania; a practice enabling TASWO to facilitate and promote the continued professional development of social workers in Tanzania.

On the other hand, TASWO has been associated with social workers working for the DSW and as such, has a close relationship with the Ministry of Health and Social Welfare. TASWO has many activities that mostly focus on two main objectives:

▻ first, to advocate social work practice as a profession, and

▻ second, to develop professional management practices, including the association's budget and administration for its further development.

---

17    Institute of Social Work, 2012.

18    Ibid.

19    Ibid.

These objectives helped TASWO to enhance members' ownership of the organisation, as well as to maintain and sustain management and administration transparency. In addition to programmes offered at the ISW, the DSW within the Ministry of Health and Social Welfare, and in collaboration with the ISW, offers the Social Welfare Assistant Certificate Programme, a para social workers' certificate programme with graduates to be employed as the new cadre of welfare assistants at ward level.

Due to increased demand for social work professionals in Tanzania, the ISW and the Jane Addams College of Social Work at Illinois, USA, realised that while social work education was offered at various academic institutions in Tanzania; it was important that universities and colleges bring the quality of social work education in line with the social work profession's international standards. They could do this by sharing information; harmonising, and standardising curricula. Therefore, the Tanzania Emerging Schools of Social Work Programme (TESWEP) was developed to review social work curricula in colleges and universities and to enhance social work faculty and development opportunities. Most recently, 12 academic institutions, including universities, are members of TESWEP. Already, bachelor degree curricula have been harmonised, and four other institutions, including the ISW, offer a Master's degree in Social Work. TESWEP has been reconstituted into the Association of Schools of Social Work in Tanzania (ASSWOT), operating under the umbrella of TASWO, with the support from the President's Emergency Plan For Aids Relief through a partnership project with the American International Health Alliance; the Jane Addams College of Social Work; and the Midwest Aids Training and Education Centre at the University of Illinois, USA. ASSWOT's objectives are to:

➤ Maintain high standards among all institutions engaged in different levels of social work education.

➤ Ensure high standards of ethical conduct in social work.

➤ Advance the professional education of social work educators and practitioners.

➤ Enhance the status of social work.

Nevertheless, the social work profession in Tanzania faces challenges and is mostly confused with other disciplines such as sociology and community development. Traditionally, social work in Tanzania mainly focused on providing services to people in need, mostly at individual, family, group and community level, and more recently at organisational level. The social worker is called upon when something in the basic social functioning area threatens the life and development of a person as a social human being. Currently, the Government of Tanzania is using the decentralisation policy, to recruit and place SWOs at the district level. Local authorities are responsible for recruiting a new cadre of social welfare assistants at ward level, for supervising and supporting principal social workers at the village level. District SWOs, government employees, then supervise and support social welfare assistants.

Furthermore, efforts to strengthen the social welfare workforce in Tanzania have encountered difficulties, including the shortage of social workers at district, ward, and village level. The few trained social workers mostly choose to work in the private sector, such as in NGOs and other better-paying industries and programmes and thus negatively affecting the government's work. Another challenge is related to the unknown profile of the DSW and its roles and functions, and how social welfare services contribute to the overall development agenda in Tanzania. The social work profession has been continuously confused with other fields such as development studies, community development and sociology, as mentioned earlier. Hence, creating more confusion regarding social welfare delivery and resource distribution to the vulnerable groups in Tanzania. Social welfare services remain a low priority for government investment; a continuation of the underutilisation of social welfare services in Tanzania.

The DSW is facing the challenge of not having a social welfare policy that could enable SWOs, including social workers, to deliver quality and essential services to the people. It has been challenging to meet the needs of the vulnerable groups, including children, older persons and the disabled, through social services. An insufficient budget from the government has slowed the expansion and retention of social workers as SWOs to strengthen the social welfare workforce, making the DSW dependent on funds from the donor community. This dependency has affected the existing community care and support models (indigenous care) in our society, in dealing with arising contemporary social problems in the community because of social change and increased technology transfers within and outside Tanzania. The Ministry of Health and Social Welfare has been working closely with the ISW in strengthening the social welfare workforce. The Government of Tanzania is using the decentralisation policy to recruit and employ social workers at various levels; the same policy the Ministry of Health and Social Welfare used to recruit and place SWOs at district and ward level. Local authorities must recruit a new cadre of social welfare assistants at ward level, to supervise and support principal social workers at the village level.

NGOs that employ social workers at various levels have created an expectation of employment opportunities for many SWOs after they complete their degrees. The expectation has increased because the government does not offer good salaries, and therefore SWOs move to better-paying jobs at potential employers like NGOs. Another challenge is that in Tanzania, indigenous social work literature is missing, and thus there is a need to focus on the local context, especially on the problems and solutions that reflect the Tanzanian society.[20] This deficit makes Tanzania reliant on Western literature, concepts and approaches, not reflecting the country's realities. The social work profession's growth is thus stunted, and it fails to intervene effectively in delivering services in the changing contexts of complex and new forms of social problems needing attention. It is proposed that all stakeholders in social work education follow the cultural and ethical values emerging from local Tanzanian conditions and reflect Tanzanian society – where its people are playing a role in social work's development.

## Conclusion

This chapter sought to trace the development of the social welfare system in Tanzania, changing over time. Since the colonial era, the profession has not been recognised as one that could help individuals, groups, and communities solve their problems. Poverty, especially, influenced by the country's economic situation, shaped the development of the profession. SWOs and social workers have played major roles in the provision of social welfare services, including care and support to OVCs, older persons, people with disabilities and other vulnerable people in Tanzania. As part of the improvement of the indigenous system of social welfare and social work, it is important to observe ethical issues that pertain to the provision of care and support, where children and their families have received such services. Social workers have been able to identify direct services. A social work professional in Tanzania works to improve the health and wellbeing of individuals and communities where they live and work. Tanzania is working hard with paid and unpaid government and non-governmental workers to deliver social work services, who are undervalued and not given priority at the grassroots level.

---

20    Mabeyo, Ndung'u & Riedl, 2014.

# References

AIHA (American International Health Alliance). 2012. *Para Social Workers Training Manual and Curriculum: Learning to Work with Orphans and Vulnerable Children.* [https://bit.ly/2H3PEys].

Aikaeli, J. & Moshi, H. 2016. *Social Policy in a Historical Perspective: Shifting Approaches to Social Provisioning.* THDR 2017: Background Paper 6; ESRF Discussion Paper 67. Dar es Salaam, Tanzania: Economic and Social Research Foundation. [http://esrf.or.tz/docs/THDR2017BP-6.pdf]. (Accessed 15 March 2017).

Boddy-Evans, A. 2019a. *Biography of Julius Kambarage Nyerere, Father of Tanzania.* [https://bit.ly/33WKCN6]. (Accessed 12 March 2019).

Boddy-Evans, A. 2019b. *What Was Ujamaa and How Did It Affect Tanzania? Nyerere's Social and Economic Policy in 1960s and 1970s Tanzania.* [https://www.thoughtco.com/what-was-ujamaa-44589]. (Accessed 12 March 2019).

Chitereka, C. 2009. Social Work Practice in a Developing Continent: The Case of Africa. *Advances in Social Work*, 10(2):144-156.

Eyong, C.T. 2007. Indigenous Knowledge and Sustainable Development in Africa: Case Study on Central Africa. In: E.K. Boon & L. Hens (eds). *Indigenous Knowledge Systems and Sustainable Development: Relevance for Africa.* Edition: Tribes and Tribals Special, 1. New Delhi, India: Kamla-Raj Enterprises.

Guyer, L., Singleton, D. & Linsk, N.L. 2012. *Situational analysis of the Twinning Center Para-Social Worker Training Programme in Tanzania, Ethiopia, and Nigeria.* Intrahealth: Capacity Plus Project. [https://bit.ly/33WOfCN]. (Accessed 27 October 2015).

Linsk, N., Mabeyo, Z., Omari, L.N., Petras, D., Lubin, B., Abate, A.A., Steinitz, L., Kaijage, T. & Mason, S. 2010. Para Social Work to Address Most Vulnerable Children in Sub-Sahara Africa: A Case Example in Tanzania. *Children and Youth Service Review*, 32(7):990-997.

Linsk, N., Mason, S., Omari, L.N. & Lubin, B. 2017. Partner approaches to developing, scaling up and sustaining HIV/AIDS Para-professional social work programs in Africa. In: A.K. Butterfield, C.S. Cohen (eds). *Practicing as a social work educator in international collaboration.* Alexandria, VA: Council on Social Work Education Press.

Mabeyo, Z. 2014. The Development of Social Work Education and Practice in Tanzania. In: Spitzer, H. & Twikirize, J.M. *Professional Social Work in East Africa: Towards Social Development, Poverty Reduction and Gender Equality.* Oxford, UK: African Books Collective.

Mabeyo, Z.M., Ndung'u, E.M. & Riedl, S. 2014. *The Role of Social work in Poverty Reduction and the Realization of Millennium Development Goals in Tanzania.* Kampala: Fountain Publishers.

Mbise, A., Bickel, S., Mngodo, S. & Mngodo, J. 2012. *Para Social Workers Training Manual and Curriculum: Learning to work with orphans and vulnerable children*. Dar es Salaam, Tanzania: American International Health Alliance. [https://bit.ly/2SQGzvx]. (Accessed 2 September 2013).

Njimba, C.C. 2011. The History of Social work in Tanzania. A paper presented at Annual Social work General Meeting, Morogoro, Tanzania, 13/10/2011.

Odetola, T.O., Oloruntimehin, O. & Aweda, D.A. 1983. *Man and Society in Africa: Introduction to Sociology*. Harlow, United Kingdom: Longman Group.

Omari, L.N. 2014. *Strengthening Tanzania's social welfare workforce: Training Para social workers to provide ongoing support services to vulnerable children and families*. Unpublished Paper.

Omari, L.N., Linsk, N. & Mason, S. 2016. Strengthening Tanzania's social welfare workforce to provide ongoing paraprofessional support services to vulnerable children and families. In: M. Gray (ed). *The Handbook of Social Work and Social Development in Africa*. Washington, DC: Taylor & Francis Group.

Rwomire, A. & Raditlhokwa, L. 1996. Social Work in Africa: Issues and Challenges. *Journal of Social Development in Africa*, 2(2):5-19. [https://bit.ly/3113s3R]. (Accessed 12 March 2017).

Shizha, E. 2013. Reclaiming Our Indigenous Voices: The Problem with Postcolonial Sub-Saharan African School Curriculum. *Journal of Indigenous Social Development*, 2(1):1-18.

Tanzania Education Network. 2020. *Topic 2: Colonial Administrative System*. [https://bit.ly/3dnZE1A]. (Accessed 12 March 2017).

United Republic of Tanzania. DSW (Department of Social Work). 2011. *Reviewed Curriculum for Basic Technician Certificate in Social Work. NTA, Level 4*. Institute of Social Work. [https://www.isw.ac.tz/social.php]. (Accessed 12 March 2017).

United Republic of Tanzania. DSW. 2015. *Students Annual Report*. Dar es Salaam: Institute of Social Work, Examination Office.

United Republic of Tanzania. Ministry of Health and Social Welfare. 2009. *Assessment of Social Welfare Workforce in Tanzania, Final report*. Dar es Salaam: Department of Social Welfare (DSW).

United Republic of Tanzania. Ministry of Health and Social Welfare. 2014a. *Human Resource for Health and Social Welfare Strategic plan 2014-2019*. Dar es Salaam: DSW.

United Republic of Tanzania. Ministry of Health and Social Welfare. 2014b. *The Simplified Version of the National Costed Plan of Action for Most Vulnerable Children 2013-2014*. Dar es Salaam, Tanzania: DSW. [https://bit.ly/34YZIkj]. (Accessed 12 March 2017).

# 12

# ORIGINS AND DEVELOPMENT OF SOCIAL WELFARE AND SOCIAL WORK IN ZAMBIA

*Ndangwa Noyoo*

## Introduction

This chapter describes the origins of social welfare and social work in Zambia. It begins by examining the work of Western Christian missionaries, and close to what is now regarded the domain of social welfare officers (SWOs) and social workers. The chapter discusses the social welfare services of colonial authorities and the mining companies in the area known as the Copperbelt. These eventually led to the rise of early social welfare and social work practice in colonial Zambia, then known as Northern Rhodesia. After that, the chapter focuses on the post-colonial period from 1964, when Zambia became independent, to the recent past. The present era is highlighted in the first section of the chapter. It is critical to mention that the development of Zambian social welfare and social work are inextricably intertwined with the rise of nationalist politics that emerged in this country, to challenge colonial rule and eventually guided Zambia to Independence. Therefore, social welfare issues in Zambia, despite their Christian inkling have a strong political dimension.

## Zambia at a Glance

Zambia is a landlocked country in southern Africa that shares borders with eight countries: Angola (west), Botswana (south), the Democratic Republic of the Congo (DRC) (north-west), Malawi (east), Namibia (south-west), Tanzania (north-east), and Zimbabwe (south). Zambia is a member of the Southern African Development Community and is part of the Commonwealth Group of Nations. Zambia's landmass is 752 618 km² and the capital city, Lusaka, is found in the south-central part of the country. Presently, the Patriotic Front (PF) government governs Zambia with Edgar Chagwa Lungu, the president. Lungu took over from Michael Chilufya Sata who died in 2014 after being in power for less than three years. Sata had risen to power via a populist agenda that had supposedly wanted to 'put more money' in the pockets of Zambian citizens. Sata's rule was chaotic and malevolent. One issue that stands out during Sata's and the PF's rule is the squandering of financial reserves built-up during the reign of Levy Patrick Mwanawasa, late president of Zambia and the Movement for Multiparty Democracy, (2001-2008). The PF government, under Sata and Lungu, had effectively taken Zambia back into the debt hole whence it emerged after 2005 when it attained the Highly Indebted Poor Countries (HIPC) completion point. Zambia became eligible for debt forgiveness from the World Bank and International Monetary Fund (IMF) under the two organisations' heavily indebted poor countries initiative. After adhering to strict austerity conditions, these multilateral aid agencies approved the bulk of Zambia's debt amounting to about 4 billion US dollars for relief.

According to the World Bank (2019), Zambia's overall public and publicly guaranteed debt is expected to increase to 98 per cent of the Gross Domestic Product (GDP) by 2020, while external public and publicly guaranteed debt service obligations over 2019-2021 are estimated at 4.6 billion US dollars. Zambia, Africa's second-largest copper producer, achieved middle-income country status in 2011 during a decade (2004-2014) of impressive economic growth, averaging 7.4 per cent per year. However, growth only benefitted a small segment of the urban population and had a limited impact on poverty. Zambia ranks among the countries with the highest level of inequality globally. As of 2015, 58 per cent of Zambians earned less than the international poverty line of 1.90 US dollars per day (compared to 41 per cent across sub-Saharan Africa) and three-quarters of the poor living in rural areas.[1] The World Bank (2019) further notes that the current account deficit widened from 1.5 per cent of the GDP in 2017 to 2.6 per cent in 2018, reflecting increased deficits in income and services accounts amidst a narrowing trade surplus. With reduced capital inflows, a drawdown in official reserves financed the overall balance of payments. Gross official reserves, therefore, fell to 1.6 billion US dollars (1.8 months of imports) at the end of December 2018 from 2.1 billion US dollars at the end of 2017. Thus, the current account registered a deficit of 414 million US dollars in 2019, partly reflecting higher interest payments on public debt, outweighing the recorded trade surplus. Correspondingly, the exchange rate faced some pressures during 2019, depreciating by about 10 per cent to about 13 Zambian kwacha to 1 US dollar through August, and reserves fell further to 1.4 billion US dollars (1.7 months of imports).[2]

It needs to be stated that the PF government created this new debt 'crisis' through highly imprudent economic policies and questionable public policies. These, mainly emanated from heavy borrowing to support its inchoate infrastructure development programme, which was not strategically driven, among other missteps. Due to the depressed economy, the country's social welfare system is strained. Nevertheless, it can be noted that the Zambian social welfare system is presently leaning more towards social protection in the form of cash transfers.

## Present Social Welfare and Social Work Scenario

The Department of Social Welfare (DSW) under the auspices of the Ministry of Community Development, Mother and Child Health, oversee the Zambian social welfare system that rests on these pillars:

▻ Public Welfare Assistance Scheme

▻ Places of Safety

▻ Statutory Services, and

▻ Non-Statutory Services.

---

1    World Bank, 2019.

2    Ibid.

## Public Welfare Assistance Scheme (PWAS)

According to the Ministry of Community Development, Mother and Child Health (2016), the PWAS social assistance programme; the oldest welfare scheme in the country, emanating from the colonial era, aims to mitigate the adverse effects of socio-economic shocks on the extremely poor and vulnerable persons. The scheme targets the following vulnerable individuals:

- Older persons
- Disabled persons
- Chronically ill-persons
- Single-Headed Households
- Orphans and vulnerable children (OVCs)
- Minor Disaster Victims and
- Others, genuinely unable to support themselves.

The care for older persons forms part of the PWAS. Thus, older persons benefit from the PWAS through community or institutional care. The following are some of the older person's homes in the country:

- Maramba in Livingstone
- Chibolya in Mufulira
- Mitanda in Ndola
- Divine Providence Home in Lusaka
- Chibote in Luanshya
- Mwandi in Sesheke
- St. Theresa in Ndola
- Likulwe in Senanga.[3]

---

3    Ministry of Community Development, Mother and Child Health, 2016.

The old age homes were inherited at Independence from the British colonial regime. During colonial rule, these homes had responded to the needs of European older persons and later, mixed-race persons. During the second decade of Independence, there were plans to abolish all these homes as the ruling United National Independence Party (UNIP) and the first president of Zambia, Kenneth Kaunda deemed them 'un-African'. These plans were in line with the UNIP's and Kaunda's humanism ideology wanting to pattern the country's social and economic affairs along with Zambia's traditional and egalitarian past. To this end, it was envisaged that the extended family set-up should look after older persons. However, the realities of urbanisation, modernity, among others, sharply brought home the reality that there were black Zambian older persons who did not have extended families to look after them.

Nevertheless, the DSW collaborates with civil society and religious partners such as the Salvation Army, the Catholic Nuns and the United Church of Zambia (an amalgamation of Protestant Churches) to provide old age homes. The DSW mounts public awareness campaigns that include an observance of the International Day for Older Persons (1st October) as well as encourages initiatives in the country centred on residential and non-residential care.[4]

## Places of Safety

These are institutions that provide temporary shelter, food and care for citizens who are stranded, destitute and in difficult situations. Such institutions are found in Kabwe, Lusaka and Mansa.

## Statutory Services

Statutory services mainly focus on young people in conflict with the law. SWOs carry out the main work and provide counselling to parents/guardians of young offenders in need of maintaining contact with their children or dependants incarcerated in institutions. This work is meant to prepare young offenders for eventual reintegration into the community. The DSW runs several facilities, including the Nakambala Approved School and the Insakwe Probation Hostels for the reformation of children in conflict with the law or who exhibit disruptive behaviour. The Prisons Department, under the Ministry

---

4    Ibid.

of Home Affairs, and the DSW seconds staff to the Katombora Reformatory School. Aftercare services are offered to young offenders after being released from correctional institutions.[5] These efforts are meant to assist in preparing young former offenders for eventual reintegration into the community under the supervision of probation officers and young offenders' inspectors.

The Ministry of Community Development, Mother and Child Health (2016) points out that work in this area revolves around the building of capacity and inspection of child-care facilities. The DSW does not provide child-care facilities but works collaboratively with and provides guidelines to non-governmental organisations (NGOs) and individuals permitted to operate children's homes. The DSW provides minimal grants to some of these homes that care for the children in need: orphaned, abandoned or children whose parents or guardians are unfit to look after them. However, government policy encourages community participation in the care of these children. Thus, institutional care is viewed as a measure of last resort. The DSW provides quality assurance vis-à-vis the proliferation of children's homes; regulates service delivery and sets guidelines to all child-care service providers for better, effective and quality service provision in line with national obligations to OVCs as enshrined in international conventions, national policies and laws.[6]

Statutory services encompass adoption services to provide a permanent home, legal protection and security to children in need of care in accordance with the *Adoption Act Chapter 54 of the Laws of Zambia*. Foster care is a statutory service that endeavours to respond to children in need of care in accordance with the *Juveniles Act 4 of 1956 (Chapter 53) of the Laws of Zambia*. This service provides a temporary home to the child.

The following pieces of legislation govern statutory services in Zambia:

▻ *Probation of Offenders Act Chapter 93 of the Laws of Zambia*.

▻ *Juveniles Act Chapter 53 of the Laws of Zambia*.

▻ *Adoption Act Chapter 54 of the Laws of Zambia*.

▻ *Maintenance Orders Act Chapter 55 of the Laws of Zambia*.

---

5      Ibid.

6      Ibid.

➢ *Day Nurseries Act Chapter 313 of the Laws of Zambia.*

A further statutory service is the correctional services – forming the core of statutory services provided to young offenders. They include:

➢ Investigations for courts – SWOs, gazetted as probation officers carry-out investigations on behalf of the courts to determine and advise the courts on the sentence form, best suited for young offenders;

➢ Probation of offenders – either an institutional or community-based rehabilitation process is placing a young offender under the supervision of a probation officer in accordance with the Probation of Offenders Act; and

➢ Correctional facilities, and after-care services – institutions providing reception, care and rehabilitation of young offenders as the court ordered; such as the Nakambala Approved School in Mazabuka; the Katombora Reformatory in Kazungula; and the Insakwe Probation Hostel in Ndola for young female offenders.[7]

## Non-Statutory Services

These are services that are administered without reference to an Act of Parliament. They include the Social Cash Transfer Scheme with the main objective to reduce extreme poverty and intergenerational transfer of poverty among beneficiary households and the community. The beneficiaries receive transfers that are paid bi-monthly. Beneficiary households with persons with disabilities receive double transfers bi-monthly.

## Other Social Welfare Services:

➢ Marriage counselling – premarital and marital counselling and guidance services to couples;

➢ Medical social work – material and other forms of assistance, counselling, and tracing of relatives for/to patients mainly in districts where there are no medical social workers; and

---

7    Ibid.

▷ Prison welfare – support provided to prisoners by way of linking them to their families and preparing for integration into the communities once discharged from prison.

It is important to delve into the country's past to understand the present social welfare system in Zambia.

## Pre-Colonial Period: Meeting Human Needs

Zambia was not a homogenous society before colonial rule, but a heterogeneous spread of polities, autonomous in some cases or ruled by other stronger indigenous kingdoms. The San people initially inhabited pre-colonial Zambia. Later, immigrations from the Luba-Lunda Kingdom, in the Katanga region of present-day Democratic Republic of the Congo (DRC), resulted in many Bantu ethnic groups settling in present-day Zambia. Eventually, these groups drove out the San people. Pre-colonial Zambia was always in a state of flux as there were migrations, inter-ethnic wars, and long-distance trade unfolding in the area. During these times, almost all the different ethnic groups eked out a living by existing on a subsistence basis. They gathered fruits, dug roots, hunted, cultivated crops or in some cases, kept livestock. The land was the most important and abundant resource that people could access as well as exploit for their benefit. The main impediment to further commercial development was among other things, low technological levels. In the past, different ethnic groups rarely harmoniously coexisted, and usually, the weaker ones were susceptible to pillage from those that were powerful. To escape subjection and plunder, some ethnic groups migrated while others sought protection from powerful polities that would co-opt or assimilate them. On the eve of colonial rule, there existed four well-organised kingdoms: the Lozi or Barotse in the west; Ngoni in the east; and the Lunda; and Bemba in the north.

It is important to bear in mind that social welfare's primary objective is to respond to human needs. Therefore, social welfare can be regarded as a direct or indirect response to human needs. The goal may be to:

▷ Prevent new categories of needs from arising.

▷ Recognise categories of needs from affecting still untouched individuals or groups.

▷ Maintain people or groups at their present state of need fulfilment.

▷ Help those with unsatisfied needs or unsolved problems.

These categories are often spoken of, respectively, as the preventative, maintenance, and rehabilitative functions of social welfare.[8]

## Missionaries' Early Social Welfare Interventions in Zambia

Even though the missionary and explorer, David Livingstone had crisscrossed pre-colonial Zambia, and in 1873 died at Chitambo, Frederick Stanley Arnot, a young Scots Plymouth Brethren missionary, was the first European to establish a permanent residence in the country, specifically in Barotseland (now the Western Province of Zambia) in 1882. Historical accounts cite George Westbeech, an ivory hunter and trader, as having helped Arnot to make his way into Barotseland. Arnot left the area in 1884 without converting anyone and settled around Katanga in today's DRC. François Coillard, a French Paris Evangelical Missionary Society missionary was the next European to set up a permanent settlement in Barotseland in 1885 and convert some of the local people to Christianity. Coillard and his wife had previously worked amongst the Basotho people of present-day Lesotho. They had acquainted themselves with the Bamangwato in today's Botswana, and the linguistic factor might have influenced their choice to move to Barotseland, as they could easily communicate with the Lozis, who spoke a language that was a mixture of Sesotho and Setswana.

In 1887, the London Missionary Society opened a mission station on the southern end of Lake Tanganyika among the Mambwe people. Primitive Methodists began work in the area where the Ila people resided and arrived at Kazungula in September 1890.

Furthermore, the White Fathers, a Catholic group, began their work amongst the Bemba people from 1891. Then there was the United Free Church of Scotland, initially beginning its work in Malawi and later moving southward into Zambia; establishing four mission stations at Mwenzo in 1895 and then later at Lubwa, Serenje, and Chitambo. In 1905, after the defeat of Mpenzeni, king of the Ngoni people, the Dutch Reformed Church, from the then Orange Free State in South Africa set up a mission station at Fort Jameson,

---

8    Macarov, 1995:17.

now called Chipata. In this part of Africa, it is safe to say that the missionaries were the first Europeans to establish permanent bases in the pre-colonial period: before the hunters, traders, miners, and administrators. From there, the Plymouth Brethrens made in-roads into the northern parts of Zambia in the early 1900s.

The missionaries were initially preoccupied with providing education to the local populations and later healthcare. Kelly (1991) argues that during the British South Africa Company (BSAC) rule (1891-1924), the development of education depended upon the missionary societies' initiative, perseverance, and financial resources. The missionaries' intentions or methods might have been questionable, arguably, but for the better part, they had genuinely wanted to uplift the conditions of the indigenous people. By the turn of the twentieth century, there were about 17 missionary societies managing churches, schools, and a hospital in the land. For instance, in 1915, Miss Mabel Shaw of the London Missionary Society opened a girls' school at Mbereshi in Luapula in northern Zambia.

When mineral deposits were discovered in the area that came to be known as the Copperbelt, Europeans began to arrive in large numbers in Northern Rhodesia from 1911. Many of these were petty merchants, traders and farmers who came from South Africa and had left that country after the Anglo-Boer/South African War (1899-1902).[9] For the minerals to be exploited, infrastructure such as roads and a rail-line had to be built. The erection of a rail line from Victoria Falls to the Copperbelt led to an expansion of European settlements along its course. Fertile land was allocated to Europeans for agricultural purposes as well. In these early years of colonial rule, colonial administrators and European commercial enterprises in the territory were in dire need of construction labourers. Labour recruitment was not easy at this time, and unconventional means were used to source it. The colonialists thus forced Africans to work in the nascent money economy to provide cheap labour for the colony in the mining and emerging agricultural sectors. Since Africans were used to a subsistent type of lifestyle and were not willing to work in the new mines or other commercial enterprises, the colonial authorities worked out a tax system which forcefully incorporated them into the colonial economy:

> One of the obvious means of obtaining more money was the imposition of an African Tax. The question of taxation, in turn, was closely linked with the labour

---

9    Mwanakatwe, 2010 cited in Noyoo, 2000.

question, for the need to earn tax money was the most important incentive to induce Africans to take up paid employment.[10]

Thus in 1901, the BSAC introduced the hut and poll tax (collectively known as the African tax) which coerced Africans into wage employment. The hut tax was a form of a poll tax, based on the number of huts an African owned. Later, the colonial authorities exclusively focused on taxing the wages earned in the money economy. Tax defaulters or evaders were severely punished; some even imprisoned or forcibly recruited into labour gangs. Since most Africans did not participate in the modern economy, they could only pay this tax in kind, for example, through grain, fowls, fruit, or livestock. At the end, when these agricultural products were depleted, they had no choice but to sell their labour. Later on, in 1905, the colonialists passed a decree that compelled Africans not to pay tax by any means other than money. Following these developments, Africans migrated in large numbers to the urban areas to work in the mines and factories. Thus, the twin processes of migratory labour and rural-urban migrations became a permanent feature of the colonial era. Colonial rule had deliberately created a reserve army of labourers in the rural areas and turned villagers into wage seekers. In the same vein, urban settlements became wholly dependent on cheap labour from the hinterland. However, once the contracts were over, they would be sent back to the rural areas, and new workers would be recruited.

The migration of predominantly male Africans to the urban areas posed serious threats to the stability of the extended family and the traditional mutual-aid system, which had safeguarded the livelihoods of its members. Migrations had resulted in distorted demographic patterns in African communities in that only women, children, the old and infirm remained behind in the villages. Women had to take on new roles and responsibilities, which were previously the domains of men. In adapting, at times, it was a blessing in disguise in so far as African gender relations were concerned. Urbanisation further threatened the old order in the way that the new and young 'urbanites' quickly discarded their traditional values for modernity and assumed new social roles in the towns. Labourers, who returned from the urban centres to their respective villages, challenged the traditional authorities and the traditional value system. Urbanisation had helped to spread the money economy to the traditional sector. Previously, people had bartered and cooperated in wealth-creating activities. By and large, the process of

---

10    Gann, 1958:77.

urbanisation was drawing Africans into the modern economy's consumer-oriented and individualistic culture. By 1924, Zambia had become a British colony and colonial rule was cemented thereafter.

## The 1930s, Second World War and Afterwards

From the mid-1930s, major changes began to transpire in colonial Zambia. For instance, it was during this period that the policy of stabilisation became a colonial programme. Previously, an urban African was considered a sojourner who would return to the village once his employment was terminated. Therefore, African workers were accommodated in temporal, make-shift, or barrack-type housing. They were classified as:

▻ bonafide natives in search of work

▻ bonafide seekers after work

▻ destitute and unemployed persons, and

▻ persons otherwise occupied than working for Europeans.

The former approach had further entrenched the temporary resident status of the African worker and delayed the stabilisation of labour and the establishment of African settlements.[11] Thus, the second phase of social welfare activities in colonial Zambia was necessitated by labour stabilisation, which brought about a shift in the mining firms' welfare approach, from a pure missionary type of work to a more systematic approach. Another important factor was the changed thinking regarding urban African quarters as permanent settlements.

Nevertheless, the labour question was bound up with the rise of social problems in the African quarters:

▻ The squalid conditions of urban Africans were matched by immorality, 'juvenile delinquency', and crime.

---

11    Keith & Stephenson, 1936.

▷ The compound system in the mines at first made it impossible for unskilled men to bring their wives with them from the villages, so prostitution found ample opportunities for trade.[12]

The Europeans were the major beneficiaries of the colony's wealth with which came other life-sustaining opportunities like employment, proper healthcare and education, and social security for the settlers. Mineral production was so lucrative that at one point a ton of copper – the main export of the colony – cost about 27 pounds to mine and export to London, where it fetched about 43 pounds on that market. From 1929 onwards, the territory's total revenues – 70 per cent directly due to copper –increased four-fold because of demand.[13] Furthermore, industrial development in the colony generated economic growth, not evenly redistributed to the rest of the Northern Rhodesian society, as Europeans got rich and Africans remained impoverished. When the Second World War broke out in 1939, Northern Rhodesia was firmly inserted into the global capitalist economy through its mining ventures. It was part of the British Empire, and thus its people were mobilised for the war effort against Nazi Germany. Considerable efforts were made to persuade the Africans to participate in the war whether by volunteering for military service, increasing production or giving contributions to war-time funds in return for promises of improvement in economic, social and political conditions after the war. Posters, radio broadcasts, mobile cinema shows and information bureaux, told Africans that they were partners with their colonial 'masters' in the fight for democracy and that a brave new post-war world awaited them, notably influencing Africans' reactions during and after this war.[14]

Thus, Africans' expectations of a better life were not misplaced as the colonialists themselves raised them in the first place, but in fact they were false promises. More importantly, the new concept of the British Government's obligation for the economic and social welfare of the colonies (itself a child of the Depression) was nurtured during the war. That is why plans to develop higher education institutions in African colonies were drawn up during the war, as were those to develop trade unions.[15] Britain undertook tentative reforms, partly under pressure from her American ally, not prepared to fight

---

12    Hall, 1965:130.
13    Rotberg, 1965.
14    Crowder, 1993.
15    Ibid.

a war on her behalf merely to preserve her empire; partly in reform both within and outside the Colonial Office; and partly to avoid a repetition of the disturbances in the West Indies in 1940, caused by prevailing scandalous economic and social conditions.[16]

As mentioned earlier, British colonial policy began to shift in the early 1940s. Slowly, genuine concern replaced indifference. In the first place, the British Government and indeed ordinary Britons were reacting to the unfolding tensions in the colonies that the settlers' wanton exploitation of indigenous communities fanned. Furthermore, the settlers' outright disregard of the local people's human rights was a source of concern in certain sections of British society. On the other hand, colonies were becoming quite difficult and expensive to manage, thus:

> Welfare replaced law and order as the imperative of imperialism around this time. In 1940, following the strike and riots by African miners, the House of Commons, the Christian churches and the Aborigines Protection in Britain had identified the poverty of the labour camps as the most pressing problem in Zambia.[17]

Indeed, the term 'welfare' denoted recognition of the extent of poverty in tropical colonies, revealed at the end of the 1930s, expressed through the acceptance of the large 'welfare' element in expenditure under the 1929 Colonial Development Act. The British colonial authorities' changed approach should not be naively taken as wholesale benevolence of the British Government, but must be seen in context as a clear signal of self-preservation and a desire to shed its colonial baggage:

> ... the Colonial Development and Welfare Act of 1940, passed in time of war when the physical shortages of capital and skill were such as to make it difficult rather than advantageous to export them, had its aim the raising of the standard of living of colonial peoples and their emancipation from economic dependence on the United Kingdom. Before the funds were allocated the colonial governments were called upon to present ten-year plans of development.[18]

Similarly, the return of soldiers from the war front, during and after the Second World War, heightened the contradictions in the colonial setting with the situation necessitating the need for an increase in the welfare services of the then Northern Rhodesia. Most of these war veterans ended up destitute after serving the British Crown in the Second

---

16    Ibid:97.
17    Heisler, 1974:16.
18    Deane, 1953:6.

World War. As per the customary racial divisions in the colony, the colonial authorities provided more help, through welfare services, to war veterans of European descent. At the same time, the urban areas were experiencing huge problems stemming from urban decay such as homelessness, begging, destitution, prostitution, and disruptive youth. The colonial authorities prioritised the Copperbelt and other urban areas for social welfare service provision due to their economic importance. Also, the colonialists wrongly thought that their families would look after Africans in rural areas.

Regarding 'juvenile delinquency'; a draft report on juvenile welfare in the colonies, already completed in 1942, paid attention to the need to establish a mechanism to respond to the problem of 'juvenile delinquency'. It addressed itself to the coordination of activities related to juvenile welfare in the departments of education, health, agriculture and labour.[19] In 1949, the African Mineworkers' Union was formed to safeguard the rights of Africans working on the mines with Lawrence Katilungu elected its first president. It was quite a militant force, providing Africans with an outlet to voice out and articulate their grievances both against racial discrimination at the workplace and unequal working conditions within the territory.

## Rise of Welfare Societies and Nationalist Politics

The first well-defined form of resistance to colonial rule emerged with the formation of Welfare Societies in the mid-1930s in the main urban areas; the first wave in the rise of these organisations confronting the exploitative nature of colonialism and how this system abused Africans. It is important to note that even though Welfare Societies represented the embryonic stage of nationalistic politics in Northern Rhodesia, they had initially tackled welfare issues and mutely addressed hard political questions in the colony. For instance:

> The African Welfare Societies were anxious about the social disorder in the towns. With the help of missionaries and social workers, they organised football matches, started small libraries and run small clubs.[20]

---

19    Waddington, E.J., 1946.

20    Hall, 1965:130.

Though pragmatic, these attempts could not yield tangible results against colonial subjugation. Welfare Societies' efforts to empower local people proved futile as the colonial status quo remained intact and harsh. There was a resurgence of these organisations in the 1940s, and this development would fundamentally add momentum to Zambia's drive towards self-rule. The mid-1930s and the 1940s proved to be significant milestones in the light of increased African political consciousness. Africans were steadily beginning to interrogate the appalling inequalities and inequities embedded in the colonial socio-political and economic order, particularly those residing along the railway between Victoria Falls and the Copperbelt. However, there was another dimension to the preceding issues. It turned out that politics and social welfare had a symbiotic relationship that would foster fundamental changes in the colony. The march towards independence was raised to another level in May 1946 when Dauti Yamba, founder of the Luanshya Welfare Association, together with representatives from thirteen other urban and rural welfare organisations, called for the country's welfare organisations to unite under one body. In attendance at this meeting in Kabwe were several delegates such as:

⊳ Godwin Mbikusita Lewanika (Kitwe African Society)

⊳ Nelson Nalumango (Livingstone Welfare Society)

⊳ N.S. Liyanda (Mongu Welfare Society)

⊳ Sykes Ndilila (Broken Hill (Kabwe) Welfare Society)

⊳ Joseph Y. Mumba (Lusaka Welfare Society), and

⊳ George W.C. Kaluwa (Mazabuka Welfare Society).

All these societies were amalgamated into the Federation of African Welfare Societies with Yamba as President; Mumba as Assistant Secretary and Kaluwa, the Organising Secretary. The federation aimed to create cooperation and mutual understanding between constituent urban and rural societies of Northern Rhodesia. Two years later, in 1948, the federation was reconstituted into a political party, the Northern Rhodesia Congress under the leadership of Godwin Mbikusita Lewanika.

## Shifts Towards Professionalism in Social Welfare Activities in Colonial Zambia

As stated earlier, the period after the end of the Second World War was quite momentous for Northern Rhodesia in the light of social welfare activities. In the following 1950s decade, even the colonial authorities accelerated the welfare sector's professionalisation. During this period, the Northern Rhodesian Ministry of Local Government and Social Services was in charge of social welfare services throughout the territory. However, a critical development at the time was the appointment of Archibald H. Elwell, the first SWO in 1945 in the Copperbelt. He was posted to Kitwe, and the Provincial Commissioner of the then Western Province (Copperbelt) instructed him: "... to adopt the role of a student" by observing what was happening in the country and "learning about the conditions on the Copperbelt from a welfare point of view". Elwell's duties revolved around health, recreation and educational activities and he was expected to possess an intimate knowledge of the "African language and customs" and have the "well-being of the African at heart".[21] Also, the SWO should have had "a good knowledge of hygiene, cinema work and business". Welfare work developed largely in terms of recreational activities and other functions that revolved around: play centres; care of people with disabilities; medical social welfare; health visits and aftercare; diet (nutritional) schemes; the removal of evil social conditions; and communal feeding.[22]

Elwell had a short stay in Northern Rhodesia and was dismissed and sent back to England. One reason behind his sacking was his overt sympathy for African people. For instance, on one occasion, he attended a Kitwe African Society meeting; an action the colonial authorities took as an affront. In a letter to the Colonial Office in London, the Governor of Northern Rhodesia expressed concern that this welfare officer was not a suitable candidate for welfare work. He pointed out that the Nkana Mining Company believed

---

21    Central Province African Provincial Board, 1948.

22    Ibid.

that the welfare officer was a threat and could not allow him to enter their compounds.[23] Elwell did not impress his new employers as attested by the following comments:

> My impression at the moment is that the gentleman who is welfare officer is entirely bound up with African interests. If that is so I deprecate it. I hope he is going to deal [with] both European and African welfare.[24]

Roy Welensky, who would later become the Prime Minister of the Federation of Rhodesia and Nyasaland, made these remarks. Even though such sentiments were not unanimous in the Legislative Council, they nonetheless reflected the wider settler population's views as can be noted from the remarks of one Member of the Legislative Council during the same debate. He rightly argued that Europeans had a highly organised welfare system they had created for themselves and pointed out that they had big recreational, athletic, dramatic, women's and youth clubs as well as scout, and girl-guide movements.[25]

The year 1950 can be regarded as a watershed in social welfare matters in Zambia when the colonial government established the DSW. The colonial authorities had approached the South African Government to realise this and had solicited both advice and help to constitute an organisation that would oversee social welfare issues in Northern Rhodesia. After that, the South African Director of Social Welfare visited Northern Rhodesia to conduct a survey of social welfare services in the country and make necessary recommendations on how they could be organised, coordinated and developed. The South African DSW published the survey's findings in a report titled, *Social Welfare Services in Northern Rhodesia: A Report Presented to the Government of Northern Rhodesia* (1950) by Graham C. Bain. It is interesting to note that during this period, South Africa was entrenching institutionalised racism or apartheid, creating separate social welfare services for the white, black, coloured and Indian population groups. In this arrangement, services for blacks were minimal. A natural corollary of this set-up was a permeation of an ethos of racial inequality in social welfare service delivery. Thus, South Africa was not the best country that the Northern Rhodesian Government could have used as a model for its social welfare system given South Africa's apartheid policies. However, Northern Rhodesia had its form of apartheid known as the colour-bar system.

---

23    Waddington, 1946.
24    Legislative Council of Northern Rhodesia, 1945.
25    Ibid.

After the DSW was established, administrative secretaries and local government officials, who were colonial government representatives, oversaw the department. Initially, a skeleton staff complement was in charge of the department comprising:

▷ a director – responsible for the overall work of the department,

▷ three SWOs, responsible for the towns of Kabwe, Livingstone and Lusaka, and

▷ two wardens in charge of children's shelters in Ndola.

Before this appointment, a director, acting as an advisor on welfare matters to the Northern Rhodesian Government, headed the department. Following his employment, the colonial government undertook measures to arrive at a plan for managing social welfare services in the country, so that communities could have access. After the plan was prepared, in consultation with local authorities and the mining companies, it became the policy that delineated African and European social welfare service provision in colonial Zambia. British colonial policy after the Second World War, in the light of social welfare service provision, was quite specific when it came to the roles the different territories of the British Empire were to play. They not only had to provide social welfare services to people in various territories but recruit personnel for such work.

In this regard, respective authorities in the colonies then sought suitable local candidates for the various social welfare positions. However, this endeavour proved extremely difficult due to the non-availability of locally trained personnel, causing field workers of limited educational background to become the first indigenous social welfare workers in Northern Rhodesia. Consequently, the first trained officials in charge of social welfare were from the British Probation Service. Not surprisingly, there was a strong bias towards probation work at that time in Northern Rhodesia.

Furthermore, the Juvenile Ordinance, passed in 1953, entrenched such a tilt in social welfare matters.[26] At the time, Northern Rhodesia did not have an approved reformatory school or place of safety for non-African racial groups. Only in 1961 did these services extend to them. The colony had made use of services in Southern Rhodesia, and South Africa for European and bi-racial young people conflicted with the law. The only 'place of safety' for young Africans at Katombora near Livingstone, operating since 1950, was

---

26    Brooks & Nyirenda, 1987.

fraught with challenges such as lack of trained staff and training facilities, as well as shortages in accommodation. In 1954, the department started casework and handed over group work to the local authorities. Interestingly, the eventual recognition of the urban African family brought in its wake a new emphasis on social welfare services, especially in mitigating social change. Voluntary organisations also increased, including the Young Women's Christian Association, although their services were particularly directed towards expatriate needs.[27]

Professionalism in social welfare matters was strengthened in Zambia with the introduction of a course at Mindolo in Ndola in 1951. This training was earmarked for Africans working in social welfare organisations and a total of 14 employees from various local authorities in the towns of Chingola, Kitwe, Livingstone, Luanshya and Ndola attended. The course included theoretical and practical lessons focusing on casework and group work methods. Lecturers who conducted this course were drawn from different government departments such as the Rhodes-Livingstone Institute and the Ndola Municipal Council.[28] In Lusaka, the Lusaka Management Board organised a two-year course for its African staff. The course was more practical in outlook and laid stress on welfare work and the importance of character training in group work. Another development that added professionalism and a coherent approach to social welfare was the formation of the Northern Rhodesian Council of Social Services.[29] At the behest of the Northern Rhodesian Government, the Council was created in 1954, to coordinate the work of all social welfare agencies in colonial Zambia. The government provided annual subsidies to the Council. Despite this, the main social welfare service offered to Africans was still recreation – except for Barotseland (or western Zambia), where three orphanages for African children existed that the missionaries and the Barotse Native Government maintained.[30] As inferior educational standards remained, indigenous trained social workers could not be recruited into the DSW. After this shortfall was observed, plans got underway to establish a training centre for social welfare practice in the country.

---

27    Ibid.
28    DSW, 1952.
29    Ibid.
30    DSW, 1950.

While these activities aimed at professionalisation were unfolding in the colony, both missionary and voluntary organisations continued providing services to needy people; the missionaries' services were non-racial, while certain services voluntary organisations provided were exclusively for white and mixed-race populations. In 1953, the colonial government established a central welfare assistance programme to help vulnerable individuals and coordinate the policy governing this assistance. There were attempts made to increase both European and African staff in the department as well as find a balance between recreational activities and social work. The scope of social welfare initiatives became clearer to the administrators and policymakers once the former was achieved. The DSW established its training centre for African social workers in 1954. In 1955, serious discussions between municipalities, mining companies and the DSW were concluded. These discussions aimed to initiate a standard generic social work course for Africans.[31] The preceding endeavours culminated in concrete actions, taken to establish social work training in the country.

To this end, the Oppenheimer College of Social Services, a non-profit institute of learning, was opened in Lusaka in 1961. Before its establishment, all the training centres around the country offering social work courses were closed down to arrive at a uniform approach to social welfare training in the country. The college began training students in the same year, and the first-class graduated in 1964 after students had completed a three-year diploma. At the outset, the college endeavoured to provide quality programmes by offering an external Diploma in Social Services in conjunction with the University of London. There was an external Junior Diploma that was specifically offered to individuals already employed as social workers but who did not have any formal qualifications.[32] The Oppenheimer College recruited lecturers from the United Kingdom and the USA. The assumption underlying the hiring of such a mix of academics was that students would benefit from two distinct intellectual traditions. Initially, Oppenheimer College offered courses in the social sciences, and there was intensive training in generic social work available to students from the same college. The foreign and Western influence in social welfare and social work training was amplified with this conscious approach. This training, even though deemed advantageous, because it was generic and would enable practitioners to effectively respond to the terrain and multiplicity of social problems in

---

31    DSW, 1955.

32    DSW, 1961.

the country, nonetheless reinforced the colonial and Western heritage. Nevertheless, for social workers dealing with various social ills in Zambia, the generic approach was favoured for its holistic appraisal of social reality.

Without a specific emphasis on one type of intervention, this approach provided the practitioner with the latitude to intervene at multiple levels. Training, particularly related to skills and the development of psychiatric interventions, were prioritised. Hence, after Independence, social work education did not change at all and instructions continued as before. Due to this situation, the Oppenheimer College of Social Services was still preoccupied with the blending of American and British models. The philosophical underpinnings of both American and British social work models were pivotal in shaping the curriculum of social work in post-colonial Zambia. Efforts at introducing a social work course of a higher quality finally bore fruit in 1966, when the Faculty of Humanities and Social Sciences was opened at the University of Zambia (UNZA), incorporating the Oppenheimer College. This was two years after Zambia's independence in 1964. UNZA provided instructions in social work at both degree and diploma levels. The main advantage in taking over the Oppenheimer programme was that there was an availability of trained staff that could provide a professional social work programme.

Furthermore, the Social Work Department at UNZA had a reasonable budget for fieldwork placements and supervisory visits.[33] When UNZA began operating, there was a pressing need for trained personnel in various fields in the country. There were numerous employment opportunities for trained social workers in social welfare departments, urban municipalities and the townships of mining companies, general hospitals, mental institutions, voluntary organisations as well as in community development activities. Trained social workers were in demand in the areas of personnel and industrial relations and for positions requiring skills in the human relations field.[34] In years to come, social work educators would constantly grapple with this foreign origin of the profession, as they sought after more relevant models of social welfare and social work in a Zambian context.

When Zambia became independent on 24 October 1964, the new African government led by the United National Independence Party (UNIP) made choices in matters of national development in general and social welfare, in particular, during the First

33    Hough, 1969.
34    Ibid.

Republic from 1964-1972. When it came to social welfare, it is quite ironic that there was the congruence of approaches of the colonial government and the new government. Startlingly, in the area of the family, both the colonial government and the UNIP Government had regarded the extended family as critical to meeting the needs of its members, as earlier mentioned. Both the colonial and post-colonial policies governing the plight of the aged were not dissimilar at all, although their rationales and outcomes were different. According to UNIP's humanism ideology, old people in traditional societies were regarded as fountains of knowledge from where the community could solicit advice, especially in times of crises; they were venerated and, therefore, had to participate in numerous community activities that brought forth community cohesion; they arbitrated disputes and offered wise counsel. Whenever old persons could no longer care for themselves, the extended family took the responsibility of looking after them. Politicians and policymakers argued alike that urbanisation had played a significant role in loosening the ties of the extended family system.

## Conclusion

This chapter discussed the evolution of the social welfare system of Zambia from the pre-colonial to the post-colonial era. The biggest part of the social welfare system is still similar to the way it was in the colonial era; nevertheless, there were strong moves towards community development and social development in the 1960s and 1970s. Presently, the government emphasises the social cash transfer programme, a non-statutory service. Social work is still being offered by UNZA, as well as some new colleges and private universities. There is, however, a challenge of regulating and legislating practice; a regulatory body is still needed to govern social work practice in the country.

# References

Brooks, E. & Nyirenda, V.G. 1987. Zambia. In: J.E Dixon (ed). *Social Welfare in Africa*. Kent: Croom Helm. pp.247-279.

Central Province African Provincial Board. 1948. Sixth Council Meeting, Broken Hill, 20-21 April.

Crowder, M. 1993. Africa under British and Belgian Domination, 1935-45. In: A.A. Mazrui & C. Wondji (eds). *General History of Africa, VIII. Africa since 1935*. Paris: United Nations Educational, Scientific and Cultural Organisation. pp.76-104.

CSO (Central Statistical Office). 2018. *Zambia in Figures 2018*. Lusaka: CSO.

Deane, P. 1953. *Colonial Social Accounting*. Cambridge: Cambridge University Press.

Gann, L.H. 1958. *The Birth of a Plural Society*. Manchester: Manchester University Press.

Government of Northern Rhodesia. DSW (Department of Social Welfare). 1950. Annual Report. Lusaka: Government Printer.

Government of Northern Rhodesia. DSW. 1952. *Annual Report*. Lusaka: Government Printer.

Government of Northern Rhodesia. DSW. 1955. *Annual Report*. Lusaka: Government Printer.

Government of Northern Rhodesia. DSW. 1961. *Annual Report*. Lusaka: Government Printer.

Hall, R. 1965. *Zambia*. London: Pall Mall Press.

Heisler, H. 1971. The creation of a stabilised urban society: A turning point in the development of Northern Rhodesia/Zambia. *African Affairs*, 70(279):125-145.

Herbert, E.W. 2002. *Twilight on the Zambezi: Late Colonialism in Central Africa*. Houndsmills: Palgrave Macmillan.

Hough, M.A. 1969. Education for social work in Zambia. *Social Work/Maatskaplike Werk*, 4(69):186-191.

Keith, J.L. & Stephenson, A. 1936. *Report of the Sub-Committee on the Native Industrial Labour Advisory Board*. Lusaka: Government Printers.

Kelly, M.J. 1991. *Education in a Declining Economy: The Case of Zambia 1975-1985*. Washington, D.C: World Bank.

Legislative Council of Northern Rhodesia. 1945. *Hansard No.49*. Lusaka: Government Printer.

Macarov, D. 1995. *Social Welfare Structure and Practice*. London: Sage Publications.

Ministry of Community Development, Mother and Child Health. 2016. *Services Provided*. Lusaka: Ministry of Community Development, Mother and Child Health.

Noyoo, N. 2000. *Social Welfare in Zambia*. 1st Edition. Lusaka: Multimedia Publications.

Rotberg, R.I. 1965. *The Rise of Nationalism in Central Africa: The Making of Malawi and Zambia, 1873-1964*. Cambridge, MA: Harvard University Press.

Waddington, E.J. 1946. Correspondence from the Governor of Northern Rhodesia to George Gater, Colonial Office, London, 2 February.

World Bank. 2019. *The World Bank in Zambia: Overview*. [https://bit.ly/2STs6Po]. (Accessed 2 September 2019).

# 13

# SOCIAL WELFARE AND SOCIAL WORK IN ZIMBABWE

*Rodreck Mupedziswa and Mildred Mushunje*

## Introduction

Zimbabwe, a member of the Southern African Development Community (SADC), gained Independence from Britain in 1980. Currently, the country has a population of just over 13 million, of which approximately 48 per cent are males and 52 per cent females. About 67 per cent of the population live in rural areas.[1] For several decades leading to Independence, Zimbabwe was dubbed the breadbasket of the southern African region, as the colonial government had a viable agricultural programme. At Independence, the country boasted abundant natural resources and a diversified economy with relatively viable commercial, industrial, mining, and agricultural sectors. Since 2000, Zimbabwe has experienced a deteriorating economic, political and social environment, with the Gross Domestic Product (GDP) dropping by approximately 50 per cent in 2008.

A hyperinflationary environment, de-industrialisation marked by a sharp drop in capacity utilisation and closure of industries, large scale job losses and poor service delivery characterised the socioeconomic crisis. Thus, risk and vulnerability in Zimbabwe have emanated from a combination of intrinsically linked socio-economic, environmental and

---

1    Republic of Zimbabwe, 2012.

political factors.[2] Today the majority of the population in Zimbabwe is poor and face major vulnerabilities. It is in this suffocating environment that the social work profession is faced with the onerous service delivery task.

This chapter considers the evolution of social welfare and social work in Zimbabwe. It begins by considering the indigenous social welfare system in place before colonisation, after which it delves into discussing various elements of the colonial era social welfare system. The chapter then considers the historical evolution of social work in the country, followed by an exposé of how social work has responded to the needs and challenges of various groups. Consideration is given to social welfare and social work in the post-colonial era, including the challenges it faced and what its prospects are. Suggestions are made in respect of the way forward.

## Origins of Social Welfare and Social Work in Zimbabwe

Before Independence, social welfare mainly targeted the minority white settlers. With blacks, the expectation was that they had the extended family network to provide for them.[3] Traditionally, social welfare provision was predicated on the philosophy of what Ntseane and Solo (2007) termed, 'self-organised' informal safety nets, and these were based on membership of a particular social group which could be the extended family, a kin group or the community at large. The extended family, in particular, would provide support during difficult times in the form of cash, food, housing, and care for the sick or dependent relatives; provision of material relief, labour, and emotional support.[4] Bourdillon (1991) saw the extended family as being the main unit for providing security and support in times of distress.

In the pre-colonial era, the principles of solidarity and reciprocity guided the Zimbabwean society, with emphasis on unity and shared responsibility towards family members.[5] Community support played a key role, especially in cases where the extended family network faltered. The poor had an opportunity to work in the field or sell their labour to the well-off, especially during planting or harvesting. Destitute persons could look

---

2    Norton, Conway & Foster, 2001.

3    Moyo, 2007.

4    World Bank, 2009.

5    Mushunje, 2014.

after the cattle of the rich in return for a cow or two. The poor would look after the cattle of those who were relatively well off, using the animals as draught power, or accessing milk. Ntseane and Solo (2007) argue that "the harsh economic environment and the magnitude of needs today make it difficult for the extended family system to continue to play its social security role effectively."[6]

Support came in the form of food security provision through what was termed, *Zunde raMambo* ('chief's granary'). The granary was used to guard against drought or famine, and to mitigate the impact of any mishaps that might befall vulnerable members of the community, especially older people, the infirm and children.[7] The primary aim of *Zunde raMambo* was to ensure that a community had enough reserves which could be used in times of food shortage.[8] Some of the food would feed orphans, the chief's soldiers, subjects awaiting trial, the chief's advisors and those engaged in disputes within the community. Proceeds were used to sponsor community ceremonies. Historically, *Zunde raMambo* was used as a social, economic, and political rallying-point for the community. This concept embodied the traditional values that promoted togetherness and a sense of belonging.[9]

Over the years, developments in Zimbabwe affected the *Zunde raMambo* initiative in several ways. For instance, the land reform programme brought people from different areas into communal areas for resettlement, disrupting the age-old social order, causing conflicts culminating in the solidarity value being undermined. Mararike (2001) concurred, noting that challenges included a shortage of land; lack of agricultural inputs; and lack of control of assets such as land; as well as inadequate knowledge and organisation skills on the part of some chiefs.

However, despite these challenges, many believe that the *Zunde raMambo* concept can bring together community members, particularly in the wake of the debilitating socio-economic and political hardships. Currently, there is talk of the need to revive this practice, especially in the wake of the HIV/Aids scourge.[10] Kaseke (2002) argues that this

---

6    Ntseane & Solo, 2007:52.
7    Mushunje, 2006.
8    Mararike, 2001; Patel et al., 2012.
9    Mararike, 2001.
10   Patel et al., 2012.

traditional support system is still relevant, although the weakening of the extended family system eroded its effectiveness. The weakened extended family system is essentially due to urbanisation, modernisation and industrialisation that resulted in the adoption of new value systems that do not promote traditional support systems. Another strategy that communities utilised, to meet their basic needs, during the period, was the promotion of burial societies. These were local indigenous organisations, providing mutual help and assistance to community members in the event of death or illness.[11] These entities are a type of non-formal or indigenous social security arrangement and have been seen to offer a measure of financial security, especially in the event of bereavement. Cormack (1983) notes that burial societies evolved to provide aid, especially to migrant workers who faced serious deprivation and social insecurity.

In Zimbabwe, burial societies are known to have been in existence as far back as 1919. Pioneers included the Sena Burial Society and the Gazaland Burial Society that the then migrant labourers from Mozambique organised. By 1973 there were 248 registered burial societies and probably an equal number not registered, in Bulawayo alone.[12] Over the years, the role of burial societies has become even more pronounced given the limited access to formal systems such as funeral insurance, for the majority of the Zimbabwean population. Dhemba, Gumbo and Nyamusara (2002) state that burial societies provide immediate assistance to the bereaved in the form of cash and other benefits such as a coffin. However, due to Zimbabwe's economic woes, the viability of burial societies may be under serious threat as members may increasingly find it difficult to maintain their monthly contributions.

Another initiative that Zimbabwean communities used to meet needs during the colonial period was that of rotating and savings clubs. These refer to a form of non-formal social support system in both the colonial and post-colonial periods. Rotating and savings clubs constitute a member-based organisation system (i.e. non-kinship-based). They operate based on balanced reciprocity and can be described as a self-organised mutual support system predicated on the solidarity principle. Usually, the money they generate is saved with formal banks. With many rotating and savings clubs, benefits include credit

---

11    Hall, 1987.

12    Cormack, 1983.

facilities, low-interest loans, and a share of the profits. The associations play a key role in meeting the financial needs of especially people with limited sources of income.[13]

## Colonial Incursion

Zimbabwe was under British colonial (white) rule between 1890-1980 when the country gained political Independence. The policies, the various pre-Independence regimes that ruled (the then Rhodesia) at different points, adopted were based on dualism. To this end, various pieces of legislation were promulgated, aiming essentially at alienating the best land to the settler community and entrenching the policy of separate development of races. These laws included the Land Apportionment Act (1931), the Land Husbandry Act (1951) and the Land Tenure Act (1969). Hall and Mupedziswa (1995) noted that under these pieces of legislation: "Social services, e.g. social welfare, education, health, housing were as a matter of course provided on colour lines with the white community enjoying superior services to those of their black counterparts."[14]

The white settlers effected a unilateral declaration of Independence in 1965, incensing the colonial masters in the UK and resulting in the country being isolated. The then ruling Rhodesia Front Party promoted a philosophy of separate development, modelled after the apartheid system in South Africa. During this period, white areas continued to flourish while indigenous blacks languished in poverty. Naturally, this infuriated the black majority and this would lead to a protracted armed struggle for Independence. When in 1972, the armed struggle commenced in earnest, there was a massive disruption of the social order, negatively impacting social welfare provision, especially for the majority black population. The extended family network continued to play a key role even as the colonial regime was promulgating all manner of legislation aimed at denying blacks' basic social welfare services. However, the impact of the extended family increasingly became negligible as resources dwindled.

---

13    Ntseane & Solo, 2007.

14    Hall & Mupedziswa, 1995:13.

## Characteristics of Colonial Welfare

The first official effort at organised welfare provision in the then Rhodesia occurred in 1936 when a 'probation and school attendance officer' programme was introduced. The first probation officer was recruited from the UK, and the programme catered solely for the white population. A non-contributory, means-tested old-age pension scheme was introduced in 1936, and it made provisions for non-Africans only. In 1948, a duly constituted Department of Social Welfare (DSW) was established, serviced exclusively with white officers. The first black probation officer, however, was recruited in 1949. The functions of the DSW included the investigation of juvenile delinquency cases among all ethnic groups.[15] With time, appropriate structures for welfare provision were put in place in major cities and towns including Harare, Bulawayo, Gweru and Mutare.

In 1964, the DSW introduced a public assistance programme, but less than 400 black families were adjudged eligible for assistance in the first four years. Assistance this Department offered included rations (or cash equivalent) and rental allowances. With time, the base for social welfare provision widened, when several local authorities, mines and other private organisations began to offer social services, albeit to a limited extent. By the mid-1970s, several non-governmental organisations (NGOs) had emerged and were offering a variety of social welfare services. In 1976, a Welfare Organisations Act was passed, and this required all voluntary organisations providing social services to register with the Department of Social Services (DSS).[16] Despite the increase in the number of organisations offering social welfare services, coverage remained rather limited.

## Social Work's Response: Pre- and Post-Independence

For many years, during the colonial era, no social work training institution existed in the country. Social workers were therefore trained in countries like Zambia and South Africa, but some were recruited without a social work qualification. It was not unusual to find a newspaper advert for the position of a social worker whose qualifications were a retired nurse or a retired school teacher. There was thus a warped idea that anyone could practice as a social worker; even without a formal qualification. In 1964 the Jesuit

---

15   Hall & Mupedziswa, 1995.

16   Mupedziswa, 1995.

Fathers, a Catholic order, initiated the establishment of a School of Social Work (SSW). Initially, the institution only offered a course in group work. With time, as demand for qualified social workers increased, the SSW launched a Diploma in Social Work. In 1975, the Bachelor degree in Social Work (BSW) was launched, followed by an Honours and a Master of Social Work degree. A Clinical Social Work degree programme was offered for a few years. The SSW offered a one-year Certificate in Social Work and ran short courses on an ad-hoc basis.[17] Cadres trained at the SSW immersed themselves in social welfare work.

The transition from white colonial rule to Independence was a torturous experience. At Independence, social work adopted an unambiguous commitment to the social justice and equity policies in healthcare, relief and resettlement programmes, education, and personal social services intended to be free of racial and discriminatory practices.[18] The new government stated that it sought to establish a society founded on socialist, democratic and egalitarian principles. In a policy document titled, *Growth with Equity*, the government stated that it was determined to embark on policies and programmes designed to involve the entire population fully in the development process.[19] There would be an emphasis on rebuilding the country, ravaged by war. Decentralisation was adopted as a catalyst, especially for community development. Much more funding went towards programmes targeting the black population as the new government initiated some form of 'positive' discrimination. Areas that had borne the brunt of the war needed rehabilitation, and hence the government embarked on a massive reconstruction programme. Thus, in the first decade of Independence, considerable progress was realised regarding social welfare delivery.

## Recent Efforts of the Post-Independence Government

However, these fortunes took a nose-dive from the onset of the second decade of Independence.[20] Two hotly contested events occurred in 2000: the launch of a controversial land reform programme and a disputed presidential election, creating massive political

---

17   Hall & Mupedziswa, 1995.
18   Kaseke, 2001.
19   Republic of Zimbabwe, 1981.
20   Kaseke & Dhemba, 2007.

polarisation, earning Zimbabwe pariah state status internationally. Commercial white farmers were forcibly dispossessed of the land they farmed, and this land was reallocated to both peasant farmers and emerging black commercial farmers, as part of the national resettlement programme. A substantial chunk of land so acquired was, however, reportedly parcelled out to a select few political elite individuals aligned to the ruling party. During this period of turmoil, a considerable proportion of the population left the country, either to seek greener pastures or to flee the charged political environment characterised by a culture of violence.[21] The 'brain drain' saw an estimated 2-3 million of the country's citizens leaving the country for the Diaspora by 2010.[22]

Since then, the country has experienced severe socioeconomic and political challenges, and these have impacted negatively on the citizens' quality of life, with poverty having both deepened and widened. To address the declining economy, the government through different institutions developed several short, medium and long-term policies and programmes:

➤ the Millennium Economic Recovery Programme (2002)

➤ the National Economic Revival Programme (2003)

➤ the National Economic Priority Development Programme (2006)

➤ the Short-Term Emergency Recovery Programme (2009)

➤ the Three-Year Budget and Macro-Economic Policy Framework (2010).

While the government came up with a raft of new legislation, social welfare services essentially remained residual and largely urban-based. As Hall and Mupedziswa (1995) noted: "Admittedly there have been efforts to redress the imbalances through the introduction of mechanisms that have resulted in the considerable spread of services to rural areas, but this has, by and large, been an uphill struggle."[23] Currently, the country has several social welfare programmes in place. These can be classified as follows:

➤ Social assistance (e.g. cash transfers, fee waivers for basic services)

---

21    Mupedziswa, 2015.

22    Crush & Frayne, 2010.

23    Hall and Mupedziswa, 1995:84.

⊳ Social insurance (e.g. old age and disability pensions, health insurance, unemployment insurance)

⊳ Labour market-based interventions.

While various organisations outside of government spearheaded a number of these initiatives (e.g. agriculture-based inputs support, school feeding), for purposes of this discussion, the focus will be confined to the government's non-contributory social welfare services provided through the DSS.

## Public Assistance Monthly Maintenance Allowances

Although this dates to the pre-Independence era, the *Social Welfare Assistance Act of 1988* (Chapter 17.06) established the legal framework for the programme's current configuration; programme objectives were to "provide relief to individuals and households in distress". Beneficiaries are provided with unconditional cash transfer after means-testing.[24] The programme is implemented only in districts that the Harmonised Social Cash Transfer programme has not yet reached. Target groups include older people (above 60 years), vulnerable families and people with disabilities. Clients receive the support of 20 US dollars per month. The coverage in 2015 of the DSS implemented programme was 6 688 households with the programme expenditure topping 831 222 US dollars. The social assistance initiatives such as the Public Assistance (PA) interventions have been extremely underfunded.

According to Mupedziswa (1995), the problem with Zimbabwe's public assistance scheme is that it is operated following the residual approach which holds that the family or market system should meet the individual's needs, with the State only assisting when these systems break down. A means-test has, therefore, been applied to determine eligibility for assistance. The public assistance allowance of 20 US dollars a month (as at 10 November 2012) was far below the United Nations' (UN) 'official' poverty line of 1.25 US dollars per day.[25] According to Kaseke (1998), potential beneficiaries have been discouraged from applying because they have had to contend with transport and related costs. Disbursement has also been erratic owing to perennial underfunding of

---

24     Garcia & Moore, 2012.
25     Government of Zimbabwe & United Nations, 2012.

the DSS. In January to September 2012, for instance, beneficiaries only got one-month allowances.[26] Furthermore, Kaseke (1998) maintained that there was a general lack of awareness of the existence of the public assistance scheme in some areas, and as a result, many potential beneficiaries did not apply for assistance. Dhemba (2013) noted that the application of a means-test, effectively restricted the number of beneficiaries of the public assistance scheme.

## Harmonised Social Cash Transfer

The Ministry of Labour and Social Services reportedly launched the Harmonised Social Cash Transfer initiative in 2011 to "strengthen the purchasing power of 55 000 ultra-poor households that are labour constrained through cash transfer". This programme replaced the Public Assistance Programme which was phased out. The objective was to increase households' consumption to a level above the food poverty line; reduce the number of ultra-poor households; help beneficiaries avoid risky coping strategies (such as child labour and early marriage).[27] The cash transfers are unconditional, and the programme beneficiaries are entitled to educational fee waivers, the Basic Education Assistance Module (BEAM) and non-contributory health insurance.[28] Recipients are means-tested with the aid of community verification.

By 2012, ten districts had been enrolled while the figure rose to 19 districts by 2016. The target population included ultra-poor, labour-constrained and food-poor households, with recipients re-assessed every two years together with the head beneficiary of the household. Benefits ranged from 10-25 US dollars per month paid bi-monthly through cash-in-transit means and delivered at pay points. Programme coverage as at 2015 was 52 049 beneficiary households, translating into 236 013 individual beneficiaries. Programme expenditure in 2011 was 6.9 million US dollars, while in 2016 annual expenditure was estimated at 14.5 million US dollars. The Government of Zimbabwe and the UN International Children's Fund (UNICEF) jointly fund the Harmonised Social Cash Transfer through the multi-donor aligned Child Protection Fund. Challenges have

---

26    Ibid.
27    Chikova, 2013.
28    DFID & FAO, 2013.

included delays and uncertainty surrounding payments. According to Schubert (2016), operational costs are approximately 12.5 per cent signalling high cost-effectiveness.

## Assisted Medical Treatment Order

This programme was introduced in the late 1960s, and its primary objective is to "enhance health care among vulnerable populations".[29] It is a non-contributory health insurance, and beneficiaries include older people, people with disabilities, people who are chronically ill and vulnerable children.[30] The scheme intervenes by settling hospital bills. In 2011, 25 000 beneficiaries were reached at an expenditure of 700 000 US dollars.[31] Institutions and agencies participating in this programme have included the Ministry of Public Service, Labour and Social Welfare and selected mission hospitals. Kaseke (1998) observed that older people tended not to benefit much from free health services as the hospitals and clinics were always congested, and there was often an acute shortage of drugs and medical personnel. Government policy stipulates that children get priority in accessing medical care ahead of adults, and this has always prejudiced older people. Thus, this scheme has suffered from targeting challenges.

## Basic Education Assistance Module

The literacy levels in Zimbabwe continue to be among the best on the African continent, with the 2012 Census putting the rate at 96 per cent. Even so, the rate of school drop-outs has been alarming. A study on School Dropout and Repetition established that failure to pay fees had been one of the major reasons for dropping out of school while other reasons included early marriage and pregnancy, as well as the absence of a school within walking distance.[32] The education sector has faced some challenges, essentially due to a reduction in budgetary allocation as a result of political, economic and social factors.[33] The government, therefore, introduced BEAM to "enhance access to primary and secondary education for orphans and vulnerable children".[34] BEAM was first rolled

---

29    Cirrilo & Tebeldi, 2016:158.
30    UN Zimbabwe, 2014.
31    World Bank, 2011.
32    Republic of Zimbabwe, 2014.
33    UNESCO, 2013.
34    Cirillo & Tebaldi, 2016:159.

out in 2001 with nearly 600 000 beneficiaries (6-18-year-olds) in primary and secondary schools. The programme comprises a waiver of fees for both primary and secondary education.[35] Beneficiaries have included orphans and vulnerable children and children with disabilities. The programme caters for children who have never been to school, who have dropped out due to poverty and who are currently in school but failing to pay fees. A target to assist 10 per cent has been mooted for children with disabilities. By 2005, the programme had a budget of around 35 million US dollars and was assisting 970 000 pupils, representing 27 per cent of enrolment. The coverage and the resources allocated to the programme have diminished substantially because of fiscal challenges.

During the hyperinflation years, the programme ceased to operate because the money channelled to schools was being rendered useless even before it reached beneficiaries. A new funding partnership between the government and UNICEF revitalised BEAM in 2009, to support primary (560 000 pupils) and secondary (243 000 students) education. Coverage in 2015 was 194 000, with a programme expenditure of 8.2 million US dollars. An evaluation conducted in 2012 showed that the programme had made an impact in terms of increasing school coverage and contributed to retaining children in school, especially orphans.[36] Challenges that the BEAM initiative faced have included poor targeting and a limited resource base. There have been reports of children with disabilities being left out of the programme, while some undeserving children benefitted.

## How Zimbabwe Evolved since Independence

Since 2000, Zimbabwe has faced serious socio-economic and political challenges. Life expectancy fell to 44 years for men and 43 years for women.[37] According to Kaseke and Dhemba (2007), the middle class consequently disappeared, and many are now classified poor and in need of government support. Unprecedented levels of political violence characterised the year 2008, and most economic activities virtually grounded to a halt. Inflation rose to unprecedented levels. In June 2008, for instance, as the economy virtually imploded, inflation increased to 11.2 million per cent. By 2012, the UN Office for the Coordination of Human Affairs reported that Zimbabwe's inflation

---

35    Smith, Chiroro & Musker, 2012.
36    Ibid.
37    UNAIDS & WHO, 2005.

stood at a mind-boggling '6.5 quintdecillion novemdecillion' per cent.[38] Consequently, the country suffered from critical food, fuel, and foreign currency shortages, while many more professionals sought to flee the country for greener pastures. Over 75 per cent of the Zimbabwean population was reportedly poor, while 47 per cent were adjudged very-poor.[39]

There was a serious depletion of essential drugs in the country, resulting in many highly experienced health professionals abandoning the health sector. Some schools failed to re-open for the better part of 2008 and the beginning of 2009. Many teachers abandoned their posts and left the country in search of greener better opportunities or safer operating environments. Unemployment reportedly topped the 90 per cent mark.[40] HIV/Aids caused an upsurge in the numbers not only of orphaned children but of female-headed and child-headed households, as well. A Government of National Unity (dubbed inclusive government), formed in early 2009, and comprising members of both the ruling Zimbabwe African National Union-Patriotic Front (ZANU-PF) party and the main opposition parties (in particular the Movement for Democratic Change), introduced a raft of measures aimed at resuscitating the country's economy, including suspension of the Zimbabwe dollar and introduction of multiple currencies, including the US dollar. The move helped wipe out inflation and somewhat helped to stabilise the economy. The year 2013 witnessed the end of the inclusive government and the return to power of the ZANU-PF government. The inclusive government's gains gradually began to disappear.

Today the country's economy remains in dire straits, with erratic water supplies, power shortages, and a serious liquidity crisis. External debt has reportedly ballooned to over 10 billion US dollars, with economic deflation firmly taking root.[41] This deflation has been attributed to the government's lack of a durable land reform policy, lack of respect for human rights and the rule of law, and poor agricultural policies. The poor performance of the economy has led to poorer households, as poverty has been both increasing and deepening. The HIV/Aids Report (2013) noted that adult prevalence was still high, at 15 per cent, and this had had a greater impact on women and adolescents.

---

38    Mupedziswa & Mushunje, 2012.

39    Kisner, 2008.

40    Kachembere & Majaka, 2017.

41    Ibid.

The dependency ratio had worsened with an estimated 25 per cent of children orphaned and vulnerable – mostly under the care of older people. High drop-out rates have been witnessed particularly at a secondary school level due to lack of financial resources. The deterioration in basic social services, including in the health sector, and clean water and sanitation meant that health and human capital development were compromised.[42]

Given the poor social indicators and the increased vulnerability of the Zimbabwean populace, the impetus for comprehensive social welfare programmes is evident. The 2013 Constitution of Zimbabwe has in Section 30 taken the lead in constitutionally providing for the right to social security and social care. The Government of Zimbabwe was reportedly in the process of developing a National Social Protection Policy aimed to "strengthen existing social protection systems, increase harmonisation across programmes, strengthen administration and ensure overall policy coherence to effectively address the varied vulnerabilities of the population".[43] Serious shortages of financial and related resources, however, keep the government seriously hamstrung.

A national social protection framework was launched in the said period, but government expenditure on social protection and safety nets has represented only a small proportion of spending in the social sectors, amounting to 1.3 per cent of GDP and 2.9 per cent of the government budget in 2011. More than half of the resources allocated towards social protection have been spent on administrative costs.[44] Public expenditures on safety nets (1.5 per cent of total government expenditure) has mainly concentrated on payment of school fees for vulnerable children. Given the weak state of the public social service delivery system today, donors and NGOs have taken the lead in financing the sector through the provision of agricultural inputs, food, medicine, and school fees. Thus, enormous challenges have been experienced in the area of social welfare provision, particularly since the year 2000, when the country earned its pariah status.

---

42  World Bank, 2014.
43  Republic of Zimbabwe, 2014b.
44  Ibid.

## Current Social Welfare and Social Work Challenges

The cited developments and challenges had a major impact on Zimbabwe's overall family and household viability.[45] The impact on human security and welfare has been enormous, resulting in numerous challenges for the social work profession, particularly regarding the development of social welfare services. These challenges can be subdivided into two broad categories – poor resource base and poor deliverables.

### Human Resources Shortages

Resources can be sub-divided into human power and material aspects. It has been noted elsewhere that the socioeconomic and political meltdown, a key feature of Zimbabwe since around 2000, resulted in many people 'voting with their feet' and skipping the country and thus precipitating a brain drain of immense magnitude. Many went to neighbouring countries like Botswana and South Africa, while a considerable number flocked to countries like the UK, USA, Canada, and New Zealand. Among those who left were qualified social workers, most of whom had been in government service. Mupedziswa and Ushamba (2006) report that one key social welfare office in Bulawayo, in the space of three months, lost no less than 13 officers through resignations. The loss was so bad that, in the early 2000s, more than 30 Zimbabwe-trained social workers were working for Birmingham City in the UK alone, while Leeds, reportedly had no less than six social workers – all former classmates at the University of Zimbabwe's (UZ) SSW – sharing the same office.[46] Of those who remained, the majority elected to perform secondary social work roles in NGOs and other sectors where remuneration packages were relatively better. The DSS was thus deprived of a large number of officers, including its most experienced senior-level staff.

The human resources crisis forced the government to employ non-social workers from cognate disciplines such as sociology, psychology and political science. In some cases, the performance of the non-social workers has been abysmal.[47] The training arena has equally been affected as personnel with no social work qualifications have, at times, supervised social work students undertaking fieldwork placement. At times, people with

---

45    Mupedziswa & Mushunje, 2012.

46    Mupedziswa, 2005.

47    Ibid.

295

lower qualifications (e.g. diploma) have been obliged to supervise degree students; little wonder the quality of graduates has not been as expected. Thus, while there has been an increase in the number of social work training institutions in the country, there is some concern regarding the quality of the product (due to ineffective classroom training methods, inadequate fieldwork supervision, and inappropriate fieldwork placements). Thus, the mass qualified social workers' exodus from Zimbabwe that the unstable socio-economic and political environment occasioned has negatively impacted on social welfare service delivery in the country.

## Limited Material Resources

Lack of financial and other resources for programming has been a critical challenge in respect of social welfare services delivery in Zimbabwe. Coupled with delays in disbursement of funds, the inconsistency of the support provided has resulted in some BEAM recipients withdrawing from school because their benefits had been discontinued. Added problems are lack of office space and office furniture, working telephones, computers, photocopiers, stationery, and transportation. Staff accommodation has been identified as a perennial issue of concern.[48]

Staffing levels have always posed a challenge, with the officer-to-client ratio often being unfavourable. The Government of Zimbabwe has not shown enough appetite to recruit new officers in sufficiently large numbers, mostly due to resource constraints. The few social workers in posts have often been underpaid and overworked, dealing a terrible blow to their morale. During an Institutional Capacity Assessment conducted by Wyatt et al. (2010), one respondent had this to say:

> The social workers within the DSS have become destitute with nothing at hand for them to assist others in need of assistance. It is a shame to our country. Something needs to be urgently done to rescue the DSS. How do you expect a destitute to assist another destitute?[49]

The social workers earn modest salaries, and hence their welfare is a cause for concern, as this negatively impacts on efficient service delivery. Some have, consequently, ended up quitting their jobs for greener pastures. The problem of human power shortages has

---

48    Wyatt, Mupedziswa & Rayment, 2010.
49    Wyatt et al., 2010:42.

rendered social welfare services delivery extremely difficult, with beneficiaries often short-changed, as the services rendered across the country have quantitatively reduced and qualitatively deteriorated. Social workers in Zimbabwe have thus, often found themselves failing to render meaningful welfare services to vulnerable populations.

## Deliverables: Disjointed Welfare Programmes

A common challenge in respect of social work in Africa – Zimbabwe included – is that of the lack of relevance and appropriateness, essentially because of the philosophy of the profession's colonial legacy predicated on the remedial orientation which tends to drive the programmes. Consequently, the profession has found itself promoting programmes that do not improve the circumstances of the lot of the poor. The social welfare programmes have taken insufficient cognisance of the social and economic situation in the country, resulting in shoddy delivery of services. Programmes have tended to be disjointed, have lacked funding, as well as lack a coherent framework to address the broad spectrum of risk and vulnerability factors.[50] Vulnerable populations have faced significant challenges with the lengthy application processes and related costs for applicants for assistance. There has been an overemphasis on relief as opposed to initiatives that promote empowerment, capacity building and self-reliance.

## Present Status of Social Welfare and Social Work

In Zimbabwe, social work is still a young profession and relatively unknown; hence some of the challenges faced are a function of teething problems. However, the profession is increasingly gaining traction, with three institutions now 'mass-producing' social work professionals. As part of regulating the work of the social work profession in the country, the Parliament of Zimbabwe enacted the Social Workers Act, establishing the Council of Social Workers that will be responsible for the registration of social workers and regulating their conduct.[51] On paper, social workers are key players in the crafting of social welfare policy, the promulgation of related legislation (limited in scope) and perhaps more importantly, in the implementation and delivery of social welfare services. To fulfil the welfare delivery obligation, social workers are, as noted, employed in a variety

---

50    Wyatt et al., 2010.

51    Republic of Zimbabwe, 2001.

of both government and non-governmental agencies. Under the Social Workers Act, for one to qualify to register as a social worker, one must meet these stipulated requirements:

▷ Be over the age of twenty-one years

▷ Be resident in Zimbabwe

▷ Have obtained:

- a Bachelor of Social Work degree from the UZ; or

- a Diploma in Social Work from the UZ.

Equivalent qualifications attained in other local tertiary institutions (like the Bindura University and Women's University in Africa) or from outside Zimbabwe can be considered, providing they satisfy the stipulations of the Council of Social Workers' Act.

## Prospects for Social Welfare and Social Work in Zimbabwe

While on paper the Zimbabwean Government, local authorities, NGOs and faith-based organisations are all charged with the duty of social welfare service delivery across the country; in reality, social exclusion has become the order of the day. Due to dwindling resources, and a charged political environment, the various institutions, including both those of the State and the NGO community, have retreated, leaving the poor virtually vulnerable. Several steps will need to be taken to strengthen social welfare provision in Zimbabwe. First, the political and socio-economic environment will need to stabilise, before the social work profession can realise efficient social welfare services delivery. Second, the human resource base will need to be revamped, both in terms of quality of the social work graduates churned out and the numbers of officers deployed, especially in government service. Third, the remuneration packages of the social work profession will need attention, not only to lift morale but to inject a modicum of self-belief and self-confidence in the officers.

Fourth, the philosophical foundations of social work in Zimbabwe will equally need revisiting. As the country continues to evolve and to mature, it is imperative that the social work profession responds according to the emerging needs of the country and finds a way of 'decolonising' itself. This decolonisation implies the need for social workers to engage in continuing education so that the profession remains relevant, using appropriate strategies. Social work education must be relevant if the practitioners are to address the current socio-economic challenges meaningfully. To this end, the social work profession would need to make deliberate efforts towards a paradigm shift, to facilitate the shedding of the remedial approach in favour of a developmental approach. The developmental approach (as opposed to remedial) can reach more people and empower them to influence their life circumstances positively.[52] The proposed approach (i.e. developmental) will promote social justice, capacity building and empowerment of citizens, leading towards the often elusive goal of self-reliance.

## Conclusion

In Zimbabwe, the demand for social welfare services has tended to be enormous, essentially because of the political and subsequent economic meltdown of the country since around 2000. Social welfare programmes have remained largely underfunded, resulting in the increased vulnerability of most of the population. Donors have stepped in, profoundly, but donor dependence is not sustainable given donor fatigue that in the long run, will almost always set in. Efforts, therefore, ought to be made to ensure that the government raises its resources to finance the recruitment and retention of qualified social work professionals in adequate numbers. Other than that, the material resource base needs to be strengthened.

However, for this to be realised, the investment climate needs correction so that the economic and political climate becomes conducive, implying a serious paradigm shift on the part of the Zimbabwean Government, particularly to facilitate the diffusion of the perennial uncertainties evident especially on the political front. Without a marked improvement in the country's economic and political performance, social welfare programmes will continue to suffer from perennial under-funding, while social work professionals will continue to perform way below capacity. Social work is an evolving profession, and it needs to strategically position itself, to be responsive to emerging social challenges across the country. Indeed, a paradigm shift all-around would be the surest way of guaranteeing social and economic progress for the benefit of all, most importantly, the vulnerable in society.

---

52    Louw, 1993.

# References

Blank, L. 2014. *Zimbabwe: Crafting a Coherent Social Protection System.* Policy Note. Harare Zimbabwe: Ministry of Public Service, Labour and Social Welfare.

Bourdillon, M.F.C. 1991. *The Shona Peoples.* Gweru, Zimbabwe: Mambo Press.

Chikova, H. 2013. Social Protection Social Protection and Informal Workers in Zimbabwe. Paper presented at the SASPEN – FES International Conference: Social Protection for Those Working Informally, Johannesburg, South Africa, 16-17 September. [https://bit.ly/2IkD9ir]. (Accessed 26 February 2016).

Cirillo, C. & Tebaldi, R. 2016. *Social protection in Africa: Inventory of non-contributory programmes.* International Policy Centre for Inclusive Growth: United Nations Development Programme.

Cormack, I.R.N. 1983. *Towards Self-Reliance: Urban Social Development in Zimbabwe.* Gweru, Zimbabwe: Mambo Press.

Crush, J. & Frayne, B. 2010. *The Invisible Crisis: Urban Food Security in Southern Africa.* Cape Town: African Food Security Urban Network (AFSUN).

DFID (UK Department for International Development) & FAO (United Nations' Food and Agriculture Organisation). 2013. *Impacts of the Harmonised Social Cash Transfer Programme on Community Dynamics in Zimbabwe.* Rome: FAO. [https://bit.ly/2SQCaIU]. (Accessed 13 January 2017).

Dhemba, J. 2013. Social Protection for the Elderly in Zimbabwe: Issues, Challenges and Prospects. *African Journal of Social Welfare,* 3(1):1-22.

Dhemba, J., Gumbo, P. & Nyamusara, J. 2002. Social security systems in Zimbabwe. *Journal of Social Development in Africa,* 17(2):132-153.

Garcia, M. & Moore, C.M.T. 2012. *The Cash Dividend: The Rise of Cash Transfer Programs in Sub-Saharan Africa.* Washington, DC: World Bank. [https://bit.ly/3nRocok]. (Accessed 20 January 2017).

Government of Zimbabwe & United Nations. 2012. *Zimbabwe 2012: Millennium Development Goals Progress.* Harare: Government of Zimbabwe and United Nations.

Hall, N.P. 1987. Self-Reliance in Practice: A Study of Burial Societies in Harare, Zimbabwe. *Journal of Social Development in Africa,* 2:49-71.

Hall, N. & Mupedziswa, R. (eds). 1995. *Social policy and administration in Zimbabwe.* Harare: School of Social Work.

Kaseke, E. 2001. Informal social security in Eastern and Southern Africa. Paper presented at the Towards the development of social protection in the SADC Region Conference, Helderfontein, Johannesburg, 17-19 October.

Kaseke, E. & Dhemba, J. 2007. Community mobilisation, voluntarism and the fight against HIV and AIDS in Zimbabwe. In: L. Patel & R. Mupedziswa (eds). *Research partnerships build the service field.* Johannesburg: Volunteer and Service Enquiry Southern Africa. pp.85-99.

Kaseke, E. Dhemba, J., Gumbo, P. & Kasere, C. 1998. The state and dynamics of social policy practice and research in Zimbabwe. *Journal of Social Development in Africa*, 13(2):21-34.

Kisner, C. 2008. Case studies: Harare, Zimbabwe. In: Kisner, C. *Green Roofs for Food Security and Environmental Sustainability.* Chicago: Climate Institute.

Louw, L. 1993. Process and pre-requisites necessary for successful implementation and management of community development projects. *Social Work/Maatskaplike Werk*, 29(2):94-99.

Mararike, C. 2001. Revival of indigenous food security strategies at the village level: the human factor implications. *Review of Human Factor Studies*, 6(2):93-104.

Moyo, O.N. 2007. *Tramped no more: Voices from Bulawayo's townships about families, life, survival, and social change in Zimbabwe.* Langham, MD: University Press of America.

Mupedziswa, R. 1995. Social welfare services. In: N. Hall & R. Mupedziswa (eds). *Social policy and administration in Zimbabwe.* Harare: School of Social Work. pp.81-106.

Mupedziswa, R. 2005. Challenges and prospects of social work services in Africa. In: J.C. Okeibunor & E.E. Anugwom (eds). *The social sciences and socioeconomic transformation in Africa.* Nsukka, Nigeria: Great AP Express Publications. pp.271-317.

Mupedziswa, R. 2015. We have no social life to write home about: Job opportunities experiences of exiled Zimbabwe nationals in the UK. *Global Development Studies: International Development Options*, 7(3-4):1-39.

Mupedziswa, R. & Mushunje, M. 2012. Between a rock and a hard place: Care of orphaned children in Zimbabwe and social work roles. In: J. Daugherty Bailey (ed). *Orphan Care: The Social Work Role.* Sterling, Virginia: Kumarian Press. pp.123-154.

Mupedziswa, R. & Ushamba, A. 2006. Challenges & Prospects: Social work practice in Zimbabwe in an environment of economic meltdown. In: N. Hall (ed). Social Work: making a world of difference: *Social Work Around the World IV in the Year of IFSW's 50th Jubilee*, 4:163-172.

Mushunje, M.T. 2006. Child Protection in Zimbabwe: Past, Present and Future. *Journal of Social Development in Africa*, 21(1):12-34.

Mushunje, M.T. 2014. Interrogating the relevance of the extended family as a social safety net for vulnerable children in Zimbabwe. *African Journal of Social Work*, 4(2):101-133.

Ndubiwa, M.M. 1974. *Bulawayo Municipal African Townships*. Occasional Paper 2. Bulawayo, Zimbabwe: City of Bulawayo Housing and Amenities Department.

Norton, A., Conway, T. & Foster, M. 2001. *Social Protection Concepts and Approaches: Implications for policy and practice in International Development*. Working Paper 143. London: Centre for Aid and Public Expenditure. [https://bit.ly/373SMoX]. (Accessed 15 January 2017).

Ntseane, D. & Solo, K. 2007. *Social Security and Social Protection in Botswana*. Gaborone: Bay Publishing.

Patel, L., Kaseke, E. & Midgley, J. 2012. Indigenous Welfare and Community-Based Social Development: Lessons from African Innovations. *Journal of Community Practice*, 20(1):12-31.

Republic of Zimbabwe. 1981. *Transitional National Development Plan*: 1982/3-1984/5. Harare: Amalgamated Press. p.12.

Republic of Zimbabwe. 2001. *Social Workers Act 9 of 2001*, 27:21. Harare: Government Printers. [http://www.veritaszim.net/node/257]. (Accessed 2 September 2011).

Republic of Zimbabwe. 2012. *Census 2012: National Report*. Harare: Zimbabwe National Statistics Agency. [https://bit.ly/313nhrm]. (Accessed 2 September 2013).

Republic of Zimbabwe. 2013. *National HIV and AIDS Estimates Report 2013*. Harare: Government Printers.

Republic of Zimbabwe. 2014a. *Zimbabwe Country Analysis Working Document Final Draft*. Harare: United Nations Zimbabwe. [https://bit.ly/3167Sq8]. (Accessed 20 January 2017).

Republic of Zimbabwe. 2014b. *Zimbabwe Multiple Indicator Cluster Survey (MICS): 2019 Survey Findings Report*. Harare: Zimstats. [https://uni.cf/2H8acpC]. (Accessed 12 May 2015).

Smith, H., Chiroro, P. & Musker, P. 2012. *2012 Zimbabwe: Evaluation of the Basic Education Assistance Module Programme*. Evaluation report. New York: United Nations Children's Fund. [https://uni.cf/33XRcDe]. (Accessed 13 January 2017).

Staff Editor. 2017. Zim rot spirals as 'chefs' fight. *Daily News Zimbabwe*. [https://bit.ly/314JK7p]. (Accessed 13 January 2017).

UNESCO. 2013. Cited in: Republic of Zimbabwe. 2014. *Zimbabwe Country Analysis Working Document Final Draft*. Harare: United Nations Zimbabwe. [https://bit.ly/3167Sq8]. (Accessed 20 January 2017).

UN Zimbabwe. 2014. *Zimbabwe United Nations Development Assistance Framework: 2012-2015 ZUNDAF Snapshot*. [https://bit.ly/34WRPfh]. (Accessed 20 January 2017).

World Bank. 2009. *Realising the Full Potential of Safety Nets in Africa: Social Safety Nets: Lessons from Rich and Poor Countries.* [https://bit.ly/2H9zCmo] (Accessed 14 July 2019).

World Bank. 2011. *Zimbabwe – Public expenditure notes (Vol. 3): Challenges in financing education, health, and social protection expenditures in Zimbabwe (English).* Washington, DC: World Bank. [https://bit.ly/3nRBQrt]. (Accessed 20 January 2017).

Wyatt, A., Mupedziswa, R. & Rayment, C. 2010. *Institutional Capacity Assessment: Department of Social Services, Zimbabwe.* Harare: Ministry of Labour and Social Services. DSS.

# Conclusion

## PROSPECTS FOR SOCIAL WELFARE AND SOCIAL WORK IN SOUTHERN AFRICA

*Ndangwa Noyoo*

## Introduction

The need to have indigenous scholarly work on the origins and evolution of social welfare and social work in Southern Africa informed this book's rationale. It is based on the contributions of authors from different universities and organisations in Southern Africa; thus, the chapters examine many issues, but all of them primarily centre on the genesis and progression of social welfare and social work or allied areas of social security/ protection in the region. In this regard, the book's chapters present a panoramic view of both the historical context and contemporary trends of social welfare and social work in Southern Africa. It can be discerned from the authors' discussions that colonialism left its imprints on Southern Africa's social welfare and social work approaches, and continuing to reinforce and replicate themselves several decades after countries in the region became independent. In this regard, colonialism bequeathed these countries a legacy of different administrative and governance systems, still defining the way they arrive at policy choices and development strategies. The former influenced how different political systems run and manage social welfare systems. Therefore, in examining social welfare and social work in Southern Africa, it is important not to lose sight of these historical tangents. Part of Africa's history, that Western scholars have not given much prominence to and for centuries presented from their perspectives and continue to do so, is the pre-colonial era. Mostly, Africa's pre-colonial period that even some African academics and scholars scantly mention or perfunctorily refer to in their works, especially in social welfare and social work texts, is a crucial missing link that needs to be reified in African academic discourse. Critically, academics even in Africa seldom highlight and explore pre-colonial Africa's links to social welfare and social work.

Despite pre-colonial Africa's crucial part in the continent's past and present standing, some scholars spend less time to understand it scrupulously. For instance, a corollary of this endeavour would be to ascertain why systems and organisations in contemporary Africa, imported from Europe and imposed on Africans' structures by the colonialists, continue to be so stark in determining the development trajectory of Africa and the wellbeing of Africans. In effect, although the imported systems are hegemonic, they continue to be in dissonance with the value systems and aspirations of most African people, even though African governments in the post-colonial era have for decades unwittingly, and at times overtly, reinforced colonial systems in responding to their citizens' needs as well as to govern them. Indeed, human needs and the way societies are addressed are dependent on the mechanisms that they created. However, for Africa, what is missing in this equation are indigenous social welfare and social protection systems. Hence, social welfare and social work in this region cannot be examined without delving into this historical past.

## Southern Africa's Indigenous Past

It is worthy to note that chapters in this book refer to the pre-colonial era in their discussions, as a way of appreciating the origins of social welfare and social work systems in this part of Africa. Southern Africa's indigenous past is located in its pre-colonial era, whereby everything that was done in this part of Africa resonated with the aspirations of the people, and all aspects of life were organic, intrinsic, as well as local in content and outlook. The type of political authorities in existence at the time mainly legitimised the former. Indeed, Southern Africa's pre-colonial history shows distinct features of existence, resting on two forms of socio-political state formation, namely stateless and nomadic communities and strong, organised polities; forms of pre-colonial states that predominated most parts of Southern Africa. In colonising these polities, European powers did not always use force, in the first instance, but they had initially disarmed and beguiled Africans through the 'signing' of so-called treaties of 'cooperation' and 'trade' before they resorted to force, armed invasion and conquest. On the eve of colonial incursion, Southern Africa had huge swathes under the rule of powerful rulers and kingdoms, for instance:

- Queen Nzinga of the Ndongo and Matamba Kingdoms of the Mbundu people in present-day Angola;

- the Bamangwato kingdom in Botswana;

- the Undi kingdom in present-day Malawi, Zambia and Mozambique;

- the Gaza kingdom in Mozambique;

- Barotseland or Bulozi, Lunda, Ngoni and Bemba kingdoms in present-day Zambia;

- Mwenemutapa, Rozwi and Ndebele kingdoms in present-day Zimbabwe;

- Shaka and the Zulu nation, King Sekhukune of the ba Pedi nation, Mapungubwe, in South Africa;

- the Basuto kingdom in present-day Lesotho, and

- Sobhuza of Eswatini (Swaziland), among others.

## Emerging Trends from Chapters

Even though different issues are examined in the chapters, there are common emerging trends that anchor this book. For starters, the ubiquitous Eurocentric interventions or knowledge bases, symptomatic of post-colonial welfare systems of countries in Southern Africa, and social work seem to be the common denominator for all social welfare and social work endeavours in the region. These are inextricably bound up with the colonisation of Africa and Southern Africa. Therefore, the colonial ethos still holds sway in the way social welfare systems and the profession of social work are constituted not only in Southern Africa but across Africa. Thus, an outcome of this anomalous situation is the ill-equipped nature of social workers to respond to the realities and other challenges of Africa. This colonial legacy is the one issue cross-cutting all the countries examined in this book. Authors of this book have not just cited this issue, but other scholars have highlighted it and questioned Eurocentric models of social welfare and social work interventions' efficacy to respond to Africans' needs.[1]

Another key issue that emerges from the chapters' discussions is the paucity of both financial and human resources in almost all the region's countries, with Botswana, Mauritius, Namibia and South Africa, probably an exception, even though they also face challenges. It is easy to decipher that social welfare, and social work, do not operate independently of the political and economic structures of the countries in the region. The politics and economies of the region influence and inform the social welfare systems and social work responses. In most cases, the region's economic downturn, that saw the downward spiral of ordinary people's living conditions, eroded the capacities of social welfare systems to perform their requisite roles in these countries. In the same vein, the deteriorating economic situation in the region negatively impacted social workers. It is important to note that poor economic performance directly resulted from political challenges typified by authoritarian rule and malevolent leadership, corruption, lack of transparency and accountability. Politics plays a crucial role in the way some regional governments support, strengthen or even neglect social welfare systems. Therefore, socio-economic challenges and human deprivation exemplify the post-colonial era, despite countries in the region attaining Independence in the 1960s-1990s.

In the same vein, the deplorable economic situation led to the migration of skilled human resources to other countries in Southern Africa or other parts of the world. This scenario has not changed for the better. Thus, the state of social welfare and social work in some of the countries of the region remains quite woeful.

## Decolonisation of Social Welfare Systems and Social Work Practice

It can thus be noted that social welfare and social work still have colonial trappings and need to be decolonised in Southern Africa and Africa; work to be undertaken on both government policy and academic levels. In this regard, social welfare systems and social work practice must be in sync to search for consistent practice in Africa, arguably, one way to begin the decolonisation process in earnest. In this regard, the drive for relevant practice should be embedded with Indigenous Knowledge Systems, amplifying the need

---

1    Nyirenda, 1975; Lifanu, 1978; Ankrah, 1984.

to imbue social welfare and social work practice with these systems.[2] Social welfare and social work are development vehicles. Therefore, African development initiatives cannot be treated in isolation but must be linked to the total emancipation of Africa's peoples from the vestiges of colonial domination; neo-colonialism; post-colonial dictatorships; ethnicity, ethnic-based politics; and single-party rule. In this way, Southern Africa and Africa, in general, can begin to propel an autonomous development process, free from borrowed development formulae continuously defining African people's lives since the 1950s.[3]

## Future considerations

This book is an attempt to bring to light the origins and evolution of social welfare and social work in Southern Africa. What the authors of the chapters managed to do is to lay a basis for future work and research on social welfare systems and social work practice initiatives in the Southern African region and broadly Africa. There is already work in Southern Africa from various academics, in the aforementioned areas, and these will be helpful and useful in advancing education and practice initiatives. However, this text is one of the few efforts to bring a collection of chapters together from authors of different Southern African countries. It is hoped that such endeavours will result in much deepened and sustainable indigenous forms of social welfare and social work education and practice in the region.

---

2    Noyoo, 2019a.
3    Noyoo, 2019b.

## References

Ankrah, E.M. 1984. *The Problem of Relevance: A Study of the Perceptions of Social Work Professionals on Education and Practice in Three African Countries.* Doctoral dissertation. Nairobi, Kenya: University of Nairobi.

Lifanu, L.N. 1978. Community self-reliance and social development in Zambia's Western Province. Doctoral dissertation. Waltham, Massachusetts: Brandeis University.

Noyoo, N. 2019a. Decolonising social work practice and social work education in post-colonial Africa. In: K. Kliebl, R. Lutz, N. Noyoo, B. Bunk, A. Dittmann, & B. Seepamore (eds). *The Routledge Handbook of Post-colonial Social Work.* London: Routledge. pp.261-268.

Noyoo, N. 2019b. Pushing for autonomous African development. In: K. Kliebl, R. Lutz, N. Noyoo, B. Bunk, A. Dittmann, & B. Seepamore (eds). *The Routledge Handbook of Post-colonial Social Work.* London: Routledge. pp.244-257.

Nyirenda, V.G. 1975. Social Change and Social Policy in a Developing Country: The Zambia Case. Doctoral dissertation. Los Angeles: University of California.

www.ingramcontent.com/pod-product-compliance
Lightning Source LLC
Chambersburg PA
CBHW080643270326
41928CB00017B/3171